# The
# GOOD HEALTH COOK BOOK

OCTOPUS BOOKS

# NOTES

Standard spoon measurements are used in all recipes.

1 tablespoon = one 15 ml spoon
1 teaspoon = one 5 ml spoon
All spoon measures are level.

Fresh herbs are used unless otherwise stated. If unobtainable substitute a bouquet garni of the equivalent dried herbs, or use dried herbs instead but halve the quantities stated.

Home-made stock should be used whenever possible. Beef, chicken or ham stocks give the best flavour, but for vegetarian diets use vegetable stock or add yeast extract to water.

If fresh yeast is unobtainable, substitute dried yeast but use only half of the quantity recommended.

Ovens should be preheated for at least 5 minutes to the specified temperature.

Only one column of measures should be followed; metric and imperial columns are not interchangeable.

# CONTENTS

First published 1983 by
Octopus Books Limited
59 Grosvenor Street
London W1

© 1983 Octopus Books Limited

Reprinted 1985

ISBN 0 7064 1714 3

Printed in Hong Kong

# Nutrients in food

Food is composed of various nutrients which the body needs in order to keep healthy. There are five types of essential nutrients, each of which plays a special part in maintaining health. To ensure that the body receives these nutrients in the required proportions, it is important to follow a balanced diet.

In the following chart these nutrients are identified and their main sources are listed.

| Nutrient | Functions | Deficiency Symptoms | Prime Food Sources | Special Points |
|---|---|---|---|---|
| **CARBO-HYDRATES** | Provide the body with energy for work and warmth. May also be converted into body fat. | Reduced stamina and energy. | | |
| **Sugar Carbohydrates** | These provide a source of quick energy, but most of their prime food sources contribute little else in the way of nutrients and are therefore very fattening. | | Sugars (all types), honey, jam, syrup, dried fruit, bananas. | Excessive consumption of sugar promotes tooth decay. |
| **Starch Carbohydrates** | In addition to carbo-hydrate, starch foods also contain vegetable protein and useful amounts of minerals and B group vitamins. | | Flour, bread, cereals, pasta, rice, potatoes, pulses. | |
| **Cellulose** | This carbohydrate cannot be digested by the human body but it adds valuable bulk to the diet and aids bowel movement. | Constipation | Wholegrain cereals, raw vegetables, fruit, bran | A wholefood diet provides plenty of cellulose. |
| **FATS** | Provide the body with energy for work and warmth. May also form body fat. Supply fat-soluble vitamins A, D and E. | Reduced energy, bad skin, possible lack of fat-soluble vitamins. | *Butter, *processed cooking fats and margarines, *lard, *suet, *fat in meat, *cream, *milk, *cheese, *egg yolk, soft margarines, vegetable oils, oily fish (herrings, etc.) | Fats provide twice as much energy as carbohydrates. Fats high in saturated fatty acids (denoted*) are considered less preferable from a health viewpoint. |
| **PROTEINS** | Provide materials for growth and repair of body tissues. They can also provide energy and can sometimes be converted into fat. | Retarded growth and development, increased susceptibility to disease. | | As protein is necessary for growth, it is essential that children and pregnant women obtain an adequate amount. |
| **Animal proteins** | These contain all the essential amino acids in satisfactory proportions for human needs. | | Meat, fish, eggs, milk, cheese. | |
| **Plant proteins** | These are deficient in one or more of the amino acids required by the body. | | Cereals, bread, flour, pulses, nuts. | By eating a mixture of these at the same meal, it is possible to obtain an adequate intake of all the essential amino acids. |
| **MINERALS** | Provide material for growth and repair of the body, and for control of the body processes. | | | |

| | | | | |
|---|---|---|---|---|
| **Calcium** | Required for proper development and growth of bones and teeth; muscle and blood. Especially important for pregnant women and children. | Reduced growth, badly formed teeth, rickets. | Milk, cheese, sardines, bread. | Vitamin D helps the absorption of calcium. |
| **Iron** | Essential for blood functioning; it is present in haemoglobin which is necessary for the transport of oxygen in the body. | Fatigue, anaemia. | Liver, kidney, beef, eggs, cocoa powder, dried fruit, green vegetables. | Vitamin C helps the absorption of Iron. |
| **Sodium** | Essential for maintaining the normal balance of body fluids. | Muscular cramps. | Salt, bacon, ham, saltwater fish, cheese, bread, butter. | Extra salt is required after strenuous exercise and in hot weather to replace loss in perspiration. |
| **Iodine** | For production of thyroid hormones. | Stunted growth in children; goitre in adults. | Saltwater fish, iodized salt, watercress. | |
| **VITAMINS** | Regulate the metabolic processes. Important for energy utilization, growth, repair and protection. | | | |
| **Vitamin A** | Protects surface tissues, including hair, nails, skin and eyes. Important for eyesight. Necessary for growth of children. | Infection of eyes, respiratory tract and skin. Poor vision at night. Retarded growth. | Fish liver oils, liver, butter, margarine, cheese, eggs, herrings, sardines, almonds, peanuts. | Can be stored by the body so a daily intake is not absolutely essential. |
| **Carotene** | Converted into Vitamin A in the body. | (As Vitamin A) | Carrots, spinach, water-cress, dried apricots, tomatoes, cabbage, peas. | |
| **Vitamin B group** | B vitamins – thiamine, riboflavine and nicotinic acid form essential links in the chain of processes by which the body obtains energy from food. The other B group vitamins are also involved in metabolism. | B vitamins are generally found together in the same foods, so a dietary deficiency of one vitamin is unlikely and symptoms would probably reflect a multiple deficiency. Growth of children is checked. General weakening of body: depression, fatigue, inflamed skin, tongue and eyes; nervous disorders. | Yeast extract (Brewer's yeast) wholewheat bread, wheatgerm, cereals, liver, beef, pork, bacon, cheese, fish, pulses. | Cannot be stored by the body so a daily intake is essential. B vitamins are water-soluble and may be lost in cooking liquid. |
| **Vitamin C** | Concerned with growth and repair of tissues. Important for body's resistance to infection. | Depression, low resistance to infection, poor skin and slow healing of wounds. Chronic deficiency results in the disease scurvy. | Fresh fruit and vegetables, especially blackcurrants, lemons, oranges, grape-fruit, rose hips, Brussels sprouts, cauliflower, cabbage, parsley, tomatoes, lettuce. | Cannot be stored by the body so a daily intake is essential. Vitamin C dissolves in water and much is lost in cooking. Further losses occur after cutting foods. |
| **Vitamin D** | Important for the absorption and laying down of calcium in the bones. Especially important for developing children and expectant mothers. | Poor teeth and bones. Rickets in children. | Cod liver oil, oily fish, liver, eggs, milk, butter, margarine. | Vitamin D is also produced by the action of the sun's rays on the skin. It can be stored by the body. |

# The Essential Nutrients

Once it is known which essential nutrients are contained in which foods, a balanced diet can be planned, but it is also useful to know a little more about how the nutrients work.

## Carbohydrates

Energy can be provided by carbohydrates, fats and proteins. However, proteins are also needed for growth and maintenance of body tissues. It is therefore important, particularly for growing children, to have an adequate intake of carbohydrate to ensure that proteins are used mainly for body building rather than energy.

Sugar carbohydrates (see page 8) provide quick energy: a spoonful of glucose will give you a lift when you're flagging but little else, and if this energy is not burnt up, then they can cause overweight. People who are slimming often try to cut out *all* carbohydrates for this reason. However, this can be detrimental to health because a small intake of carbohydrate is absolutely essential for the correct breakdown of fat stores.

Starch carbohydrates, such as bread and cereal contain other vital nutrients, such as protein and minerals, and are therefore less fattening than sugar carbohydrates. The third kind of carbohydrate is cellulose, which is indigestible to the human body. Cellulose forms the cell walls of fruit and vegetables; it is also found in unrefined cereals and nuts. Although it cannot be digested, it is important as roughage in the diet.

When planning meals, remember that the body needs vitamin B, so that carbohydrates and proteins can be used completely. Also remember to combine carbohydrates and proteins, like cereals with milk, or brown bread with a boiled egg, so that the carbohydrate provides energy while the protein builds and repairs tissue.

## Fats

The body uses fats to provide energy and to form body fat for warmth and protection. Fats are a more concentrated energy food than carbohydrate, and anyone who uses a vast amount of energy needs an adequate intake to avoid a very bulky high-carbohydrate diet.

Children need a large amount of energy and, as they only have small stomachs and cannot cope with large quantities of carbohydrates, it is important that they have sufficient fat – in the form of milk, cheese and egg yolks, for example.

Fats are also important because they contain vitamins, particularly A and D. They are digested more slowly than carbohydrates, and do not provide such a quick energy source.

## Proteins

Protein is necessary for growth. It is thus particularly important for children to eat enough, as it is necessary for developing bones, muscles, skin and blood. However, adults need it for more or less the same reason – in their case, old tissue breaks down and needs to be replaced.

Proteins are composed of amino acids – there are twenty-two of these commonly found in foods, eight of which are essential for the adult and ten for the growing child. These 'essential amino acids' must be supplied by the foods we eat. Protein from animal sources usually contains all the essential amino acids; vegetable proteins are normally deficient in some essential amino acids. If all animal foods are excluded from the diet, it must be carefully planned to ensure an adequate protein intake.

*VALUABLE SOURCES OF VITAMIN C: tomatoes, lemons, tangerines, new potatoes, Brussels sprouts, strawberries, blackcurrants, rose hip syrup, oranges and grapefruit.*

## Minerals

A variety of minerals is essential to the body, but most of them are required only in minute quantities. The four most important minerals are calcium, iron, iodine and sodium.

**Calcium** is necessary for bones and teeth; children, who are growing and forming new bones and teeth, require more than adults. An adult body contains about 1 kg (2 lb) calcium, while a baby has only about 25 g (1 oz), so a large amount is accumulated in the growing years. Calcium is also important for muscles and blood functioning. Milk and cheese provide most of the calcium we need: 75 g (3 oz) Cheddar cheese contains as much calcium as 600 ml (1 pint) milk.

**Iron** is present in the haemoglobin of the blood. The amount of iron found in the body is only enough to make a very small nail, but it is very important; if you don't have enough iron in your food anaemia can develop.

**Iodine** is needed in a tiny quantity, to help the thyroid gland work properly; this gland controls the rate at which chemical changes take place in the body. If there is not enough iodine in the diet the thyroid gland becomes enlarged. Lack of iodine in children can adversely affect their development.

**Sodium** or salt is essential for body fluids. It is lost from the body in sweat and must be replaced.

## Vitamins

Vitamins are only present in very small amounts in food, but they are vital to the body – it cannot live without any one of them. They help the body to use the other nutrients in food, and protect it from illness. A good mixed diet will provide all the necessary vitamins. However, doctors may recommend that small children and expectant mothers take supplements of vitamins A and D, in particular. Only the correct amount of supplements should be taken, as the body stores excess vitamins A and D and it is possible to accumulate too much, resulting in illness.

**Vitamin A** is essential for growth; it helps the formation of bones and teeth, keeps skin and eyes healthy, and helps eye sight. It also keeps the throat and breathing passages in good working order. Vitamin A is present in animal foods which are rich in fat, and in some fruit and vegetables in the form of carotene, which is converted into vitamin A in the body. All red, orange and dark green fruits and vegetables contain carotene.

**Vitamin D** is contained in fat-rich animal foods and is also produced from the action of sunshine on the skin. It works in conjunction with calcium and phosphorus to build up bones and teeth.

**Vitamin B group** comprises a number of vitamins which are vital for metabolic processes, especially obtaining energy from carbohydrates. They cannot be stored in the body and must be taken every day.

**Vitamin C,** also known as ascorbic acid, is essential for general health and growth and also helps wounds to heal and broken bones to mend. Found in fruit and vegetables, it is easily destroyed. When plant cells are broken down, either by cutting or cooking, an enzyme is released which destroys vitamin C. Vegetables should therefore be cooked very quickly in a little boiling water, as this destroys the enzyme. Bicarbonate of soda (baking soda) also destroys vitamin C and should therefore never be added to the cooking water.

*VALUABLE SOURCES OF IRON: spinach, kidneys, steak, watercress, wholewheat bread, dried apples, dried figs, dried apricots, dates and broccoli.*

# Valuable foods

A balanced healthy diet should contain those foods which are nutritionally most beneficial to us. The range of these 'valuable foods' is enormous and, by basing our diet on a wide selection of them, we obtain the variety necessary to maintain our enjoyment of food – as well as a healthy eating pattern.

**Cereals** are a rich source of carbohydrate and therefore provide the body with energy. They also contain small amounts of useful vegetable protein and B group vitamins. The main dietary cereals are wheat, maize (corn), barley, oats, rice and rye, and their carbohydrate content ranges from about 66 per cent (oats) to 72 per cent (rye). They store well, are relatively cheap to buy, and can be combined with many other ingredients to give quick and easy meals.

As cereals are mainly carbohydrate, they are more beneficial eaten with a protein food. For example, breakfast cereal with milk provides a good balance of carbohydrate and protein. Furthermore, the protein value of the cereal is greater than if it were eaten on its own because milk supplies the amino acids which are deficient in cereal.

Breakfast cereals often have extra vitamins and minerals added, so even if this is all you eat in the morning – plus fruit for vitamin C – you will still obtain a healthy supply of nutrients.

Calcium, iron and some group B vitamins are added to flour – so bread, too, is good for you: it provides a valuable staple food containing carbohydrate, vegetable protein and fat, as well as the vitamins and minerals added to the flour.

**Meat and offal (variety meats)** are concentrated sources of protein and a variety of vitamins and minerals. Meat does, however, contain a proportion of fat under the skin and distributed between the muscle fibres.

Pork, ham and bacon are particularly rich in thiamine.

Liver is a particularly valuable food in the diet: 100 g (4 oz) calf's (veal) liver yields 45 per cent of the recommended daily ten times as much as cod.

Liver is a particularly valuable food in the diet: 100 g (4 oz) calf's (veal) liver yields 45 per cent of the recommended daily intake of protein – as well as enough iron, vitamin A and riboflavin for two days. It also contains vitamins C and D. Tongue, sweetbreads and tripe are other excellent sources of protein and are all easily digested; tripe also provides calcium. Heart and kidneys are again prime sources of protein and B group vitamins; kidneys are also a rich source of iron.

All offal (variety meat) is relatively fat-free and thus plays an important part in low-fat diets.

**Fish** is rich in animal protein, sodium, iodine and nicotinic acid. It is therefore a highly nutritious protein food, and is more tender and easily digested than meat.

Oily fish, such as herring and mackerel, are very popular and useful in the diet, providing a valuable source of protein, unsaturated fat, calcium, iron, vitamin D and the B group vitamins – riboflavin and nicotinic acid. Oil, containing vitamins A and D, is distributed throughout the flesh of these fish while most other varieties of fish only have oil in the liver which is not normally eaten. Cod and halibut liver oil are thus concentrated sources of the oil-soluble vitamins A and D, and are sometimes used as dietry supplements. Canned salmon and sardines are rich sources of protein and vitamin B group; if the bones are eaten too, they are excellent sources of calcium and phosphorus.

Shellfish – such as crabs, lobsters, prawns and shrimps – also provide protein, fat and iodine. Molluscs such as oysters, mussels and scallops, are not of such great food value, though they are useful sources of vitamins and minerals.

**Milk** is sometimes called the perfect food. It provides sufficient quantities of most of the essential nutrients in an easily digested form. It is therefore particularly valuable for babies, small children and invalids, but it is an excellent food for everybody. Milk does, however, lack iron, and is deficient in vitamin C, so these nutrients must be supplied by other sources.

**Cheese** retains the valuable constituents of milk and is a valuable source of protein, fat, calcium, vitamin A and riboflavin. Hard cheeses (Cheddar, Gruyère, etc.) are composed of about one-third protein, one-third fat and one-third water. Because of the high fat content, some people find cheese hard to digest but grated cheese is more easily digested and can be combined with a variety of other foods – in salads or cooked dishes.

**Eggs** are rich in animal protein and egg yolk contains plenty of iron; eggs are also useful sources of vitamins A, D and the B group vitamins. However, they are also a concentrated source of fat and cholesterol, and should be eaten in moderation by those on a low-cholesterol or low-fat diet.

**Vegetables** play an important part in the diet. Besides adding variety and colour to meals, they provide valuable fibre, minerals and vitamins A and C. They also contain protein and starch.

The nutritional content of vegetables varies considerably. As a rough guide, the green leafy vegetables are high in vitamin C – especially broccoli, kale, Brussels sprouts, peppers, cabbage, cauliflower, spinach and watercress. These vegetables also provide vitamin A in the form of carotene, some B group vitamins, iron, calcium and other minerals.

Root vegetables, especially carrots, are very rich in carotene. Potatoes are, of course, high in starch; although not particularly high in vitamin C, they provide an important source for those who consume large quantities. Potatoes also yield useful amounts of protein, iron and some B group vitamins. Pulses (legumes) are a rich source of vegetable protein, energy and other nutrients and are particularly valuable in a vegetarian diet.

Ideally, vegetables should be eaten absolutely fresh, and raw as often as possible. Nutritive value is normally reduced during storage, preservation, preparation and cooking. Vitamin C and the water-soluble B vitamins are most susceptible to loss.

**Fruit** is a good source of vitamin C and provides us with valuable roughage; some fruits also contain vitamin A. Rosehips, blackcurrants, redcurrants and strawberries are very rich in vitamin C; oranges, lemons, grapefruit, raspberries, gooseberries and loganberries are good sources; bananas, melon and tangerines only provide a little, while apples, pears and plums are poor sources. Vitamin C is easily lost in cooking, so eat fruit raw whenever possible. Vitamin A is found in small quantities in apricots, tomatoes and peaches.

Dried fruits are a rich source of energy and add flavour to both sweet and savoury dishes. Although the dehydration process destroys practically all vitamin C, most dried fruits are useful sources of other vitamins and minerals. Prunes and dried apricots, for example, are useful sources of carotene; dried figs supply protein and B group vitamins, as well as fibre and energy.

**Nuts** are highly nutritious. They are a rich source of vegetable protein and energy, and contain useful amounts of B group vitamins, iron and calcium.

# Our Daily Needs

Everyone needs adequate protein, vitamins, minerals and energy to keep healthy. The main sources of each nutrient have already been discussed. To make sure that you are obtaining a balanced diet, eat some food from each of the following food groups every day:

Group 1: meat, fish, poultry and eggs*
Group 2: milk, cheese and yogurt*
Group 3: fruit and vegetables
Group 4: bread and cereals
Group 5: fats

* Vegetarians, particularly those who do not eat foods in either groups 1 or 2, should include a variety of vegetable protein foods – pulses (legumes), cereals, nuts etc. – instead.

Avoid sugary foods, such as sweets and cakes, as far as possible, and remember that the foods in groups 1 and 2 are also a source of fats (group 5).

Every person's needs are slightly different and this must be borne in mind when cooking for a family.

## Young children

Children up to primary school age are growing fast and need plenty of protein, calcium, iron and vitamins. They also use a great deal of energy, but it is important to avoid supplying this in the form of sugar carbohydrates. Too many sweets, sugary cakes and sweet biscuits are detrimental to teeth – especially when eaten between meals. These foods tend to create a 'sweet tooth' which reduces the appetite for other foods rich in the vital nutrients needed for health and growth. Try to satisfy children's energy requirements with other carbohydrate sources; the chapter on Wholegrain baking provides plenty of healthy alternatives.

To establish good eating habits, avoid giving children snacks between meals as far as possible. If they are hungry, provide fruit, cheese or nuts, rather than sweets or biscuits (cookies).

Milk is not a perfect food for the growing child because it lacks iron, but it is an excellent source of other nutrients – especially protein and calcium. Babies are usually born with a store of iron which will last several months; when this supply is exhausted they need to be fed small amounts of other foods which contain iron, such as egg yolk or puréed spinach. Toddlers who refuse to drink milk on its own may well enjoy a milkshake, prepared with puréed fruit, honey and milk, such as Banana flip (page 31). Small children should be encouraged to eat plenty of fruit and vegetables; a lack of these may lower their resistance to colds and other infections. For children who don't like fresh vegetables, try serving them in a sauce or in wholewheat pancakes (crêpes); for example Broccoli pancakes (crêpes) (page 163).

## Teenagers

Many children have very large appetites when they reach adolescence, not surprisingly since their nutrient requirements are high. It is most important that teenagers satisfy their appetites with well balanced meals. Too many of them consume large quantities of 'empty calorie foods', like sweets and crisps. As a result they develop spotty skins and some have a weight problem. Girls often become figure conscious at this age and develop food fads. Often they cut out breakfast in an attempt to slim, then become so hungry by mid-morning that they resort to mid-morning empty-calorie snacks.

Always try to persuade children to eat breakfast and encourage them to eat plenty of raw fruits, vegetables and high protein foods.

## The elderly

Because the elderly are less active, their energy needs are lower than those of younger adults, so they require less of the energy-giving foods – fats and carbohydrates. Older bodies do not digest food as quickly, or absorb nutrients as effectively, so it is particularly important for elderly people to have a carefully balanced diet, which provides enough of the nutrients required to maintain and repair the body tissues, without excess energy. Meals should therefore be based primarily on protein foods, fresh fruit and vegetables. Fish and eggs are more easily digested than meat; cheese, yogurt, milk, liver and kidney are also valuable and can be purchased in small quantities.

Elderly people usually have smaller appetites because they are less active, and are often tempted to nibble at biscuits (cookies) rather than prepare fresh and balanced meals daily. This can result in nutrient deficiencies and must be avoided.

*DAILY SUMMER MENU (see page 232): Breakfast – Muesli; Lunch – Baked crab, Peach yogurt shake; Dinner – Cucumber, lemon and mint soup, Spring beef casserole, Hot berry snow.*

## Pregnancy

The idea of 'eating for two' during pregnancy is old-fashioned and ill-advised. Stoking up on carbohydrate foods when expecting a baby will only result in excess weight gain; doctors recommend that weight should increase by only 11 kg (24 lb) during the total pregnancy period. A carefully balanced diet is the answer. Pregnant women require extra iron, calcium and vitamin C. Liver, kidney, eggs, milk, cheese, yogurt, fish, fresh vegetables and fruit will supply these extra nutrients.

## At work all day

Anyone who goes to work needs a good breakfast; even if it has to be a quick one. A carefully balanced evening meal is also important. Lunchtime can be a problem though, particularly if heavy business meals are regularly eaten or if a meal has to be taken to work. Packed lunches can, however, be as nutritious as other meals, providing the ingredients are chosen carefully (see page 19). When eating out at lunchtime, try to avoid the high energy foods on the menu and don't drink too much alcohol with your meal – as it is also full of 'empty calories'!

# Dietary Considerations

Cholesterol, insufficient fibre and excess calorie intake are sometimes termed 'The diseases of the modern Western diet', yet the reasons for the description are frequently misunderstood.

## Dietary Fibre

The fibrous part of plant foods, called cellulose, is a starch carbohydrate. It was once thought to be useless to the body because it cannot be digested but it is now accepted that this dietary fibre provides the roughage which is essential to the healthy working of the digestive system. Fibre carries plenty of moisture and cleans the intestine and bowels, thus helping to eliminate waste products of the foods we eat.

Many of today's foods are preserved or processed in such a way that the fibre originally present is lost. For example, all the fibre supplied by the bran in cereal is lost when white flour is refined. It is therefore important to avoid over-refined foods as much as possible. Choose wholewheat bread and flour in preference to refined varieties and eat plenty of fresh fruit and vegetables, particularly the outer leaves and skins.

## Cholesterol

This is a fatty substance which is essential to the body. It is present in all body cells and body fluids, including blood. It is a normal constituent of animal tissue, so that all food of animal origin may contain it. The body manufactures all of the cholesterol it requires so a dietary intake is not essential.

Cholesterol-rich foods include egg yolk, dairy produce, brains, liver and kidney. Plants contain no cholesterol and therefore neither do vegetable oils.

Studies indicate that a high blood cholesterol level increases the risk of coronary disease. In view of this, it is wise to know a little about the various types of fat we use in our diet. Fats are composed of fatty acids which may be 'saturated' or 'unsaturated'. Saturated fatty acids markedly raise the blood cholesterol level; these saturated fatty acids form a large proportion of animal fats, such as butter, lard and beef fat.

Unsaturated fatty acids do not raise the blood cholesterol level and highly unsaturated ones, called 'polyunsaturated fatty acids', actually tend to lower the level. Vegetable oils, particularly soy bean, sunflower and cotton seed oil, and vegetable margarine, contain a high proportion of polyunsaturated fatty acids. By using these vegetable fats in preference to animal fats it is possible to lower the blood cholesterol level considerably, which is highly beneficial for health.

If cholesterol intake has to be cut down for health reasons, the total amount of fat eaten – including food prepared from fats, such as ice-cream and pastry – must be cut. Dairy produce and eggs should be restricted, and chicken, veal and fish eaten instead of pork, lamb and beef. Vegetable oils may be used for cooking, and vegetable margarine may be used for baking and spreading.

Vegetable fats provide as many calories as animal fats and should also be cut down if calorie intake is to be restricted.

## Calories

The amount of energy provided by the food we eat is measured in calories. Energy is required to maintain the normal processes of the body, such as breathing, heartbeat and circulation. On average, a woman uses 1300 to 1400 calories a day, and a man uses about 1600 to 1800 calories simply staying alive. In addition, about 700 to 1200 calories are needed for everyday activities, such as standing, walking, eating or running.

The energy we obtain from the food we eat should balance the energy used; if it doesn't the surplus calories will be converted into fat and stored in the body.

Starches, sugars and proteins yield 4 calories per gram, while fats – a more concentrated form of energy – supply 9 calories per gram. By using these values the energy content of any food can be calculated from the proportion of nutrients it contains. So-called 'empty' calorie foods, such as sugar, simply provide energy but no other nutrients. The Calorie Chart (pages 26-27) provides a comprehensive list of food calorie values – a useful reference for those who are concerned about their weight. By following a diet which provides less calories than needed, surplus fat is used up as energy and you are on the way to a slimmer figure. (See also page 10.)

## Vegetarianism

Vegetarianism is frequently associated with food faddism, yet the vegetarian diet can be a perfectly acceptable one. Most people in the Western world who choose to follow a vegetarian diet, do so either because they feel it is ethically wrong to eat flesh, or because they simply find meat unpalatable.

There are two main types of vegetarian diet. The vegan diet excludes all food from animal sources, including dairy produce. Their sources of protein are therefore restricted to cereals, nuts, pulses (legumes) and other vegetables. Lacto-vegetarians will, however, eat milk, cheese and eggs.

A vegetarian diet can supply all the necessary nutrients, but it must be carefully planned to do so. Vegans, in particular, must eat an assortment of vegetable proteins at each meal to ensure that they obtain an adequate supply of all the essential amino acids. Vegetable proteins may be incomplete eaten alone, but they are perfectly capable of supplementing each other's amino acid deficiencies when eaten together. Essential minerals, vitamins and fats can be provided from vegetable sources, but care must be taken that sufficient iron is included in the diet.

*PACKED LUNCH: Prawn (shrimp) quiche (page 68); Potato and courgette (zucchini) salad (page 128); wholewheat bread and fruit.*

# Planning your Meals

Many people do not bother to plan meals ahead because they feel it is not worth the effort and they don't have time anyway. But planning several meals at a time – ideally, for a week – need only take a few minutes to do and can actually save you time in the long run. If you know what you're going to cook for the following few days, you can shop just once and avoid waste. Most important, you can ensure that all essential nutritional needs are met, and such mineral rich foods as liver and oily fish are included regularly. Planning ahead is likely to provide more interesting and varied meals, as well as more healthy ones.

Three meals a day – breakfast, a light meal and a main meal – should be sufficient for a healthy, balanced diet. A milk drink at bedtime will encourage a good night's sleep.

**Too busy to cook**

All too frequently there doesn't seem to be a spare minute to cook, or the effort involved hardly seems worthwhile. The answer is often a quick high-calorie snack which may give instant energy and sustain appetite for a while, but, as a habit, it may build up overweight.

If life is always hectic, try to build up a regular meal pattern so that some dishes can be prepared in advance when there is time for cooking. If there's no time to cook vegetables, wholewheat bread and a crunchy vegetable salad are delicious replacements. When an instant snack is inevitable, choose fruit, cheese and wholewheat bread, rather than sweets, crisps (fries) or biscuits (cookies).

**Breakfast**

So often this first meal of the day is rushed or missed completely. But it is important to start the day with breakfast – to provide the body with sufficient energy to last the morning, and avoid the temptation of a mid-morning snack.

Breakfast need not be a heavy meal, or take long to prepare. Fresh fruit or fruit juice, wholewheat toast, an egg and a drink will provide a well-balanced meal. Cereals are popular, especially with children; accompany them with a hot milk drink – such as cocoa or drinking chocolate which will add valuable iron – and they will have a good start to the day.

### Light meal

This may be eaten at midday or in the evening. Include eggs, or cheese – in wholewheat sandwiches or toasted snacks – if they haven't been served at another meal. Wholewheat flans, a cheeseboard, or pancakes (crêpes) with savoury fillings will provide a tasty, nourishing meal. Finish with fresh fruit or yogurt and a refreshing drink. If time is again a problem, a meal-in-a-glass is an excellent quick nourishing snack.

### Main meal

Each main meal should contain some foods rich in protein and plenty of fruit and vegetables, as these are rich sources of vitamins and minerals. If serving a first course, keep it simple – clear soup, grapefruit, fruit juice or salad. For the main course, include a wide variety of dishes in your weekly menu – casseroles, grilled (broiled) meat, fish, egg and cheese dishes. Make sure that meat is lean and aim to serve offal (variety meats) once a week. Always serve vegetables or salad – as an accompaniment – if they do not form the basis of the main course. Complete the meal with cheese and fresh fruit as often as possible. Limit rich puddings and cream to special occasions, and avoid over-sweetening desserts.

### Single meals

It is not difficult to plan well-balanced meals for a family, but catering for oneself can create problems. Some single people take great pleasure in cooking for themselves, but many find it a chore and rely on convenience foods, pre-packed meals or carbohydrate snacks instead. The occasional snack meal, lacking in nutritional value, rarely does any harm because dietary needs are usually made up later in the day. However, if detrimental to health. Even on a shoestring budget, it is still possible to enjoy nutritionally sound meals.

Look at the list of five basic food groups (see page 14) and see which foods can be bought in small portions, and which will store well. In group one, for example, meat may be expensive, or not obtainable in small enough portions, but a single chicken quarter, a portion of liver, kidneys and eggs are all relatively cheap and can be cooked in a variety of appetizing ways. Cheese and yogurt can also be bought in small quantities. Margarine keeps well and can be used for spreading as well as cooking, while a stock of cereals, crispbreads and pulses (legumes) is also useful and can be stored easily. Only fruit and vegetables need to be bought regularly.

Most of the recipes in this book can be prepared in small quantities, or used for several meals. All of the breakfast dishes are easily adapted for single portions and many are suitable for other meals, too. Salads are good for an individual meal – especially if they contain a protein food.

A dessert always makes a meal on your own more appealing, and if you halve the recipes in the fruit and nuts chapter there will be enough for two meals. Try to make a single meal more interesting too, by starting with fruit juice, for example.

### Office meals

Canteen meals tend to be stodgy, pub snacks are usually inadequate, and restaurant meals are expensive, so the answer to a workday lunch is often something eaten at a desk. A packed meal can be a nourishing stop-gap between breakfast and the main evening meal. Be sure to eat something at midday, or tiredness ensues and work suffers.

A packed meal doesn't have to be a dull sandwich, nor just a bunch of lettuce leaves. Ideally it should include something from each of the food groups (see page 14). Pack the meal attractively in a polythene (plastic) box to avoid crushing. Use margarine tubs for salads or fruit and take home-made soup in a flask, or buy milk to drink.

Many of the recipes in this book are perfect for packed meals – especially the salads and savoury flans. Finish with fresh fruit and you will have a nourishing, satisfying meal.

### School meals

Some children prefer a packed lunch for school, and the same general rules apply as for office meals. Children must have easily-handled food, so sandwiches or bread rolls are ideal, but the filling must be adequate and a good source of protein. Use wholewheat bread sandwiched with eggs, cheese, fish and meat, and avoid sweet fillings like jam or bananas as they are low in protein. Do give plenty of variety during the week so that lunch doesn't become dull and unappetizing. Instead of making sandwiches – for example – provide wholewheat rolls, a hard-boiled (cooked) egg and a wedge of cheese, or fingers of lean cold meat to make a change. Complete the meal with fruit and a yogurt, rather than sweets or chocolate biscuits (cookies).

*LIGHT MEAL: Broccoli pancakes (crêpes) (page 163); fruit and cheese.*

# Adding Flavour

One of the problems of changing to a controlled healthy diet is that you may find the food less appetizing at first. When a palate is used to rich sauces and artificial flavours, it is sometimes difficult for it to accept plainly grilled (broiled) meat or fish, simple cakes, or vegetables without butter or creamy dressings, with the same enthusiasm. Careful seasoning and the use of juices, herbs, spices and low-calorie vegetables can, however, make all the difference between a bland diet and one which is tempting but still healthy.

### Extracts and pastes

Yeast or meat extracts can be used to flavour gravy or soup, or they may be spread on toast or bread as a base for an egg or cheese topping. If there is a temptation to eat something sweet with a cup of tea or coffee mid-morning or afternoon, try a thin slice of wholewheat toast lightly spread with a savoury extract or anchovy paste instead.

### Stock (bouillon) cubes

Stock (bouillon) cubes and powders are available in a variety of flavours to suit most savoury dishes. Home-made stock gives the best flavour, but when none is available a stock (bouillon) cube may be used instead, providing the seasoning is carefully adjusted.

### Fruit juices and rinds

Lemon juice is invaluable in the kitchen as it brings out all the natural flavours of the foods with which it is used. A wedge of lemon with fish is a well known accompaniment, but it is also good with veal, chicken and rabbit, and goes well with salads and lightly cooked vegetables. Orange juice is less well-known as an accompaniment, but it may be used for salad dressings and in pork, veal or duck dishes. The sharp juice of Seville oranges is particularly good with fish. Grated orange and lemon rinds also add flavour to dishes as well as providing additional Vitamin C.

### Wine, cider and tomato juice

Thick gravy and sauces will not be missed if meat and fish are cooked in a dry wine, dry (hard) cider or tomato juice instead. These give flavour and colour to food, and the alcohol content is negligible as alcohol is driven off during the cooking process. A few drops of dry sherry, stirred in just before serving, will improve a clear soup or gravy.

### Sugars and syrups

Refined sugar and syrup sweeten foods but add no particular flavouring. Honey, black treacle (molasses) and natural brown sugars, such as Muscovado and molasses sugar, will add a rich flavour and colour to desserts, cakes and other baked goods.

### Vegetables

A few low-calorie vegetables are very useful for adding flavour to savoury dishes. A small quantity of chopped green or red peppers, celery or onions will add colour and texture, while mushrooms or tomatoes make a perfect garnish.

**Salt** is indispensable in the kitchen for it makes all food more palatable and helps to bring out subtle flavours. Sea salt has the finest flavour; it may be bought in flake form, or finely ground, or it may be freshly ground in a salt mill at the table.

**Vanilla** is a fragrant pod (bean) which may be used to flavour sugar, milk and desserts. For convenience it is usually bought in its less expensive, and less subtle form – vanilla essence (extract).

### Herbs

Fresh, frozen or dried herbs will enhance the flavour of most savoury dishes and some sweet ones. Fresh herbs should preferably be used when available. Dried herbs must be used with discretion as their flavour is less subtle; use half of the recommended quantity of fresh herbs in the recipe. A small selection of the most popular herbs will make a world of difference to simple foods.

**Basil** has a fairly strong flavour and is delicious with tomatoes, kebabs, fish and seafood. It is also very good sprinkled sparingly on grilled (broiled) meat or fish.

**Bay** is combined with thyme and parsley in the classic 'bouquet garni', used to flavour all kinds of soups and stews. Bay leaves are also used in marinades, with oily fish, such as mackerel and salmon, and they impart a delicious spicy flavour to milk puddings and egg custards.

**Caraway** seeds are often used to flavour cakes, but they are delicious in cabbage dishes too.

**Chervil** looks like rather delicate parsley. It has a refreshing spicy flavour and is good for light soups and egg dishes.

**Dill** leaves impart a delicious flavour to new potatoes, and to fish. The seeds are used, whole or ground, in lamb stews, soups and in pickled cucumber.

**Fennel** is sometimes known as 'the fish herb' because its slight flavour of aniseed goes so well with all fish dishes.

**Garlic,** used with discretion, is a splendid addition to meat and poultry dishes, and to salads. It should be crushed with a little salt to release the full flavour. Garlic powder is available for those who prefer a mild garlic flavour.

**Horseradish** – grated into cream – is a traditional accompaniment to beef, but it can also be grated and added to beetroot (beet), or coleslaw.

**Marjoram** has a sweet, slightly spicy flavour which improves stuffings, meat and tomato dishes.

**Mint** is usually made into a sauce to serve with lamb, but chopped fresh mint is good with new potatoes, peas and vegetable salads, and can also be used in fruit salads.

**Oregano** is a strongly-flavoured variety of wild marjoram, used extensively in Italian dishes – especially in sauces to serve with pasta.

**Parsley** is often only used as a garnish, but it can be added generously to many dishes, and it is rich in Vitamin C. Add chopped parsley liberally to soups, sauces and cooked vegetables – especially to broad (lima) beans, peas, potatoes and carrots.

**Rosemary** has a sweet, pungent flavour. Traditionally used with lamb, it is also good with beef, pork, chicken and white fish.

**Sage** is a strongly-flavoured herb which goes particularly well with fatty meat, especially pork and duck.

**Savory** looks like thyme, but gives a more subtle flavour to fish and broad (lima) beans.

**Tarragon** gives an excellent flavour to chicken, fish and egg dishes. Make tarragon vinegar by steeping a few sprigs in white wine vinegar and use in salad dressing for a subtle flavour.

**Thyme** is used in bouquet garni and to flavour savoury dishes of all kinds. It has a strong flavour and needs to be used sparingly.

## Spices

A hint of spice helps to bring out the flavour in both sweet and savoury dishes. Freshly ground spice has a far better flavour than ready-ground.

**Allspice** is also known as pimento or Jamaica pepper. It is called allspice because the flavour is like a mixture of cloves, cinnamon and nutmeg. It is not, however, the same as mixed spice.

**Cayenne** is a hot and stimulating ground pepper.

**Cinnamon** is a spice from the bark of an evergreen tree.

Ground cinnamon is a favourite flavouring for cakes. Cinnamon sticks gives a subtle flavour to many desserts, savoury dishes and drinks.

**Cloves** are very pungent and may be used, whole or ground, in sweet and savoury dishes; the flavour goes particularly well with apples.

**Curry Powder** is a mixture of many spices and varies widely in composition. Many people prefer to grind the different spices freshly and mix them just before use. A pinch of ready-made curry powder will spice up savoury dishes, sauces and salad dressings.

**Ginger** has a distinctive flavour which is very popular for cakes and biscuits; it is also an important ingredient in curries and Chinese dishes. For a pleasant flavour, sprinkle a little on meat or chicken before grilling (broiling).

**Mace** is the outer husk of nutmeg and has a similar, though milder flavour. A pinch of mace will help to bring out the flavour of cold meat and poultry dishes.

**Nutmeg** is used to flavour cakes, desserts and vegetables, as well as hot drinks.

**Paprika** is made from the fruit of the sweet pepper and has a slightly sweet flavour. It is good in meat and poultry dishes, and its bright red colouring makes it a useful garnish.

**Pepper** tastes best when freshly ground. Black pepper suits most dishes, but use white pepper in delicate dishes and sauces which will be spoiled by specks of black.

# Cooking for Healthy Eating

Having chosen the right foods for a healthy diet, it is just as important to make sure that they are not then ruined by poor preparation and cooking. The most perfect vegetable will be tasteless and of little nutritional value if it is boiled for an hour in a large pan of water; delicate fish will be spoiled if boiled furiously in liquid, or fried in a bath of fat; and crisp, fresh-tasting apples will be unrecognizable if stewed endlessly in sweetened water. For maximum nutrient retention, eat fruit and vegetables raw as often as possible.

It is very easy to become careless about basic cooking methods, and not to bother about the required quantity of cooking liquid, or exact cooking time. To ensure you really do get the optimum value from the dishes in this book, check that you are preparing foods in the best possible way to retain their nutritional value.

### Boiling and Simmering

Many foods which are referred to as 'boiled' are best cooked at a temperature below boiling point, termed simmering. Meat, fish and chicken will be tough if boiled fast; the liquid should be brought to boiling point at a steady pace, then the temperature should be lowered so that the liquid only just bubbles – or simmers. Vegetables should be added to boiling water and cooked quickly; always use minimum liquid.

### Poaching

This process is similar to simmering, but is even more gentle; the liquid should only just be quivering. This method is used for food of a delicate consistency which would be spoiled by high heat. It is a particularly good way of cooking fish, eggs and fruit so that their texture and shape are retained. The liquid used for poaching can often be used in an accompanying sauce for the finished dish, so that no flavour is lost from the main ingredient.

### Stewing

This may take place on top of the cooker in a flameproof casserole or heavy-based saucepan, or in the oven. Meat and vegetables are cooked very gently in just enough liquid to cover them. It is an ideal method for cooking cheaper cuts of meat so that they become really tender. Meat for stewing must have a small quantity of fat otherwise it may become hard and dry during cooking.

For a brown stew, first seal the meat in a little oil; this helps the meat keep its shape and retain all its flavour, as well as lightly colouring the finished casserole. For a white stew, cover the meat with cold water and bring slowly to the boil, then skim off any scum so that the liquid remains clear and the meat is pale. Add vegetables and flavourings when the liquid comes to the boil, then cover and simmer until tender. The latter process is always carried out on top of the cooker.

## Braising

This is similar to stewing, but is used for better cuts of meat. The ideal pan to use is an iron casserole so that it can be used on top of the cooker and in the oven. Brown the meat on all sides in a little oil and then remove from the pan. Add a selection of diced vegetables to the pan – onions, carrots, celery, etc. – and cook gently without browning. Place the

meat on top of the vegetables, and add a little liquid – just enough to cover about a quarter of the meat. Cover the pan tightly and simmer for about 45 minutes on top of the cooker, then continue cooking in a moderate oven (170°C/325°F, Gas Mark 3) for about 2 hours. Serve the meat with a gravy made from the pan juices.

Vegetables, such as chicory (endive) and celery hearts, can be braised in a similar way – in a little stock or water, seasoned and flavoured with herbs.

## Steaming

This long, slow, thorough method of cooking is especially suitable for vegetables, fish and puddings. The food – cooked in a special steamer over a pan of water and covered with a tight fitting lid – is exposed to and surrounded by concentrated steam. The water in the saucepan must never stop boiling, or cooking ceases, and more boiling water should be added once or twice during cooking.

## Roasting

True roasting is carried out in front of an open fire and the meat has to be regularly turned and basted. Today we 'roast' meat in an oven, but this dry all-round heat actually bakes food, and the semblance of a roast is only achieved by basting, which keeps the meat moist and juicy. As the meat is generally surrounded by fat, it is not really suitable for those who wish to avoid animal fats in their diet. The meat can, however, be placed on a rack in the pan so that some of the fat drains away from the meat.

Vegetables such as potatoes, parsnips and onions can be added to the roasting pan to cook in the meat juices. When the meat is cooked, skim the juices and use to make gravy.

## Grilling (Broiling)

This is an excellent method of cooking good quality meat, poultry and fish, particularly where fat is to be avoided. When grilling (broiling) red meat – such as steak, lamb chops, liver or kidney – brush lightly with oil and place under a high heat to seal in the juices. Reduce the heat and cook according to taste; if the meat is to be well done, lower the grill (broiler) pan from the heat to prevent it becoming hard and dry. Turn once or twice during cooking, using tongs so that the surface is not pierced and juices released and lost.

White meat – such as veal, chicken or pork – and fish should be grilled (broiled) at a moderate heat throughout. These foods need longer cooking than red meats, and if sealed first, the hard outer surface will prevent heat from reaching the inner meat. Cook them further from the heat, too, to prevent them drying.

The best thickness for grilled meat is about 2.5 cm (1 inch), though fish may obviously be a little thinner. Do not use salt on meat when grilling (broiling) as it tends to harden the meat.

Tomatoes and mushrooms are traditional accompaniments to grilled (broiled) food: place mushrooms on grill (broiler) rack to cook in the meat juices; brush tomatoes lightly with oil and add to the pan when the heat is lowered, or serve raw.

## Frying

Frying, as we all know, means cooking food in preheated shallow or deep fat. People who wish to follow a healthy eating pattern should try to avoid fried food, as a certain amount of fat is bound to be absorbed by the food during frying. If you do have to fry food – for example, to brown meat before stewing – then oil is the best frying medium. Heat the oil before adding food, and only fry a little food at a time, as too much will cool the oil and the food will become heavy and greasy; reheat the oil before adding more food. Always drain fried food thoroughly on a wire rack or crumpled kitchen paper towels and serve at once.

# The Healthy Way to a Slimmer Figure

Overweight or obesity is simply the result of consuming too much food, the excess being stored as body fat. It is most important to avoid excess weight. Apart from being unattractive and depressing, statistics show that fat people are more likely to suffer from heart disease, circulatory problems, kidney diseases and diabetes. Obesity also aggravates a range of other disorders, such as arthritis, respiratory diseases and back problems.

Extra weight does not, of course, appear overnight; it accumulates over an extended period of eating more food than the body requires. If you are overweight, it does not necessarily mean that you eat a lot but you are eating more than you need. Many factors – such as age, sex, height and the amount of physical activity you do – all affect energy needs, so individual calorie requirements vary considerably. Some people are inclined to put on weight more easily than others simply because they have a low metabolic rate; i.e. they require less energy than most people to maintain basic living processes, such as heartbeat, breathing and circulation. So each person's calorie requirements will be slightly different.

The only way to lose weight is to eat foods which provide less energy than the body needs so that the body will draw on fat reserves for energy. The safest and most effective way to slim is to cut down on energy-rich foods and follow a diet based on fresh wholefoods – rich in the vital nutrients required to keep you healthy. Extra physical activity will also help you to slim – and keep you fit. You could lose weight by disregarding this advice and eating your daily calorie allowance in chocolate, for instance, but you would soon begin to miss some important nutrients and health would inevitably suffer.

Avoid 'crash diets' designed to bring about a rapid weight loss. Followed for a few days they may slim off extra inches for a special occasion but they rarely bring about a permanent weight loss. If crash diets are followed for any length of time they can deprive the body of essential nutrients, resulting in tiredness, irritability and such unpleasant disorders as ketosis.

If you intend to lose a considerable amount of weight, it is always advisable to see a doctor first. For those who want to trim off a little surplus fat – a carefully calorie-controlled diet which includes sufficient quantities of the necessary nutrients will maintain general health.

## Calorie Allowances

|  | Daily calorie needs for weight maintenance | Daily calorie allowance for weight loss |
|---|---|---|
| Average Man | 2500 to 3500 | 1400 to 1600 |
| Average Woman | 1800 to 2500 | 1000 to 1200 |
| Active Teenager | 2300 to 2800 | 1400 to 1600 |

If you stick to the appropriate calorie allowance for weight loss by cutting down on energy-rich foods, your body will draw on fat reserves and you will start to lose weight. About 800 to 1000 calories will be taken from body fat each day, and this should give an average weight loss of 0.5 to 1 kg (1½ to 2lb) each week.

To start with, weight loss is often quite dramatic but then adopts a slower steady rate. The initial quick weight losses are largely fluid losses; subsequent slower losses are generally fat losses.

To check your progress, weigh yourself once or twice a week on the same scales and at roughly the same time of day. After the first week, aim for a gradual weight loss as this is better for health and is more likely to result in a permanently lowered calorie intake.

## Planning your slimming diet

Never miss a meal completely – several small meals are better than one large meal each day. When you start dieting, relieve hunger pangs by nibbling small pieces of raw carrot, celery, cucumber, radish and apple. If you have a family to cook for, you can enjoy the dishes in this book, but omit the accompanying potatoes or bread. Don't add extra fat or oil when cooking, leave gravy unthickened, and have fresh fruit instead of a pudding. Eat plenty of citrus fruits, berry fruits, melon, rhubarb, tomatoes, celery, Brussels sprouts, lettuce, cress and cucumber.

Don't try to lose weight by giving up liquids. Water is calorie-free and is needed for normal functioning of the body. Herbal and lemon teas, black coffee, low-calorie fruit juices and low-calorie soft drinks may be taken throughout the day.

Avoid foods which contain starch and sugar. Cut out sweets, jam, sugar in drinks, puddings, cakes, biscuits (cookies), canned fruit, thickened soups and sauces, and pasta. Bread and cereals contain valuable minerals and vitamins and some protein, so eat a moderate amount of them which will also help to reduce your appetite for sweet foods. Avoid fatty foods, such as fried foods, cream, fat, meat, oil and mayonnaise dressings. Use a low-fat spread for bread, glazing vegetables and making sauces; use a liquid or powder sweetener instead of sugar.

If possible, cut out alcoholic drinks completely as they are high in calories. If you have to drink socially – a small glass of dry white wine is the best choice – or have a low calorie tonic water with a slice of lemon and ice cubes if you can manage without alcohol.

To ensure good health, it is advisable to eat the following foods every day: 300 ml (½ pint) milk, 25 g (1 oz) cheese, 1 egg, 75 g (3 oz) bread, 1 orange and up to 15 g (½ oz) butter. Have at least one portion of liver and oily fish each week, and be sure to have enough iron-rich foods – such as egg, sardines, red meat and leafy green vegetables.

Your main meal of the day should include a high protein food – such as meat, poultry or fish – and the other should contain cheese or eggs, unless of course you are a vegetarian.

Use a calorie chart to check your shopping. Cottage cheese and curd cheese are lower in calories than hard cheeses. Look for labels which say 'low-fat' or 'medium-fat' on dairy products, such as cheeses and yogurt, and use those for the recipes in this book.

Fat is a concentrated source of calories – so always drain excess fat or oil from food. Trim fat from meat and avoid frying – bake, boil, poach, steam, braise or grill (broil) instead. As far as possible, eat vegetables and fruit raw so that none of their nutrients are lost during cooking.

# Calorie Chart

The following chart provides a comprehensive list of food calorie (kcal) and kilojoule (kJ) values. Unless otherwise stated, the values refer to a quantity of 25 g/ 1 oz and this is the edible portion, i.e. without bone, skin, etc.

| Food | Calories | Kilojoules (kJ) | Food | Calories | Kilojoules (kJ) |
|---|---|---|---|---|---|
| Almonds, ground | 180 | 800 | Chives | 10 | 50 |
| shelled | 170 | 750 | Chocolate, milk | 165 | 700 |
| paste | 115 | 500 | plain | 155 | 650 |
| Anchovy fillets (6 fillets) | 40 | 150 | Chutney, average | 50 | 200 |
| Apples (1 medium) | 40 | 150 | Cod, raw | 20 | 90 |
| Apricots, canned (1 medium) | 30 | 150 | Cod's roe, raw | 35 | 150 |
| dried | 50 | 200 | Consommé, canned (300 ml/ ½ pint) | 40-65 | 150-250 |
| fresh (1 medium) | 5 | 20 | Cornflakes, and most cereals | 105 | 450 |
| Artichokes, Globe | 5 | 20 | Cornflour (Cornstarch) | 100 | 450 |
| Jerusalem | 5 | 20 | Corn Kernels, see Sweetcorn | | |
| Asparagus | 5 | 20 | Courgettes (Zucchini) | 2 | 10 |
| Aubergines (Eggplants) | 5 | 20 | Crabmeat, boiled | 35 | 150 |
| Avocado Pear (1 medium) | 250 | 1,050 | Cream, double (heavy) (2 tablespoons) | 130 | 550 |
| Bacon, lean raw | 115 | 500 | single (light) (2 tablespoons) | 60 | 250 |
| gammon raw | 90 | 400 | soured (sour) (2 tablespoons) | 55 | 200 |
| Bamboo Shoots, canned | 8 | 30 | Cucumber | 3 | 10 |
| Bananas (1 medium) | 60 | 250 | Currants | 70 | 300 |
| Bass, steamed | 20 | 80 | Damsons | 10 | 50 |
| Bean Sprouts, raw | 8 | 30 | Duck, meat only, raw | 70 | 300 |
| Beans, baked | 25 | 100 | Eggplant, see Aubergines | | |
| broad (lima beans) | 10 | 50 | Eggs, whole (1 small) | 70 | 300 |
| butter | 75 | 300 | (1 large) | 90 | 400 |
| French | 5 | 20 | white | 10 | 50 |
| haricot (navy beans) | 75 | 300 | yolk | 100 | 450 |
| runner | 5 | 20 | Flour | 100 | 450 |
| Beef, very lean | 75 | 300 | Garlic (1 clove) | 2 | 10 |
| Beetroot (beet) raw | 10 | 50 | Gelatine (Gelatin) powder (8 teaspoons) | 100 | 450 |
| Bilberries, raw | 10 | 50 | Ginger, fresh stem | 85 | 350 |
| Blackberries | 10 | 50 | Gooseberries, raw | 10 | 45 |
| Blackcurrants | 10 | 50 | Grapefruit, flesh | 5 | 20 |
| Blueberries, see Bilberries | | | whole (1 medium) | 30 | 150 |
| Bread, white or brown | 70 | 300 | Grapes | 15 | 60 |
| (average slice, large loaf) | 80 | 350 | Haddock, fresh, raw | 20 | 90 |
| (average slice, small loaf) | 50 | 200 | smoked | 20 | 90 |
| Broccoli | 5 | 20 | Hake fillets, raw | 25 | 100 |
| Brussels Sprouts | 10 | 50 | Halibut, raw | 30 | 150 |
| Butter | 225 | 950 | Ham, lean only, boiled | 60 | 250 |
| Buttermilk (600 ml/ 1 pint) | 235 | 1,000 | York, raw | 145 | 600 |
| Cabbage, red or white | 5 | 20 | Herrings, raw | 65 | 280 |
| Carrots | 5 | 20 | Honey | 80 | 350 |
| Cauliflower | 5 | 20 | Ice Cream | 55 | 250 |
| Celery | 3 | 10 | Jam | 75 | 300 |
| Cheese, Austrian smoked | 80 | 350 | Jelly, made up (600 ml/ 1 pint) | 420 | 1,800 |
| Camembert | 90 | 400 | cubes | 75 | 300 |
| Cheddar | 120 | 500 | Kidneys, raw | 30-35 | 150 |
| Cheshire | 110 | 450 | Kippers, raw | 30 | 150 |
| Cottage | 30 | 150 | Lamb, very lean only | 75 | 300 |
| Cream | 230 | 950 | Lard | 260 | 1,100 |
| Curd | 40 | 150 | Leeks, raw | 10 | 50 |
| Danish Blue | 105 | 450 | Lemon, raw | 5 | 20 |
| Edam | 90 | 400 | juice (2 tablespoons) | 2 | 10 |
| Gouda | 95 | 400 | Lentils, raw | 85 | 350 |
| Gruyère | 130 | 550 | Lettuce, raw | 3 | 10 |
| Leicester | 110 | 450 | Liver, raw | 40-45 | 150-200 |
| Parmesan | 120 | 500 | Loganberries | 5 | 20 |
| Stilton | 135 | 600 | Macaroni, raw | 100 | 400 |
| Cherries, fresh | 10 | 50 | boiled | 30 | 150 |
| glacé | 60 | 250 | Mackerel | 30 | 150 |
| Chicken, flesh only, raw | 35 | 150 | Margarine | 225 | 1,000 |
| Chicory (Belgian endive) | 3 | 10 | Marmalade | 75 | 300 |

| Food | Calories | Kilojoules (kJ) |
|---|---|---|
| Marrow (Squash), boiled | 2 | 10 |
| Melon | 5 | 20 |
| Milk, whole (600 ml / 1 pint) | 380 | 1,600 |
| skimmed (600 ml / 1 pint) | 190 | 800 |
| Mushrooms, dried | | |
| fresh | 2 | 10 |
| Nuts, Almonds, shelled | 170 | 750 |
| Brazils, shelled | 180 | 800 |
| Chestnuts, shelled | 50 | 200 |
| Peanuts, shelled | 170 | 750 |
| Peanuts, shelled, roasted and salted | 180 | 800 |
| Walnuts, shelled | 155 | 650 |
| Oil, vegetable (30 ml / 1 fl oz) | 250 | 1,050 |
| olive (30 ml / 1 fl oz) | 265 | 1,100 |
| Olives (8-10) | 25 | 100 |
| Onions, raw | 5 | 20 |
| Oranges (1 medium) | 40 | 150 |
| juice (30 ml / 1 fl oz) | 11 | 50 |
| Parsnips, raw | 5 | 20 |
| Peaches, raw (1 medium) | 40 | 150 |
| Pears, raw (1 medium) | 40 | 150 |
| Peas, canned | 20 | 90 |
| canned, processed | 25 | 100 |
| dried | 30 | 150 |
| fresh, boiled | 15 | 60 |
| frozen | 20 | 90 |
| Peppers, red or green | 10 | 50 |
| Pickles, sweet | 37 | 150 |
| Pineapple, canned | 20 | 90 |
| fresh | 15 | 60 |
| Plaice, raw | 15 | 60 |
| Plums, raw | 10 | 50 |
| Pork, very lean only | 35 | 150 |
| Potatoes, raw | 25 | 100 |
| old, boiled | 23 | 100 |
| old, chips (French fries) | 68 | 290 |
| old, roast | 35 | 150 |
| new, boiled | 21 | 90 |
| crisps (chips) | 159 | 650 |
| sweet, boiled | 23 | 100 |
| Prawns (Shrimps), flesh only | 30 | 150 |
| whole, raw | 10 | 50 |
| Rabbit, meat only, raw | 50 | 200 |
| Radishes, raw | 5 | 20 |
| Raspberries, raw | 5 | 20 |
| Redcurrants, raw | 5 | 20 |
| Rhubarb, raw | 2 | 10 |
| Rice, raw | 100 | 450 |
| boiled | 35 | 150 |
| Salmon, canned | 40 | 150 |
| fresh, raw | 55 | 250 |
| smoked | 45 | 200 |
| Sardines, canned | 85 | 350 |
| Sausages, average, raw | 100 | 400 |
| Scallions, see Spring Onions | | |
| Scallops (Sea Scallops) | 30 | 150 |
| Sole, raw | 15 | 60 |
| Soup, consommé (300 ml / ½ pint) | 40-65 | 150-250 |
| thin, e.g. chicken noodle (300 ml / ½ pint) | 65-100 | 300-400 |
| thick (300 ml / ½ pint) | 90-200 | 400-800 |
| Spaghetti, boiled | 35 | 150 |
| raw | 105 | 400 |
| Spinach | 5 | 20 |
| Spring Greens | 3 | 10 |
| Spring Onions (Scallions) | 10 | 50 |
| Squash, see Marrow | | |

| Food | Calories | Kilojoules (kJ) |
|---|---|---|
| Stock Cube (each) | 15 | 60 |
| Strawberries | 5 | 20 |
| Suet | 260 | 1,100 |
| Sugar, white and brown | 110 | 500 |
| Sweetcorn, canned or frozen | 25 | 100 |
| on the cob | 35 | 150 |
| Syrup | 85 | 350 |
| Tangerines | 5 | 20 |
| Tomatoes, ketchup (catsup) (30 ml / 1 fl oz) | 28 | 130 |
| purée (paste) | 40 | 150 |
| raw | 5 | 20 |
| Tongue | 85 | 350 |
| Trout, raw | 25 | 100 |
| Tuna, canned in oil | 75 | 300 |
| Turbot, steamed | 30 | 150 |
| Turkey, meat only, raw | 35 | 150 |
| Turnips, raw | 5 | 20 |
| Veal fillet, raw | 30 | 150 |
| Vinegar (30 ml / 1 fl oz) | 1 | 5 |
| Water Chestnuts | 23 | 90 |
| Watercress | 5 | 20 |
| Watermelon | 5 | 20 |
| Whiting, raw | 15 | 60 |
| Yogurt, natural (unflavored) low fat | | |
| (30 ml / 1 fl oz) | 15 | 50 |
| (142 g / 5 oz carton) | 75 | 300 |
| fruit flavored (142 g / 5 oz carton) | 125 | 500 |
| Zucchini, see Courgettes | | |

**Drinks**

| Food | Calories | Kilojoules (kJ) |
|---|---|---|
| Bacardi (1 measure) | 63 | 250 |
| Beer, bottle stout (600 ml / 1 pint) | 200 | 800 |
| brown ale (600 ml / 1 pint) | 160 | 650 |
| draught bitter (600 ml / 1 pint) | 180 | 800 |
| draught mild (600 ml / 1 pint) | 140 | 600 |
| lager (600 ml / 1 pint) | 150 | 600 |
| pale ale (600 ml / 1 pint) | 180 | 800 |
| Brandy (liqueur glass) | 75 | 300 |
| Bourbon (liqueur glass) | 65 | 280 |
| Campari (1 measure) | 120 | 500 |
| Cider, dry (600 ml / 1 pint) | 200 | 800 |
| sweet (600 ml / 1 pint) | 240 | 1,000 |
| Cocktails (vary according to ingredients) | 115-300 | 500-1,000 |
| Gin (1 measure) | 55 | 200 |
| Liqueurs (vary according to type) | 65-90 | 300-400 |
| Port (1 measure) | 75 | 300 |
| Rum (1 measure) | 75 | 300 |
| Sherry, dry (1 measure) | 55 | 200 |
| sweet (1 measure) | 65 | 280 |
| Vermouth, dry (1 measure) | 55 | 200 |
| sweet (1 measure) | 75 | 300 |
| Vodka (1 measure) | 65 | 280 |
| Whisky (1 measure) | 60 | 250 |
| Wine, dry (150 ml / ¼ pint) | 90 | 400 |
| sweet (150 ml / ¼ pint) | 115 | 500 |

**Soft Drinks**

| Food | Calories | Kilojoules (kJ) |
|---|---|---|
| Apple Juice, unsweetened (small glass) | 50 | 200 |
| Blackcurrant concentrate (1 tablespoon) | 35 | 150 |
| Grapefruit juice, unsweetened (small glass) | 55 | 200 |
| Lemonade (600 ml / 1 pint) | 120 | 500 |
| Orange Juice, unsweetened (small glass) | 60 | 250 |
| Tomato Juice (small glass) | 25 | 100 |
| Low-calorie Minerals | 0 | 0 |
| Low-calorie Orange Squash (30 ml / 1 fl oz) | 5 | 20 |
| Low-calorie Lemon Squash (30 ml / 1 fl oz) | 2 | 10 |

# BREAKFASTS

Many nutritionists believe breakfast to be the most important meal of the day, yet a great number of people go without it, including children. Some people cannot face food in the morning, others are trying to slim, and some say they simply haven't the time to prepare and eat a meal at breakfast time.

Breakfast comes at the end of an 8 to 10 hour 'fast'. If it is ignored, the body may not receive any food for a further 4 to 5 hours until the midday meal. Not surprisingly, the body cannot function as effectively if it is deprived of nourishment. The findings of a 10-year research project, known as The Iowa Breakfast Studies show just how important this first meal of the day is.

121 people took part in the project, including men and women of all ages, and older boys and girls, from a variety of occupations and different social and economic groups. Over a period of weeks they were given different breakfasts and asked to perform a series of physical and mental tests. The same tests were also performed by the subjects when they had eaten no breakfast at all.

The study showed that people were most energetic and mentally alert after eating a breakfast which provided a quarter of their daily recommended intake of protein and energy. They were able to work well, reacted quickly and did not tire easily. When the same people missed breakfast completely, their work output was lower, they were less mentally alert, less energetic and were very hungry by mid-morning. A small breakfast containing less than the recommended intake of calories and protein produced less efficient work and the subjects were hungry by mid

morning; similar results were found if breakfast provided sufficient energy but not enough protein.

So it is important to start the day with a good supply of nutrients for sufficient mental and physical energy to take you through until lunchtime. If you enjoy a cooked breakfast, it is well worth the little extra time required to prepare and cook one. Try a Country grill (broil) (page 37) or Farmhouse scramble (page 34) as a healthy change from traditional fried eggs and bacon.

If however, you haven't the time or appetite for a cooked meal first thing in the morning, necessary nutrients can equally well be obtained from cereals and fruit. Meusli (page 32) can be made in advance and stored ready for use. Served with milk or yogurt, cereals provide valuable protein, B group vitamins and minerals. A little natural brown sugar or honey can be added for sweetening. Top with fresh citrus fruit or serve with a glass of fruit juice and you will obtain a good supply of Vitamin C – which is not only essential in itself, it helps the body to absorb valuable iron from cereals and bread. Wholewheat bread or toast to round off breakfast ensures a good addition of dietry fibre to aid digestion.

If appetite is completely lacking early in the morning, it may be due to a late meal the night before, or it may simply be a bad habit which needs breaking. For a light sustaining start to the day try a Banana flip (page 31) or Breakfast in a glass (page 30) rather than avoiding food altogether. As your body gets used to the idea of breakfast, you will find your appetite will improve and you will be able to increase the quantity and variety of food you consume, so breakfast becomes as enjoyable as any other meal of the day.

*Citrus starter (page 30); Farmhouse scramble (page 32); Baked stuffed tomatoes (page 41); Bran bread (page 136)*

# Citrus Starter

| Metric/Imperial | American |
| --- | --- |
| 2 oranges, peel and pith removed and divided into segments | 2 oranges, peel and pith removed and divided into segments |
| 1 grapefruit, peel and pith removed and divided into segments | 1 grapefruit, peel and pith removed and divided into segments |
| 25 g / 1 oz seedless raisins | 3 tablespoons seedless raisins |
| 25 g / 1 oz walnuts, chopped | ¼ cup chopped walnuts |
| 2 tablespoons clear honey | 2 tablespoons clear honey |

Put all the ingredients in a bowl and mix well. Cover and leave in the refrigerator overnight.

The next morning, divide equally between 4 individual serving bowls.

**Serves 4**

# Spiced Grapefruit Refresher

*This makes an excellent breakfast starter, but may also be served as a first course for a more formal meal.*

| Metric/Imperial | American |
| --- | --- |
| 2 grapefruit | 2 grapefruit |
| 25 g / 1 oz Muscovado sugar | 1½ tablespoons Barbados sugar |
| pinch of ground ginger | pinch of ground ginger |
| pinch of ground cinnamon | pinch of ground cinnamon |

Cut the grapefruit in half, then separate the segments from the surrounding skin. Mix together the sugar and spices, then sprinkle over the grapefruit.

Cover with plastic cling film, then chill in the refrigerator overnight before serving.

**Serves 4**

# Prune Fluff

*This makes a delicious starter for breakfast for those who like fruit but may dislike the idea of prunes.*

| Metric/Imperial | American |
| --- | --- |
| 225 g / 8 oz prunes | 1⅓ cups prunes |
| juice of ½ orange | juice of ½ orange |
| 40 g / 1½ oz Muscovado sugar | 2 tablespoons Barbados sugar |
| 300 ml / ½ pint natural yogurt | 1¼ cups unflavored yogurt |

Put the prunes in a bowl, then pour on enough boiling water to just cover. Leave to stand overnight until the prunes are plump and have absorbed the liquid.

The next morning, remove the stones (seeds) and work the flesh in an electric blender with the remaining ingredients for 45 seconds until thoroughly mixed and creamy.

Divide equally between 4 individual serving dishes and serve chilled.

**Serves 4**

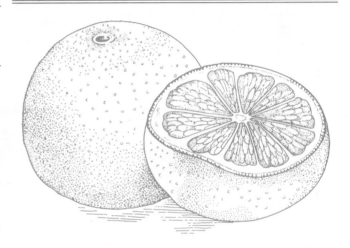

# Breakfast in a Glass

*This makes a quick breakfast or lunch which is both refreshing and sustaining and is ideal if you are eating alone.*

| Metric/Imperial | American |
| --- | --- |
| 300 ml / ½ pint orange juice | 1¼ cups orange juice |
| 1 tablespoon lemon juice | 1 tablespoon lemon juice |
| 1 tablespoon clear honey | 1 tablespoon clear honey |
| 1 tablespoon wheatgerm | 1 tablespoon wheatgerm |
| 1 egg | 1 egg |

Put all the ingredients in an electric blender and blend for 30 seconds. Pour into a chilled glass and serve immediately.

**Serves 1**

# Banana Flip

*This makes a tempting and nourishing breakfast, particularly for children who refuse to eat a cooked meal; it is equally good for a quick light lunch.*

| Metric/Imperial | American |
|---|---|
| 4 bananas | 4 bananas |
| 600 ml / 1 pint milk | 2½ cups milk |
| 225 g / 8 oz cottage cheese | 1 cup cottage cheese |
| 25 g / 1 oz Muscovado sugar | 1½ tablespoons Barbados sugar |
| pinch of ground cinnamon | pinch of ground cinnamon |

Peel the bananas, then cut them into small pieces. Place the chopped bananas and milk in an electric blender. Blend for 30 seconds. Add the cottage cheese and sugar and blend for a further 30 seconds.

Pour into chilled glasses and sprinkle with cinnamon. Serve immediately.

**Serves 4**

# Banana Honey Shake

| Metric/Imperial | American |
|---|---|
| 2 bananas | 2 bananas |
| 1 tablespoon wheatgerm | 1 tablespoon wheatgerm |
| 600 ml / 1 pint milk | 2½ cups milk |
| 2 tablespoons clear honey | 2 tablespoons clear honey |

Peel the bananas, then cut them into small pieces. Work to a purée with the remaining ingredients in an electric blender for 30 seconds.

Pour into chilled glasses and serve immediately.

**Serves 2**

# Morning Starter

| Metric/Imperial | American |
|---|---|
| 300 ml / ½ pint orange or grapefruit juice | 1¼ cups orange or grapefruit juice |
| 2 tablespoons clear honey | 2 tablespoons clear honey |

Chill the fruit juice in the refrigerator overnight.

The next morning, put 1 tablespoon honey into each of 2 chilled glasses, pour in the fruit juice, then stir briskly until well mixed.

Serve before muesli, wholewheat toast or a cooked breakfast dish.

**Serves 2**

# Muesli

*For a good muesli base, it is advisable to use a mixture of different grains and seeds. Bran is very dry, wheatgerm has a strong flavour and sesame seeds are very hard, so ingredients should be used sparingly.*

| Metric/Imperial | American |
|---|---|
| 225 g / 8 oz rolled oats | 2¼ cups rolled oats |
| 225 g / 8 oz barley flakes or kernels, sesame and sunflower seeds, bran and wheatgerm, mixed according to taste | 2¼ cups barley flakes or kernels, sesame and sunflower seeds, bran and wheatgerm, mixed according to taste |
| 50 g / 2 oz mixed nuts, chopped | ½ cup mixed chopped nuts |
| 50 g / 2 oz seedless raisins and coarsely chopped dried fruit (apples, apricots, dates, figs), mixed according to taste | ⅓ cup seedless raisins and coarsely chopped dried fruit (apples, apricots, dates, figs), mixed according to taste |

Put the oats in a bowl, then stir in the remaining ingredients.

Store in a tin or other airtight container and use as required. Serve with brown sugar or honey and milk, cream or yogurt. Fresh fruit may be added according to season.

**Makes 500 g / 1¼ lb / 5¼ cups muesli**

# Swiss Breakfast

| Metric/Imperial | American |
|---|---|
| 1 tablespoon wheatgerm | 1 tablespoon wheatgerm |
| 1 tablespoon rolled oats | 1 tablespoon rolled oats |
| 4 tablespoons water | ¼ cup water |
| 1 teaspoon lemon juice | 1 teaspoon lemon juice |
| 1 dessert apple | 1 dessert apple |
| 1 tablespoon clear honey | 1 tablespoon clear honey |
| 2 tablespoons single cream | 2 tablespoons light cream |
| 25 g / 1 oz hazelnuts, chopped | ¼ cup chopped filberts |
| TO SERVE: | TO SERVE: |
| fresh fruit in season (bananas, grapes, peaches, raspberries, strawberries, etc.) | fresh fruit in season (bananas, grapes, peaches, raspberries, strawberries, etc.) |

Put the wheatgerm, oats and water in a serving bowl. Cover and leave in the refrigerator overnight.

The next morning, stir in the lemon juice. Do not peel the apple but grate it coarsely, then stir into the oat mixture with the honey and cream. Sprinkle on the nuts and serve immediately, with fresh fruit in season.

**Serves 1**

*ABOVE RIGHT: Granola; Fruit muesli with yogurt*
*BELOW: Swiss breakfast; Muesli*

# Fruit Muesli with Yogurt

| Metric/Imperial | American |
|---|---|
| 90 g / 3½ oz rolled oats | 1 cup rolled oats |
| 4 tablespoons wheatgerm | ¼ cup wheatgerm |
| 2 tablespoons dried milk powder | 2 tablespoons dried milk solids |
| 2 tablespoons clear honey | 2 tablespoons clear honey |
| 450 ml / ¾ pint milk | 2 cups milk |
| 50 g / 2 oz prunes, stoned and chopped | ⅓ cup prunes, pitted and chopped |
| 50 g / 2 oz stoned dates, chopped | ⅓ cup pitted dates, chopped |
| 25 g / 1 oz seedless raisins | 3 tablespoons seedless raisins |
| 25 g / 1 oz walnuts, chopped | ¼ cup chopped walnuts |
| 1 orange, peel and pith removed and divided into segments | 1 orange, peel and pith removed and divided into segments |
| 1 grapefruit, peel and pith removed and divided into segments | 1 grapefruit, peel and pith removed and divided into segments |
| 100 g / 4 oz grapes, halved and seeded | 1 cup grapes, halved and seeded |
| 300 ml / ½ pint natural yogurt (optional) | 1¼ cups unflavored yogurt (optional) |

Put the oats in a bowl, add the wheatgerm, milk powder (solids), honey, milk, dried fruit and nuts and stir well to mix. Cover and leave in the refrigerator overnight.

The next morning, divide the muesli equally between 4 individual serving bowls, then arrange the prepared fruit on top. Serve immediately, topped with yogurt, if liked.

**Serves 4**

# Granola

| Metric/Imperial | American |
|---|---|
| muesli base (see page 32) | muesli base (see page 32) |
| 100 g / 4 oz desiccated coconut | 1⅓ cups shredded coconut |
| 100 g / 4 oz vegetable margarine | ½ cup vegetable margarine |
| 100 g / 4 oz clear honey | ⅓ cup clear honey |

Put the muesli base in a bowl, add the coconut and stir well to mix.

Put the margarine and honey in a pan and heat very gently until just melted, stirring occasionally. Pour into the dry mixture and stir well to mix.

Sprinkle the mixture into a roasting pan and bake in a preheated moderately hot oven (190°C / 375°F, Gas Mark 5) for about 20 minutes until golden and crisp. Stir the mixture once or twice during baking, so that it does not burn on top.

Leave the granola to cool, then store in a tin or other airtight container and use as required. Serve as for muesli base with milk, cream or yogurt and fresh fruit according to season.

**Makes about 1 kg / 2 lb / 9 cups granola**

# Poached Eggs on Wholewheat Toast

**Metric/Imperial**
300 ml / ½ pint water
pinch of salt
4 eggs
4 slices wholewheat bread
25 g / 1 oz vegetable
    margarine
1 teaspoon yeast extract

**American**
1¼ cups water
pinch of salt
4 eggs
4 slices wholewheat bread
2 tablespoons vegetable
    margarine
1 teaspoon Brewer's yeast

Put the water and salt in a small pan and bring to the boil. Crack one egg into a cup. Using a spoon, stir the water very quickly to create a 'whirlpool'. Slide the egg into the water, then simmer for 3 minutes until the egg is firmly set.

Toast one slice of bread lightly on both sides, then spread with margarine and a little yeast extract. Remove the egg from the pan with a slotted spoon and place on top of the toast. Serve immediately. Repeat with the remaining eggs and bread.

**Serves 4**

# Farmhouse Scramble

**Metric/Imperial**
100 g / 4 oz lean bacon
    rashers, derinded and
    chopped
3 eggs
salt
freshly ground white pepper
175 g / 6 oz cottage cheese
4 slices wholemeal bread
25 g / 1 oz vegetable
    margarine
watercress sprigs to garnish

**American**
½ cup chopped Canadian
    bacon
3 eggs
salt
freshly ground white pepper
¾ cup cottage cheese
4 slices wholewheat bread
2 tablespoons vegetable
    margarine
watercress sprigs to garnish

Put the bacon in a small pan and fry gently until the fat runs, stirring frequently. Fry for a further 4 minutes, then remove from the pan with a slotted spoon and keep hot.

Crack the eggs into a bowl. Add salt and pepper to taste, then whisk with a fork until lightly mixed.

Pour into the pan and cook gently until the eggs begin to coagulate but are not fully set, stirring and lifting constantly. Stir in the cottage cheese and continue cooking until the mixture is just firm.

Meanwhile, toast the bread lightly on both sides, then spread with the margarine. Arrange on warmed, individual serving plates. Stir the bacon into the egg mixture, then pile onto the toast and garnish with watercress. Serve immediately.

**Serves 4**

# Baked Tomato Eggs

*Each tomato should be large enough to hold an egg.*

| Metric/Imperial | American |
|---|---|
| 4 large tomatoes | 4 large tomatoes |
| 100 g / 4 oz cooked ham, finely chopped | ½ cup finely chopped cooked ham |
| 1 teaspoon chopped parsley | 1 teaspoon chopped parsley |
| salt | salt |
| freshly ground black pepper | freshly ground black pepper |
| 4 eggs | 4 eggs |

Cut the tops off the tomatoes, then scoop out the pulp and seeds. Work the pulp through a sieve (strainer) to remove the seeds. Put the pulp in a bowl with the ham, parsley and salt and pepper to taste. Stir well.

Divide the mixture equally between the tomatoes, pressing it down well. Stand the tomatoes in a baking dish and crack one egg into each tomato. Sprinkle lightly with salt and pepper.

Bake in a preheated moderately hot oven (190°C / 375°F, Gas Mark 5) for 15 minutes until the eggs are set. Serve immediately.

**Serves 4**

# Scrambled Eggs

| Metric/Imperial | American |
|---|---|
| 4 eggs | 4 eggs |
| 4 tablespoons single cream | ¼ cup light cream |
| salt | salt |
| freshly ground white pepper | freshly ground white pepper |
| 50 g / 2 oz vegetable margarine | ¼ cup vegetable margarine |
| 4 slices wholemeal bread | 4 slices wholewheat bread |
| 1 teaspoon snipped chives | 1 teaspoon snipped chives |
| 1 teaspoon chopped parsley | 1 teaspoon chopped parsley |

Crack the eggs into a bowl, add the cream and salt and pepper to taste, then whisk with a fork until lightly mixed.

Melt half the margarine in a small pan. Add the egg mixture and cook gently until the eggs begin to coagulate but are not fully set, stirring and lifting constantly.

Meanwhile, toast the bread lightly on both sides, then spread with the remaining margarine. Arrange on warmed individual serving plates. When the eggs are only just set, but still very creamy, stir in the chives and parsley. Pile onto the toast and serve immediately.

**Serves 4**

# Breakfast Omelette

*Vary the filling for this delicious, quick-to-prepare breakfast by adding a little lean chopped ham, or a few chopped walnuts, to the cottage (curd) cheese filling.*

| Metric/Imperial | American |
|---|---|
| 2 eggs | 2 eggs |
| salt | salt |
| freshly ground black pepper | freshly ground black pepper |
| 100 g / 4 oz cottage cheese | ¼ lb cottage cheese |
| 1 tablespoon vegetable oil | 1 tablespoon vegetable oil |

Break the eggs into a bowl. Add salt and pepper to taste and whisk until light and frothy. Stir in half of the cottage cheese and mix well.

Heat the oil in a small omelette pan and pour in the egg mixture. Cook over moderate heat, drawing the edge of the omelette into the centre with a knife, as it becomes firm.

When the omelette is lightly set, spread the remaining cottage cheese over the top and continue to cook gently for 1 minute. Fold the omelette in half and transfer to a hot serving plate. Serve immediately, with wholewheat toast and a glass of orange juice, if liked.

**Serves 1**

# Country Grill (Broil)

| Metric/Imperial | American |
|---|---|
| 3 tablespoons oil | 3 tablespoons oil |
| 4 slices lambs' liver | 4 slices lamb liver |
| 4 lambs' kidneys, skin and cores removed and split lengthways | 4 lamb kidneys, skin and cores removed and split lengthways |
| salt | salt |
| freshly ground black pepper | freshly ground black pepper |
| 4 tomatoes, halved | 4 tomatoes, halved |
| 8 large mushrooms | 8 large mushrooms |
| 2 teaspoons chopped parsley to garnish | 2 teaspoons chopped parsley to garnish |

Remove the rack from the grill (broiler) pan, then line the pan with foil and brush with a little of the oil.

Put the liver in the centre of the pan, then arrange the kidneys around the liver. Brush with a little oil.

Grill (broil) under medium heat for 3 minutes until the liver and kidneys change colour then turn them over carefully and sprinkle with salt and pepper

Arrange the tomatoes around the kidneys, cut sides uppermost. Put the mushrooms in the pan, caps uppermost.

Sprinkle both the tomatoes and mushrooms lightly with salt and pepper and brush with oil.

Return the pan to the grill (broiler) for a further 5 minutes. Sprinkle with parsley and serve hot.

**Serves 4**

# Wholewheat Crêpes

| Metric/Imperial | American |
|---|---|
| 100 g / 4 oz wholemeal self-raising flour | 1 cup wholewheat self-rising flour |
| 1 egg, beaten | 1 egg, beaten |
| 300 ml / ½ pint milk | 1¼ cups milk |
| 4 tablespoons clear honey | ¼ cup clear honey |
| 50 g / 2 oz seedless raisins | ⅓ cup seedless raisins |
| pinch of grated nutmeg | pinch of grated nutmeg |
| oil for frying | oil for frying |

Put the flour in a bowl and make a well in the centre. Pour in the egg and milk and beat well to give a smooth batter.

Mix the honey, raisins and nutmeg in a separate bowl.

Heat a little oil in a 20 cm / 8 inch frying pan (skillet). When the oil is hot, quickly pour in enough batter to thinly coat the bottom of the pan, tilting the pan to spread the batter evenly. Cook until the top of the batter is set and the underside is golden brown. Turn and cook the other side.

*Spiced grapefruit refresher (page 30); Country grill (broil)*

Slide onto a warm plate, cover and keep warm by standing the plate over a pan of hot water. Continue until all the batter has been used up, making 8 crêpes in all.

Spread each crêpe with a spoonful of the honey mixture, then fold to form wedge-shaped parcels. Serve immediately.

**Serves 4**

*Wholewheat crêpes*

# Poached Haddock and Eggs

| Metric/Imperial | American |
|---|---|
| 450 g / 1 lb smoked haddock fillets, cut into 4 pieces | 1 lb smoked haddock fillets, cut into 4 pieces |
| 600 ml / 1 pint water | 2½ cups water |
| 4 eggs | 4 eggs |
| freshly ground black pepper | freshly ground black pepper |
| 25 g / 1 oz vegetable margarine | 2 tablespoons vegetable margarine |

Put the fish in a frying pan (skillet) and cover with the water. Bring slowly to the boil, then simmer for about 10 minutes or until the fish is tender but not breaking up. Transfer with a slotted spoon to warmed serving plates and keep hot.

Bring the cooking liquid to the boil. Using a spoon, stir the water very quickly to create a 'whirlpool'. Crack one egg into a cup, then slide it carefully into the water. Repeat with the remaining eggs. Simmer for 3 minutes until each egg is firmly set.

Meanwhile, sprinkle the fish with pepper to taste and put a little margarine on each piece. Keep hot.

Remove the eggs from the pan with a slotted spoon and place one on each piece of fish. Serve immediately.

**Serves 4**

# HORS D'OEUVRE

It isn't absolutely necessary to start a meal with an appetiser, but it is an agreeable custom.

One of the prettiest and best ways to start a meal is with a selection of what the French call crudités – raw, morning-fresh, crisp vegetables served with a dip. Avoid serving with mayonnaise and instead try a cottage cheese dip, spiced with curry powder or herbs or garlic.

Melon, of one variety or another, is available all the year round and makes an equally refreshing starter. So, too, does fresh grapefruit, or a large orange treated in the same way. Why not try a mixture of these two?

But whatever you choose, take time to present your first course prettily. Remember that at a dinner party it is your guests' first impression of your talent and can set – or upset – the whole tone of the meal.

## Tomato and Mushroom Vinaigrette

| Metric/Imperial | American |
|---|---|
| 100 g/4 oz button mushrooms, sliced | 1 cup sliced button mushrooms |
| 100 g/4 oz tomatoes, peeled and sliced | ½ cup peeled and sliced tomatoes |
| 2 tablespoons chopped parsley to garnish | 2 tablespoons chopped parsley to garnish |
| SAUCE: | SAUCE: |
| ½ teaspoon prepared mustard | ½ teaspoon prepared mustard |
| 3 tablespoons corn oil | 3 tablespoons corn oil |
| ½ tablespoon lemon juice | ½ tablespoon lemon juice |
| ½ tablespoon wine vinegar or cider vinegar | ½ tablespoon wine vinegar or cider vinegar |
| 1 garlic clove, crushed (optional) | 1 garlic clove, crushed (optional) |
| ½ teaspoon salt | ½ teaspoon salt |
| freshly ground black pepper | freshly ground black pepper |

Put the mushrooms in a shallow dish. To make the sauce: whisk together the mustard, oil, lemon juice, vinegar, garlic, salt and pepper, or shake them in a screw-topped jar.

Pour this sauce over the mushrooms and allow to marinate for 30 minutes.

Arrange a layer of tomato in each of four individual serving dishes. Using a perforated spoon, lift out the mushrooms and arrange them on top of the tomatoes. Whisk the sauce again, and pour it over each serving. Garnish with parsley.

**Serves 4**

*LEFT: Tomato and mushroom vinaigrette*

# Cottage Cheese and Ham Bake

| Metric/Imperial | American |
| --- | --- |
| 225 g / 8 oz cottage cheese | 1 cup cottage cheese |
| 2 eggs, beaten | 2 eggs, beaten |
| pinch of salt | pinch of salt |
| freshly ground black pepper | freshly ground black pepper |
| 50 g / 2 oz lean boiled ham, diced | 1/4 cup diced lean cured ham |
| 1/2 teaspoon prepared mustard | 1/2 teaspoon prepared mustard |
| 1/2 tablespoon vegetable margarine, melted | 1/2 tablespoon vegetable margarine, melted |
| TO GARNISH: | TO GARNISH: |
| 1 mushroom, sliced | 1 mushroom, sliced |
| 1/2 green pepper, cored, seeded and sliced | 1/2 green pepper, cored, seeded and sliced |

Blend together the cottage cheese, eggs, salt, pepper, ham and mustard. Grease an ovenproof dish. Pour in the cheese mixture and bake in a preheated moderate oven (180°C/350°F, Gas Mark 4) for 20 to 25 minutes, adding the mushroom and green pepper 5 minutes before cooking is complete.

**Serves 4**

# Mushroom Salad

| Metric/Imperial | American |
| --- | --- |
| 225 g / 8 oz button mushrooms | 2 cups button mushrooms |
| SAUCE: | SAUCE: |
| 3 tablespoons corn oil | 3 tablespoons corn oil |
| 1 tablespoon lemon juice | 1 tablespoon lemon juice |
| 1 garlic clove, crushed (optional) | 1 garlic clove, crushed (optional) |
| 1/2 teaspoon prepared French mustard | 1/2 teaspoon prepared French mustard |
| 1/2 teaspoon salt | 1/2 teaspoon salt |
| freshly ground black pepper | freshly ground black pepper |
| 1 tablespoon finely chopped parsley | 1 tablespoon finely chopped parsley |

Wipe the mushrooms with a clean, damp cloth. Leave them whole and do not remove the stalks. Whisk together the oil, lemon juice, garlic (if used), mustard, salt, pepper and parsley, or shake them together in a screw-topped jar.

Pour the dressing over the mushrooms. Toss them well to make sure that each mushroom is coated with the dressing. Chill, covered, for 2 hours before serving.

**Serves 4**

# Raw Vegetables with Cottage Cheese Dip

| Metric/Imperial | American |
| --- | --- |
| DIP: | DIP: |
| 450 g / 1 lb cottage cheese | 2 cups cottage cheese |
| 1 teaspoon caraway seeds | 1 teaspoon caraway seeds |
| 1/2 green pepper, cored, seeded and finely chopped | 1/4 cup cored, seeded and finely chopped green pepper |
| 2 tablespoons finely chopped watercress | 2 tablespoons finely chopped watercress |
| 1/2 teaspoon salt | 1/2 teaspoon salt |
| freshly ground black pepper | freshly ground black pepper |
| 1 garlic clove, crushed (optional) | 1 garlic clove, crushed (optional) |
| 1/2 teaspoon paprika to garnish | 1/2 teaspoon paprika to garnish |
| SUGGESTED DIPPERS: | SUGGESTED DIPPERS: |
| Spring onions, trimmed; celery, cut into strips; radishes, trimmed; carrots, peeled and cut into strips; chicory leaves; melon, cut into cubes or balls; olives; florets of raw cauliflower; very young whole French beans; tiny whole button mushrooms; strips of green pepper, cored and seeded; cucumber, cut into strips | scallions, trimmed; celery, cut into strips; radishes, trimmed; carrots, peeled and cut into strips; Belgian endive leaves; melon, cut into cubes or balls; olives; florets of raw cauliflower; very young whole French beans; tiny whole button mushrooms; strips of green pepper, cored and seeded; cucumber, cut into strips |

Blend together the cottage cheese, caraway seeds, green pepper, watercress, salt, pepper and garlic, sieving (straining) the cottage cheese if a smoother dip is preferred. Pile it into a bowl and sprinkle it with paprika.

Stand the bowl in the centre of a serving dish and surround it with the prepared vegetables.

**Serves 4**

*Mushroom salad (page 41)*

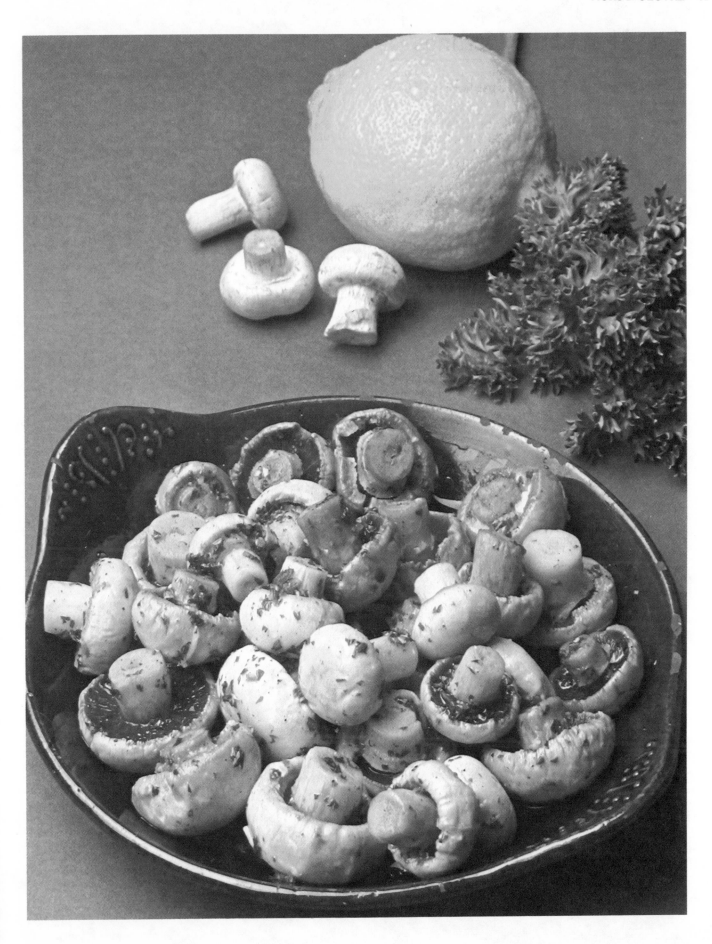

# Normandy Herrings

| Metric/Imperial | American |
| --- | --- |
| 4 small herrings | 4 small herrings |
| ½ teaspoon salt | ½ teaspoon salt |
| freshly ground black pepper | freshly ground black pepper |
| 1 large onion, peeled and sliced | 1 cup peeled and sliced onion |
| freshly grated nutmeg | freshly grated nutmeg |
| ½ tablespoon vegetable oil | ½ tablespoon vegetable oil |
| 2 dessert apples, sliced | 1½ cups sliced dessert apple |
| 1 clove | 1 clove |

Cut the heads off the fish. Split the fish down the back, open out and clean. Wash the herrings well and dry them on kitchen paper towels. Season them, inside and outside, with salt and pepper.

Simmer the onion in boiling salted water until tender. Drain well and season with salt, pepper and nutmeg.

Stuff each herring with cooked onion, and close them up again. Brush them very lightly with oil and place on a grill (broiler) rack. Cook under a preheated moderate grill (broiler) for 6 to 8 minutes, turning them during cooking.

Meanwhile, poach the apples and clove gently in boiling water until tender but still firm. Discard the clove. Arrange the hot cooked apple around the herrings and serve.

**Serves 4**

NOTE: Herrings are not the least fattening of fish, but the same recipe could be used for other fish, such as whiting or trout, which are less oily.

## Fish Tips

Whenever possible, buy fish on the day when you intend to eat it. Choose carefully, looking for:

*a fishmonger with a fast turnover
*fish with bright, clear eyes
*a clean, inoffensive smell
*fish with firm and springy flesh
*gills of a clear, red colour

*BELOW: Normandy herrings*

# Melon with Smoked Ham

| Metric/Imperial | American |
|---|---|
| 1 small melon – Ogen, Canteloup or Charentais | 1 small melon – Ogen, Canteloup or Charentais |
| 100 g / 4 oz raw smoked ham, thinly sliced | ¼ lb raw smoked ham, thinly sliced |
| freshly ground black pepper | freshly ground black pepper |
| black olives to garnish | ripe olives to garnish |

Chill the melon well before cutting it into portions. Remove and discard the seeds. Arrange rolled slices of smoked ham on each melon portion. Sprinkle with pepper and serve garnished with olives.

**Serves 4**

# Celeriac Remoulade

| Metric/Imperial | American |
|---|---|
| 4 lettuce leaves | 4 lettuce leaves |
| salt and black pepper | salt and black pepper |
| 1 celeriac about 225 g / 8 oz peeled and coarsely grated | 1 celeriac, about ½ lb, peeled and coarsely grated |
| ½ small onion, peeled and finely chopped | ½ small onion, finely chopped |
| 225 ml / 8 fl oz thick mayonnaise | 1 cup thick mayonnaise |
| 2 teaspoons lemon juice | 2 teaspoons lemon juice |
| 1 tablespoon snipped chives | 1 tablespoon snipped chives |

Arrange the lettuce leaves on individual serving plates and season each one with salt and pepper.

Combine all the other ingredients together, except the chives, then season to taste. Divide the mixture between the plates, heaping up in the centre of the lettuce. Garnish with chives and chill gently before serving.

**Serves 4**

# Tuna Pâté

| Metric/Imperial | American |
|---|---|
| 225 g / 8 oz canned tuna, drained | ½ lb canned tuna, drained |
| 2 tablespoons soured cream | 2 tablespoons sour cream |
| 2 tablespoons cottage cheese | 2 tablespoons cottage cheese |
| salt | salt |
| freshly ground black pepper | freshly ground black pepper |
| cayenne pepper | cayenne pepper |
| juice of ½ lemon | juice of ½ lemon |
| chopped chives | chopped chives |

Put the tuna fish, cream and cottage cheese in an electric blender and work to a purée.

Season to taste with salt, pepper and cayenne pepper, and blend in the lemon juice and chopped chives.

Chill well before serving with celery, radishes and cucumber, instead of the usual toast.

**Serves 4**

# Cod Steaks in Tomato Sauce

| Metric/Imperial | American |
|---|---|
| 4 cod steaks | 4 cod steaks |
| salt and pepper | salt and pepper |
| 2 teaspoons lemon juice | 2 teaspoons lemon juice |
| 15 g / ½ oz vegetable margarine | 1 tablespoon vegetable margarine |
| 1 onion, peeled and finely chopped | 1 onion, peeled and finely chopped |
| 1 green pepper, cored, seeded and finely chopped | 1 green pepper, cored, seeded and finely chopped |
| 3 celery sticks, finely chopped | 3 celery stalks, finely chopped |
| 6 tomatoes, blanched, peeled and finely chopped | 6 tomatoes, blanched, peeled and finely chopped |
| 1 garlic clove, crushed | 1 garlic clove, crushed |
| pinch of oregano | pinch of oregano |

Arrange the fish steaks on a plate. Season them with salt and pepper and sprinkle over the lemon juice.

Melt the margarine in a shallow flameproof casserole and add the onion, green pepper and celery. Cook gently until the onion is soft but not brown. Stir in the tomatoes, garlic and oregano, and season to taste with salt and pepper. Bring to the boil, reduce the heat to low, cover and simmer for 10 to 15 minutes.

Arrange the fish steaks over the tomato mixture, cover with foil and bake in a preheated moderate oven (180°C / 350°F, Gas Mark 4) for about 30 minutes, or until the fish is tender.

**Serves 4**

# Mussels in White Wine

| Metric/Imperial | American |
|---|---|
| 48 mussels | 48 mussels or clams |
| 150 ml / ¼ pint white wine | ⅔ cup white wine |
| 1 bouquet garni | 1 bouquet garni |
| 1 carrot, finely chopped | 1 carrot, finely chopped |
| 4 shallots or spring onions, finely chopped | 4 shallots or scallions, finely chopped |
| 1 garlic clove, crushed | 1 garlic clove, crushed |
| salt and black pepper | salt and black pepper |
| 1 tablespoon chopped parsley | 1 tablespoon chopped parsley |
| 3 tablespoons single cream | 3 tablespoons light cream |

Wash the mussels (or clams) and scrub them very thoroughly.

Put them into a heavy pan with the wine, bouquet garni, carrot, shallots or spring onions (scallions), garlic and salt and pepper to taste. Cover and bring to the boil, then simmer for 5 minutes until all the mussels or clams have opened; discard any shells which are still closed.

Transfer the mussels or clams to a warmed serving bowl, then stir the remaining ingredients into the cooking liquid. Pour the liquid over the mussels and serve hot.

**Serves 4**

# Flaked Fish with Garlic Sauce

| Metric/Imperial | American |
|---|---|
| 350 g / 12 oz white fish | ¾ lb white fish |
| 1 hard-boiled egg, shelled | 1 hard-cooked egg, shelled |
| 175 g / 6 oz cottage cheese | ¾ cup cottage cheese |
| 1 garlic clove, crushed | 1 garlic clove, crushed |
| 2 tablespoons finely chopped parsley | 2 tablespoons finely chopped parsley |
| salt | salt |
| freshly ground black pepper | freshly ground black pepper |
| 50 g / 2 oz shelled prawns | ⅓ cup peeled shrimp |
| 2 tablespoons capers | 2 tablespoons capers |
| shredded lettuce | shredded lettuce |

Choose any white fish – it need not have a delicate flavour since the sauce is quite powerful.

Steam the fish quite plainly. Allow it to cool, then flake it, discarding any skin or bones.

Press the egg and cottage cheese through a sieve (strainer). Blend in the garlic and parsley, and season to taste.

Gently mix the flaked fish, prawns (shrimp), capers and egg sauce. Serve on a bed of shredded lettuce.

**Serves 4**

*RIGHT: Mussels in white wine*

# SOUPS

There is such a wide range of soups that you are sure to find one to suit every occasion throughout the year.

You will still be able to have creamy looking soups, like the Chilled Summer Soup. And you can give a richer texture to a fairly thin vegetable soup by blending just half of it, so that the background is mildly creamy but there are still pieces of vegetable floating in it.

Serve wholewheat bread with this course, either as hot rolls or garlic bread, or in the form of croûtons – fried bread is, however, very fattening – but tiny cubes of cucumber, green pepper, celery, or finely sliced raw mushroom are an attractive alternative.

If you can manage with less than the quantity of oil or margarine recommended in the recipe, then do so.

## Chilled Tomato Soup

| Metric/Imperial | American |
|---|---|
| 450 g / 1 lb stewed fresh tomatoes or canned tomatoes | 2 cups stewed fresh tomatoes or canned tomatoes |
| ¹/₂ teaspoon Worcestershire sauce | ¹/₂ teaspoon Worcestershire sauce |
| juice of ¹/₂ lemon | juice of ¹/₂ lemon |
| 1 onion, peeled and sliced | 1 onion, peeled and sliced |
| 1 teaspoon salt | 1 teaspoon salt |
| 4 sprigs of parsley | 4 sprigs of parsley |
| 1 × 425 g / 15 oz can condensed consommé | 15 oz can condensed consommé |
| TO GARNISH: | TO GARNISH: |
| 2 tablespoons chopped parsley | 2 tablespoons chopped parsley |
| 2 tablespoons chopped celery | 2 tablespoons chopped celery |

Place the tomatoes, Worcestershire sauce, lemon juice, onion, salt and parsley in an electric blender and work to a purée. Stir in the consommé. Chill well and serve garnished with parsley and celery.

**Serves 4**

## Carrot and Watercress Soup

| Metric/Imperial | American |
|---|---|
| 25 g / 1 oz vegetable margarine | 2 tablespoons vegetable margarine |
| 225 g / 8 oz onions, peeled and chopped | 2 cups peeled and chopped onion |
| 450 g / 1 lb carrots, peeled and chopped | 4 cups peeled and chopped carrot |
| 1 teaspoon caraway seeds | 1 teaspoon caraway seeds |
| 1 litre / 1³/₄ pints chicken stock | 4¹/₄ cups chicken stock |
| 2 tablespoons soured cream | 2 tablespoons sour cream |
| TO GARNISH: | TO GARNISH: |
| 1 bunch watercress, finely chopped | 1¹/₂ cups finely chopped watercress |
| 1 carrot, grated | ¹/₂ cup grated carrot |

Melt the margarine in a heavy pan. Add the onions and fry for 5 minutes until soft but not brown. Add the carrots, caraway seeds and boiling stock. Bring to the boil again, cover and simmer until the carrots are quite tender. The timing will depend on the age and quality of the carrots. Cool the soup, then work to a purée in an electric blender and stir in the cream.

Serve this soup hot or cold, garnished with watercress and raw carrot.

**Serves 4**

*LEFT: Chilled tomato soup*

# Vegetable Soup Provençale

**Metric/Imperial**

1 tablespoon vegetable oil
1 large onion, peeled and
   finely chopped
50 g / 2 oz lean bacon,
   finely chopped
4 celery sticks, chopped
1.2 litres / 2 pints beef stock
salt
freshly ground black pepper
225 g / 8 oz tomatoes,
   peeled and chopped
2 tablespoons tomato purée
1 garlic clove, finely
   chopped

**American**

1 tablespoon vegetable oil
1 large onion, peeled and
   finely chopped
¼ cup finely chopped lean
   bacon
½ cup chopped celery
5 cups beef stock
salt
freshly ground black pepper
1 cup peeled and chopped
   tomatoes
2 tablespoons tomato paste
1 garlic clove, finely
   chopped

175 g / 6 oz any other diced
   vegetables in season,
   such as marrow,
   aubergine, cauliflower,
   cabbage, green pepper
   (cored and seeded), peas
   or green beans
1 teaspoon chopped fresh
   basil or thyme

1 cup any other diced
   vegetables in season,
   such as squash, eggplant,
   cauliflower, cabbage,
   green pepper (cored and
   seeded), peas or snap
   beans
1 teaspoon chopped fresh
   basil or thyme

Heat the oil in a large pan. Add the onion and fry very
gently, covered, for 5 minutes, or until soft but not brown.
Add the bacon and fry for a further 5 minutes.

Add the celery, stock, salt, pepper, tomatoes, tomato
purée (paste), garlic, diced vegetables and basil or thyme.
Bring to the boil. Cover and simmer gently for 45 minutes.
Serve very hot.

**Serves 4**

ABOVE: Vegetable soup Provençale

# Bortsch

**Metric/Imperial**

1 small onion, peeled and thinly sliced
½ tablespoon vegetable oil
100 g / 4 oz lean stewing beef (shin or chuck) cut into 1 cm / ½ inch cubes
900 ml / 1½ pints beef stock
½ teaspoon salt
freshly ground black pepper
½ bay leaf
1 teaspoon chopped fresh thyme or ½ teaspoon dried thyme
1 garlic clove, finely chopped
1 small carrot, thinly sliced
¼ small turnip, thinly sliced
⅛ cabbage, finely shredded
1 large tomato, peeled and chopped

**American**

1 small onion, peeled and thinly sliced
½ tablespoon vegetable oil
¼ lb lean stewing beef (shin or chuck) cut into ½ inch cubes
3¾ cups beef stock
½ teaspoon salt
freshly ground black pepper
½ bay leaf
1 teaspoon chopped fresh thyme or ½ teaspoon dried thyme
1 garlic clove, finely chopped
¼ cup thinly sliced carrot
¼ cup thinly sliced turnip
½ cup finely shredded cabbage
¼ cup peeled and chopped tomato

1 large beetroot, peeled and grated
4 teaspoons soured cream

2 cups peeled and grated beet
4 teaspoons sour cream

Fry the onion slowly in the oil in a heavy pan. When golden brown, add the meat. Toss it well over the heat until each cube of meat is brown all over. Add the stock, salt, pepper, bay leaf, thyme and garlic. Cover the pan, bring to the boil, then reduce the heat and allow to simmer for 5 minutes. Add the carrot, turnip and cabbage, return to the boil and simmer for 45 minutes. Add the tomato and simmer for a further 20 minutes. Add the grated beetroot (beet) 5 minutes before serving. Check the seasoning and top each portion with a spoonful of soured cream.

**Serves 4**

*BELOW: Bortsch*

# Chilled Summer Soup

| Metric/Imperial | American |
|---|---|
| 1 small onion, peeled and chopped | 1 small onion, peeled and chopped |
| 900 ml / 1 1/2 pints chicken stock | 3 3/4 cups chicken stock |
| 1/2 cucumber, chopped but unpeeled | 1 cup unpeeled, chopped cucumber |
| 1 bunch watercress | 1 bunch watercress |
| 1 small lettuce, shredded | 1 small head of lettuce, shredded |
| sprig of mint | sprig of mint |
| pinch of salt | pinch of salt |
| freshly ground black pepper | freshly ground black pepper |
| 2 tablespoons soured cream | 2 tablespoons sour cream |
| 2 tablespoons finely chopped pickled gherkin to garnish | 2 tablespoons finely chopped dill pickle to garnish |

Put the onion and chicken stock in a saucepan and bring to the boil. Reduce the heat and allow to simmer for 10 minutes. Add the cucumber, watercress, lettuce and mint. Simmer for a further 7 minutes and then leave to cool. Work the soup to a purée in an electric blender. When cold, stir in the soured cream. Chill well, and garnish with gherkins (dill pickles) just before serving.
**Serves 4**

# Iced Avocado Soup

| Metric/Imperial | American |
|---|---|
| 2 ripe avocados | 2 ripe avocados |
| 2 teaspoons lemon juice | 2 teaspoons lemon juice |
| 1 celery stick, very finely chopped | 1 celery stalk, very finely chopped |
| 1 tablespoon tomato purée | 1 tablespoon tomato paste |
| 450 ml / 3/4 pint natural yogurt | 2 cups unflavored yogurt |
| 300 ml / 1/2 pint chicken stock | 1 1/4 cups chicken stock |
| 1-2 drops Tabasco sauce | 1-2 drops Tabasco sauce |
| salt and pepper | salt and pepper |
| snipped chives to garnish | snipped chives to garnish |

Halve the avocados and remove the stones (seeds). Spoon the flesh into a bowl, add the lemon juice and beat to a smooth paste. Beat in the celery, tomato purée (paste), yogurt and Tabasco, and season to taste with salt and pepper. Add sufficient chicken stock to obtain a thick but liquid soup, then adjust the seasoning. Chill in the refrigerator, resting the bowl on a bed of ice to hasten the chilling process. Serve in chilled bowls, garnished with chives.
NOTE: Do not prepare this soup more than an hour before you intend to serve it, or the avocados may discolour.
**Serves 4**

# Iced Spanish Soup

| Metric/Imperial | American |
|---|---|
| 700 g / 1 1/2 lb tomatoes, peeled, seeded and chopped | 3 cups peeled, seeded and chopped tomatoes |
| 10 cm / 4 inch cucumber, chopped | 3/4 cup chopped cucumber |
| 3 spring onions, chopped | 1/2 cup chopped scallions |
| 1/2 green pepper, cored, seeded and chopped | 1/2 cup chopped, cored and seeded green pepper |
| 2 garlic cloves | 2 garlic cloves |
| 4 tablespoons vegetable oil | 1/4 cup vegetable oil |
| 1 1/2 tablespoons cider vinegar | 1 1/2 tablespoons hard cider vinegar |
| 1 teaspoon chopped thyme or parsley salt | 1 teaspoon chopped thyme or parsley |
| freshly ground black pepper | salt |
| iced water | freshly ground black pepper |
| TO GARNISH: | iced water |
| ice cubes | TO GARNISH: |
| 1/2 green pepper, cored, seeded and finely diced | ice cubes |
| 10 cm / 4 inch cucumber, finely chopped | 1/2 cup finely diced, cored and seeded green pepper |
| 4 celery sticks, finely chopped | 3/4 cup finely chopped cucumber |
| finely chopped parsley | 1/2 cup finely chopped celery |
| | finely chopped parsley |

Work the tomatoes, cucumber, spring onions (scallions), green pepper, garlic, oil, cider vinegar, thyme, salt and pepper together to a purée in an electric blender.

Add enough iced water to make the soup of the desired consistency. The quantity will vary according to the juiciness of the tomatoes, and your preference for a really thick or a thin soup.

Chill thoroughly. Float an ice cube in each serving and hand round the garnishes separately.
**Serves 4**

# Watermelon Soup

**Metric/Imperial**
25 g / 1 oz dried
  mushrooms, chopped
600 ml / 1 pint chicken
  stock
175 g / 6 oz chicken,
  minced
175 g / 6 oz lean pork,
  minced
100 g / 4 oz bamboo shoots,
  thinly sliced
100 g / 4 oz lean ham,
  minced
100 g / 4 oz green peas
1 × 1.75 kg / 4 lb
  watermelon

**American**
¼ cup chopped dried
  mushrooms
2½ cups chicken stock
¾ cup ground chicken
¾ cup ground lean pork
⅔ cup bamboo shoots,
  thinly sliced
½ cup ground lean ham
¾ cup green peas
4 lb watermelon

Pour boiling water over the mushrooms and allow them to
soak for 1 hour. Drain them well. Bring the stock to the boil.
Add the chicken and pork and simmer for 10 minutes. Add
the drained mushrooms, bamboo shoots, ham and peas.

Cut the top from the melon. Scoop out seeds and some of
the pulp. Pour the soup into the melon and replace top.

Stand the melon in a heatproof basin and steam it, in or
over a large pan of boiling water for about 1½ hours.

Scoop out melon flesh as well as soup for each serving.

**Serves 4**

*Watermelon soup*

# Clear Mushroom Soup

**Metric/Imperial**
2 spring onions, thinly sliced
1 cm / ½ inch slice of root
  ginger
900 ml / 1½ pints chicken
  stock
100 g / 4 oz button
  mushrooms, thinly sliced
1 tablespoon dry sherry
salt
freshly ground black pepper

**American**
2 scallions, thinly sliced
½ inch slice of fresh ginger
3¾ cups chicken stock
1 cup thinly sliced button
  mushrooms
1 tablespoon dry sherry
salt
freshly ground black pepper

Put the spring onions (scallions) and ginger in a pan with the stock. Bring to the boil and simmer, covered, for 20 minutes.

Add the mushrooms and simmer for a further 10 minutes. Remove the ginger. Add the sherry and season to taste.

**Serves 4**

ABOVE: *Clear mushroom soup*

# Prawn (Shrimp) and Egg Flower Soup

**Metric/Imperial**
2 spring onions, finely
  chopped
900 ml / 1½ pints chicken
  stock
½ tablespoon dry sherry
pinch of sugar
1 teaspoon soy sauce
175 g / 6 oz peeled prawns
1 egg, well beaten
salt

**American**
2 scallions, finely chopped
3¾ cups chicken stock
½ tablespoon dry sherry
pinch of sugar
1 teaspoon soy sauce
1½ cups shelled shrimp
1 egg, well beaten
salt

Put the spring onions (scallions) and stock in a large pan. Bring to the boil, cover, and allow to simmer for 10 minutes.

Add the sherry, sugar, soy sauce and prawns (shrimp). Reheat gently. Pour in the egg and stir until it separates into shreds. Add salt to taste. Serve immediately.

**Serves 4**

# Soup Tips

Soups need not be pale, watery affairs, even though, for healthy eating, you should avoid thickening them with flour or cream and egg yolks. If you prefer a thick, creamy looking soup, use the vegetable content to give you this effect. Simply puréed, without any additions, it will provide a soup which does not look like invalid food.

Some non-fattening garnishes:
*chopped celery
*asparagus tips
*sprigs of watercress
*finely sliced radishes
*peeled, diced cucumber

LEFT: *Chinese beef and vegetable soup*

# Chinese Beef and Vegetable Soup

| Metric/Imperial | American |
|---|---|
| 4 Chinese dried mushrooms | 4 Chinese dried mushrooms |
| 100 g / 4 oz beef (topside) | ¼ lb beef (top round) |
| 900 ml / 1½ pints beef stock | 3¾ cups beef stock |
| 1 tomato, peeled and sliced | 1 tomato, peeled and sliced |
| 2 spring onions, sliced | 2 scallions, sliced |
| 4 water chestnuts, sliced thinly | 4 water chestnuts, sliced thinly |
| 1 × 100g / 4 oz can bamboo shoots, sliced | 4 oz can bamboo shoots, sliced |
| salt | salt |
| freshly ground black pepper | freshly ground black pepper |

Soak the mushrooms in warm water for 20 minutes. Rinse them, squeeze them dry and cut them into thin strips, discarding the stalks. Cut the beef into thin strips across the grain of the meat. Bring the stock to the boil in a large pan. Add the beef and simmer for 4 to 5 minutes. Add the tomato, spring onions (scallions), water chestnuts and bamboo shoots and cook for a further 2 minutes.

. Season to taste and serve piping hot.

**Serves 4**

LEFT: *Prawn (shrimp) and egg flower soup*

# Cucumber, Lemon and Mint Soup

**Metric/Imperial**

1 tablespoon oil
1 small onion, peeled and finely chopped
½ cucumber, peeled and cut into 5 mm / ¼ inch cubes
450 ml / ¾ pint natural yogurt
300 ml / ½ pint chicken stock
finely grated rind and juice of 1 lemon
2 tablespoons chopped mint
salt
freshly ground black pepper
mint sprigs to garnish

**American**

1 tablespoon oil
1 small onion, peeled and finely chopped
½ cucumber, peeled and cut into ¼ inch cubes
2 cups unflavored yogurt
1¼ cups chicken stock
finely grated rind and juice of 1 lemon
2 tablespoons chopped mint
salt
freshly ground black pepper
mint sprigs to garnish

*Yogurt dip (page 58); Cucumber, lemon and mint soup; Slimmer's watercress soup; Summer tomato soup; Greek vegetable soup*

---

Heat the oil in a pan, add the onion and fry gently for 3 minutes. Add the cucumber and fry for a further 5 minutes. Transfer to a bowl and leave to cool.

Stir in the yogurt and stock, then the lemon rind and juice, mint and salt and pepper to taste.

Chill in the refrigerator for 1 hour. Pour into 4 individual chilled bowls, garnish with mint sprigs and serve chilled.

**Serves 4**

# Slimmer's Watercress Soup

| Metric/Imperial | American |
|---|---|
| 2 bunches watercress, trimmed | 2 bunches watercress, trimmed |
| 1 tablespoon oil | 1 tablespoon oil |
| 1 small onion, peeled and finely chopped | 1 small onion, peeled and finely chopped |
| 600 ml / 1 pint chicken stock | 2½ cups chicken stock |
| 2 egg yolks | 2 egg yolks |
| 150 ml / ¼ pint natural yogurt | ⅔ cup unflavored yogurt |
| salt | salt |
| freshly ground white pepper | freshly ground white pepper |

Remove 16 leaves from the watercress and reserve for the garnish. Chop the remaining watercress and stems.

Heat the oil in a pan, add the onion and fry gently until soft and golden. Add the watercress and the stock and bring to the boil. Lower the heat, cover and simmer for 20 minutes.

Rub the soup through a sieve (strainer), or work to a purée in an electric blender. Put the egg yolks in a bowl and whisk in the yogurt. Stir in 4 tablespoons / ¼ cup of the purée and mix well.

Pour the remaining purée into the rinsed-out pan. Add the yogurt mixture, stirring constantly, then heat through gently without boiling. Taste for seasoning.

Pour into 4 individual bowls and garnish with the reserved watercress leaves. This soup may also be served chilled.

**Serves 4**

# Summer Tomato Soup

| Metric/Imperial | American |
|---|---|
| 600 ml / 1 pint tomato juice | 2½ cups tomato juice |
| 600 ml / 1 pint natural yogurt | 2½ cups unflavored yogurt |
| finely grated rind and juice of 1 lemon | finely grated rind and juice of 1 lemon |
| ½ cucumber, peeled and cut into 5 mm / ¼ inch cubes | ½ cucumber, peeled and cut into ¼ inch cubes |
| salt | salt |
| freshly ground black pepper | freshly ground black pepper |
| TO GARNISH: | TO GARNISH: |
| 4 slices lemon | 4 slices lemon |
| 2 teaspoons snipped chives | 2 teaspoons snipped chives |

Put the tomato juice in a bowl, add the yogurt and mix well. Stir in the lemon rind and juice, then the cucumber and salt and pepper to taste.

Chill in the refrigerator for 1 hour. Pour into 4 individual bowls. Garnish with lemon slices and chives. Serve chilled.

**Serves 4**

# Greek Vegetable Soup

*Choose vegetables according to season. Peas, sweetcorn kernels, beans and chopped carrots make a good summer selection. In winter, diced root vegetables may be used, or frozen ones.*

| Metric/Imperial | American |
|---|---|
| 450 ml / ¾ pint beef stock | 2 cups beef stock |
| 100 g / 4 oz mixed vegetables, chopped | ¾ cup mixed vegetables, chopped |
| 1 egg yolk | 1 egg yolk |
| 300 ml / ½ pint natural yogurt | 1¼ cups unflavored yogurt |
| salt | salt |
| freshly ground black pepper | freshly ground black pepper |
| 1 tablespoon chopped mint leaves | 1 tablespoon chopped mint leaves |
| finely grated rind of 1 lemon | finely grated rind of 1 lemon |

Put the stock in a pan and bring to the boil. Add the vegetables, then lower the heat, cover and simmer for 10 minutes or until just tender.

Meanwhile, put the egg yolk in a bowl and whisk in the yogurt. Stir in 6 tablespoons of the hot liquid and mix well.

Add to the soup in the pan, stirring constantly, then heat through gently without boiling. Season with salt and pepper to taste.

Pour into 4 individual serving bowls, garnish with chopped mint and lemon rind and serve hot.

**Serves 4**

56

# DAIRY FOODS

With their versatility and high nutrient content, dairy foods play an important part in our diet. No single food can supply all nutrients in the required quantities but milk is the most complete of all foods, and it is easily digested. 600ml (1 pint) of milk supplies our daily calcium requirement, while the protein content is equivalent to that of 3 large eggs or 75 g (3 oz) liver, beef or white fish.

Cheese contains most of the nutrients in milk and is a particularly good source of protein and calcium. Most varieties, including both hard cheeses (Cheddar, Gruyère, etc.) and soft cheeses (Brie, Camembert, etc.) have a fairly high fat content because they are manufactured from whole milk. Cottage cheese is prepared from skimmed milk and therefore has a low fat content. It is easily digested and is very satisfying, which is a great asset in a slimming diet. Eaten in a quickly prepared salad or added to cooked dishes, it provides bulk, flavour and nutrients, but few calories.

Yogurt is another milk product, once considered only as a health food, but now a very enjoyable item in everyday meals. Over the years, some fantastic claims have been made for yogurt and what it can do, from increasing the life-span to curing any number of internal disorders. It is, in fact, a most wholesome food – high in protein, low in fat and rich in calcium. Home-made yogurt, prepared from whole milk, contains all the food value of milk. Commercially manufactured varieties usually have most of the fat removed and extra protein and vitamins added. Yogurt is almost three times as digestible as milk and makes an excellent light meal.

While all of these milk-based foods are very good to eat just as they are, they can equally well be used in cooking. Cottage cheese goes well with both vegetable and fruit salads, and can also be made into delicious cheesecakes and a variety of puddings. Its rather bland flavour can be used to advantage in fish dishes where it will enhance, rather than disguise, the delicate flavour of fish.

Yogurt is almost a miracle ingredient in the kitchen. It can be used in soups and sauces; blended into savoury mousses and salad dressings; whisked into nourishing meal-in-a-glass drinks; used as a topping for baked fish or meat dishes; used to baste kebabs or marinade poultry. It can also provide a valuable thickening agent for savoury sauces – thus avoiding the need to use flour – and can similarly be used to thicken custards. In a variety of desserts, including ices, soufflés and fruit fools, yogurt can be used as a refreshing and less fattening alternative to cream.

Of the dairy foods, the egg is the most versatile of all. Eggs are a high-quality protein food; they also supply substantial amounts of vitamins A and D and riboflavin, and egg yolk is an excellent source of iron. They do however contain a high proportion of fat and cholesterol, particularly the yolk, and should be eaten with caution by those who are cutting down on their intake of animal fats. In addition to all this goodness, an egg only contains about 80 calories, so it is a perfect food for those who are watching their weight.

Eggs can of course be cooked quickly and served in a variety of guises as a meal or snack. They are easily digested and provide goodness without bulk – a particular advantage for children and anyone with a reduced appetite through illness. When eggs are cooked, the protein 'sets' or coagulates. This property enables eggs to be used for binding dry ingredients together, thickening sauces and setting custards. An extra egg may be added to a rice pudding, or whisked into a soup or sauce, or blended into a nourishing drink.

# Borshch

| Metric/Imperial | American |
|---|---|
| 2 tablespoons oil | 2 tablespoons oil |
| 2 onions, peeled and finely chopped | 2 onions, peeled and finely chopped |
| 3 raw beetroot, peeled and roughly chopped | 3 raw beets, peeled and roughly chopped |
| 175 g / 6 oz cabbage, finely shredded | 2 cups finely shredded cabbage |
| 750 ml / 1¼ pints beef stock | 3 cups beef stock |
| 2 tablespoons vinegar | 2 tablespoons vinegar |
| ¼ teaspoon salt | ¼ teaspoon salt |
| freshly ground black pepper | freshly ground black pepper |
| 4 tablespoons natural yogurt to serve | ¼ cup unflavored yogurt to serve |

Heat the oil in a large pan, add the onions and fry gently until soft and golden. Add the remaining ingredients, except the yogurt, and bring to the boil. Lower the heat, cover and simmer for 1 hour.

Rub the soup through a sieve (strainer), or work to a purée in an electric blender. Pour the purée into the rinsed-out pan and reheat gently, adding a little stock or water if the soup is too thick.

Pour into 4 individual bowls, swirl 1 tablespoonful yogurt in the centre of each bowl and serve hot.

**Serves 4**

# Yogurt Dip

| Metric/Imperial | American |
|---|---|
| 150 ml / ¼ pint natural yogurt | ⅔ cup unflavored yogurt |
| 225 g / 8 oz cottage cheese | 1 cup cottage cheese |
| 1 tablespoon grated onion | 1 tablespoon grated onion |
| 6 pickled gherkins, very finely chopped | 6 small sweet dill pickles, very finely chopped |
| 3 celery sticks | 3 celery stalks |
| 3 carrots | 3 carrots |
| ½ cucumber | ½ cucumber |
| 1 tablespoon sea salt | 1 tablespoon coarse salt |
| 600 ml / 1 pint iced water | 2½ cups ice water |

Put the yogurt, cottage cheese, onion and gherkins (dill pickles) in a bowl and stir well to mix. Chill in the refrigerator for 1 hour.

Meanwhile, cut each celery stick (stalk) into 4 lengths. Peel the carrots and split each one lengthwise into quarters. Cut the cucumber in half, then cut each half lengthwise into 4 pieces.

Put the celery, carrots and cucumber in a bowl, sprinkle with the salt, then pour on the iced water. Chill in the refrigerator for 1 hour.

Put the yogurt dip in a serving bowl and stand the bowl on a large plate. Drain the vegetables and arrange on the plate around the dip.

**Serves 4 to 6**

# Cottage Cheese Mousse

| Metric/Imperial | American |
|---|---|
| 450 g / 1 lb cottage cheese, sieved | 2 cups cottage cheese, sieved |
| 150 ml / ¼ pint natural yogurt | ⅔ cup unflavored yogurt |
| squeeze of lemon juice | squeeze of lemon juice |
| 1 tablespoon tomato purée | 1 tablespoon tomato paste |
| salt | salt |
| freshly ground black pepper | freshly ground black pepper |
| 100 g / 4 oz peeled shrimps | ½ cup shelled shrimp |
| TO GARNISH: | TO GARNISH: |
| ½ teaspoon paprika | ½ teaspoon paprika |
| 1 teaspoon snipped chives | 1 teaspoon snipped chives |

Put the cottage cheese and yogurt in a bowl and mix together, using a fork. Add the lemon juice and tomato purée (paste) and season well with salt and pepper. Stir well.

Divide the mixture equally between 4 individual ramekins, pressing down well. Top each ramekin with shrimps, then chill in the refrigerator for 1 hour.

Sprinkle with paprika and chives before serving.

**Serves 4**

# Egg Mousse

| Metric/Imperial | American |
|---|---|
| 4 hard-boiled eggs, shelled | 4 hard-cooked eggs, shelled |
| 1 teaspoon Worcestershire sauce | 1 teaspoon Worcestershire sauce |
| dash of Tabasco sauce | dash of Tabasco sauce |
| pinch of paprika | pinch of paprika |
| salt | salt |
| freshly ground white pepper | freshly ground white pepper |
| 2 teaspoons gelatine | 2 teaspoons gelatin |
| 2 tablespoons water | 2 tablespons water |
| 150 ml / ¼ pint natural yogurt | ⅔ cup unflavored yogurt |
| 225 g / 8 oz peeled prawns | 1 cup shelled shrimp |

Cut the eggs in half lengthwise, then remove the yolks and work them through a sieve (strainer) into a bowl. Add the Worcestershire sauce, Tabasco, paprika and salt and pepper to taste. Mix well. Chop the egg whites finely. Place the gelatine and water in a cup over a pan of hot water and stir until dissolved. Whisk the yogurt into the egg yolk mixture with the gelatine, then fold in the chopped egg whites.

Pour the mixture into a 15 cm / 6 inch straight-sided serving dish, then chill in the refrigerator for 2 hours.

Pile the prawns (shrimp) in the centre of the mousse just before serving. Serve with a crisp green salad.

**Serves 4**

# Baked Stuffed Tomatoes

| Metric/Imperial | American |
|---|---|
| 4 large tomatoes | 4 large tomatoes |
| 1 small onion, peeled and grated | 1 small onion, peeled and grated |
| 1 tablespoon chopped parsley | 1 tablespoon chopped parsley |
| 175 g / 6 oz cream cheese | ¾ cup cream cheese |
| 100 g / 4 oz lean cooked ham, chopped | ½ cup chopped lean cooked ham |
| salt | salt |
| freshly ground black pepper | freshly ground black pepper |
| 2 tablespoons water | 2 tablespoons water |

Cut the tops off the tomatoes and reserve for lids. Scoop out the insides of the tomatoes, then work the pulp through a sieve (strainer) to remove the pips (seeds).

Put the tomato pulp in a bowl. Add the onion, parsley, cream cheese and ham and mix well. Add salt and pepper to taste.

Spoon the mixture into the hollowed-out tomatoes and place the lids on top. Stand the tomatoes in a baking dish, then pour in the water. Bake in a preheated hot oven (220°C / 425°F, Gas Mark 7) for 15 minutes.

Serve hot or cold.

**Serves 4**

# Cottage Bake

| Metric/Imperial | American |
|---|---|
| 1 tablespoon oil | 1 tablespoon oil |
| 1 small onion, peeled and finely chopped | 1 small onion, peeled and finely chopped |
| 100 g / 4 oz mushrooms, sliced | 1 cup sliced mushrooms |
| 225 g / 8 oz cottage cheese | 1 cup cottage cheese |
| 2 eggs | 2 eggs |
| 50 g / 2 oz cooked ham, chopped | ¼ cup chopped cooked ham |
| 2 tablespoons chopped mixed fresh herbs | 2 tablespoons chopped mixed fresh herbs |
| salt | salt |
| freshly ground black pepper | freshly ground black pepper |
| chopped parsley to garnish | chopped parsley to garnish |

Heat the oil in a pan, add the onion and fry gently until soft and golden. Add the mushrooms and fry for a further 3 minutes.

Meanwhile, put the cottage cheese and eggs in a bowl and beat together with a fork. Stir in the ham, then the cooked onions and mushrooms. Add the herbs and salt and pepper to taste.

Spoon the mixture into a lightly oiled baking dish, then bake in a preheated moderately hot oven (200°C / 400°F, Gas Mark 6) for 20 minutes. Sprinkle with chopped parsley and serve hot.

**Serves 4**

# Oriental Salad

| Metric/Imperial | American |
|---|---|
| 450 g / 1 lb cottage cheese | 2 cups cottage cheese |
| 3 tablespoons double cream, lightly whipped | 3 tablespoons heavy cream, lightly whipped |
| 225 g / 8 oz cooked chicken, diced | 1 cup diced cooked chicken |
| 1 orange, peeled, divided into segments and skinned | 1 orange, peeled, divided into segments and skinned |
| 25 g / 1 oz stem ginger, finely chopped | 3 tablespoons finely chopped preserved ginger |
| 1 small lettuce | 1 small head of lettuce |
| 1 bunch watercress | 1 bunch watercress |
| 12 black grapes, halved and pipped, to garnish | 12 purple grapes, halved and seeded, to garnish |

Put the cottage cheese, cream and chicken in a bowl and fold gently to mix. Stir in the orange segments and ginger.

Arrange a bed of lettuce and watercress on 4 individual plates. Spoon the cheese mixture on the centre of each plate. Garnish with the grapes before serving.

**Serves 4 to 6**

*Smoked haddock and yogurt mousse;*
*Fish roe stuffed eggs*

*Oriental salad*

# Fish Roe Stuffed Eggs

| Metric/Imperial | American |
|---|---|
| 8 hard-boiled eggs, shelled | 8 hard-cooked eggs, shelled |
| 150 ml / ¼ pint natural yogurt | ²/₃ cup unflavored yogurt |
| juice of 1 lemon | juice of 1 lemon |
| 100 g / 4 oz lumpfish roe | ½ cup fish roe |
| salt | salt |
| freshly ground black pepper | freshly ground black pepper |

Cut the eggs in half lengthwise, then remove the yolks. Put the yolks in a bowl with the yogurt and lemon juice and mash well together. Work in the fish roe, then add salt and pepper to taste.

Pile the mixture into the egg whites and serve on a bed of lettuce.

**Serves 4**

# Smoked Haddock and Yogurt Mousse

| Metric/Imperial | American |
|---|---|
| 225 g / 8 oz smoked haddock fillets | ½ lb smoked haddock fillets |
| 300 ml / ½ pint natural yogurt | 1 ¼ cups unflavored yogurt |
| 2 hard-boiled eggs, shelled | 2 hard-cooked eggs, shelled |
| finely grated rind of ½ lemon | finely grated rind of ½ lemon |
| 2 teaspoons lemon juice | 2 teaspoons lemon juice |
| 2 teaspoons gelatine | 2 teaspoons gelatin |
| 2 tablespoons water | 2 tablespoons water |
| salt | salt |
| freshly ground white pepper | freshly ground white pepper |
| paprika to garnish | paprika to garnish |

Poach the haddock in water to cover for 10 minutes. Drain well, then remove the skin and any bones and flake the flesh finely into a bowl. Add the yogurt and mix gently together. Chop 1 egg finely and add to the fish mixture with the lemon rind.

Put the lemon juice, gelatine and water in a small cup. Stand the cup in a pan of hot water and stir well until the gelatine becomes syrupy. Remove from the heat and cool for 2 minutes.

Stir the gelatine into the fish mixture, add salt and pepper to taste, then divide the mixture equally between 4 individual ramekins. Chill in the refrigerator for 1 hour.

Slice the remaining egg and use to decorate each ramekin, then sprinkle with paprika to garnish.

**Serves 4**

# Chicory (Belgian Endive) and Ham in Yogurt Sauce

| Metric/Imperial | American |
|---|---|
| 2 heads chicory | 2 heads Belgian endive |
| 4 thin slices cooked ham | 4 thin slices cooked ham |
| 150 ml / ¼ pint natural yogurt | ⅔ cup unflavored yogurt |
| 4 tablespoons milk | ¼ cup milk |
| 1 egg yolk | 1 egg yolk |
| salt | salt |
| freshly ground black pepper | freshly ground black pepper |
| 2 teaspoons grated Parmesan cheese | 2 teaspoons grated Parmesan cheese |
| chopped parsley to garnish | chopped parsley to garnish |

Put the chicory (Belgian endive) in a bowl and cover with boiling water. Leave to stand for 3 minutes, then drain very thoroughly.

Split each head in half lengthwise to make 4 pieces, then roll a slice of ham around each piece. Place the pieces side by side in a shallow baking dish.

Put the yogurt, milk and egg yolk in a bowl and whisk with a fork until well mixed. Add salt and pepper to taste. Pour the sauce over the ham, then sprinkle with the cheese. Bake in a preheated moderate oven (180°C / 350°F, Gas Mark 4) for 25 minutes. Serve hot, garnished with parsley.

**Serves 4**

# Cottage Cheese Cocottes

| Metric/Imperial | American |
|---|---|
| 2 eggs | 2 eggs |
| 1 large slice wholemeal bread, crusts removed | 1 large slice wholewheat bread, crusts removed |
| 3 tablespoons hot milk | 3 tablespoons hot milk |
| 100 g / 4 oz shelled prawns or shrimps | ¼ lb shelled shrimp |
| 225 g / 8 oz cottage cheese | ½ lb cottage cheese |
| 1 teaspoon made mustard | 1 teaspoon made mustard |
| salt | salt |
| freshly ground black pepper | freshly ground black pepper |
| 1 small green pepper, cored, seeded and sliced into rings | 1 small green pepper, cored, seeded and sliced into rings |

Break the eggs into a bowl and whisk with a fork until frothy. Place the bread in an electric blender and grind coarsely.

Fold the breadcrumbs, milk, prawns or shrimps and cottage cheese into the beaten eggs. Stir in the mustard and season with salt and pepper to taste.

Grease individual ovenproof ramekin dishes and divide the mixture evenly between them. Top each one with a green pepper ring.

Stand the dishes in a roasting pan, containing about 2.5 cm / 1 inch water and bake in a preheated moderately hot oven (190°C / 375°F, Gas Mark 5) for 35 minutes. Serve hot, with peas or beans and baked tomatoes, if liked.

**Serves 4**

# Cottage Pears

| Metric/Imperial | American |
|---|---|
| 4 ripe dessert pears | 4 ripe dessert pears |
| juice of ½ lemon | juice of ½ lemon |
| 225 g / 8 oz cottage cheese | 1 cup cottage cheese |
| 25 g / 1 oz walnuts, chopped | ¼ cup chopped walnuts |
| salt | salt |
| freshly ground black pepper | freshly ground black pepper |
| 2 celery sticks, cut into 2.5 cm / 1 inch slices | 2 celery stalks, cut into 1 inch slices |
| 1 carrot, peeled and coarsely grated | 1 carrot, peeled and coarsley grated |
| 1 bunch watercress, stems removed and leaves roughly chopped | 1 bunch watercress, stems removed and leaves roughly chopped |

Cut the pears in half lengthwise but do not peel them. Remove the cores, then brush the pears immediately with the lemon juice to prevent discoloration.

Put the cottage cheese and walnuts in a bowl, stir well, then add salt and pepper to taste. Fill the pears with the cheese mixture.

Mix together the celery, carrot and watercress, then arrange on individual plates. Place the pear halves on top. Serve immediately.

**Serves 4 or 8**

NOTE: Allow 1 pear half per person for a starter, 2 for a main course.

# Baked Yogurt Custard

| Metric/Imperial | American |
|---|---|
| 300 ml / ½ pint natural yogurt | 1¼ cups unflavored yogurt |
| few drops of vanilla essence | few drops of vanilla extract |
| few drops of liquid glucose | few drops of liquid glucose |
| 2 eggs, beaten | 2 eggs, beaten |
| 150 ml / ¼ pint milk | ⅔ cup milk |
| ¼ teaspoon grated nutmeg | ¼ teaspoon grated nutmeg |

Put the yogurt, vanilla and glucose in a bowl and mix well. Add the eggs and milk and beat well to an even colour. Pour into a baking dish and sprinkle with the nutmeg.

Stand the dish in a roasting pan and pour in enough water to come 2.5 cm / 1 inch up the sides of the pan. Bake in a preheated moderate oven (170°C / 325°F, Gas Mark 3) for 40 minutes.

Serve hot or cold with fresh or stewed fruit.

**Serves 4**

# Yogurt and Orange Jelly

| Metric/Imperial | American |
|---|---|
| 15 g / ½ oz gelatine | 2 envelopes gelatin |
| 1 tablespoon water | 1 tablespoon water |
| 300 ml / ½ pint orange juice | 1¼ cups orange juice |
| 150 ml / ¼ pint natural yogurt | ⅔ cup unflavored yogurt |

Put the gelatine and water in a small cup. Stand the cup in a pan of hot water and stir well until the gelatine becomes syrupy. Remove from the heat and cool for 2 minutes.

Put the orange juice and yogurt in a separate bowl, pour in the gelatine, then mix thoroughly.

Pour into a chilled 600 ml / 1 pint / 2½ cup mould. Leave to set, then chill in the refrigerator for 2 hours before serving.

**Serves 4**

# Slimmer's Coeur à la Crème

| Metric/Imperial | American |
|---|---|
| 2 teaspoons gelatine | 2 teaspoons gelatin |
| 2 tablespoons water | 2 tablespoons water |
| 350 g / 12 oz cottage cheese, sieved | 1½ cups cottage cheese, sieved |
| 150 ml / ¼ pint natural yogurt | ⅔ cup unflavored yogurt |
| juice of ½ lemon | juice of ½ lemon |
| salt | salt |
| freshly ground black pepper | freshly ground black pepper |

Put the gelatine and water in a small cup. Stand the cup in a pan of hot water and stir well until the gelatine becomes syrupy. Remove from the heat and cool for 2 minutes.

Put the cottage cheese, yogurt and lemon juice in a bowl and mix well. Add the gelatine and salt and pepper to taste; mix thoroughly.

Spoon the mixture into 4 individual ramekins, then chill in the refrigerator for 4 hours. Turn out and serve with fresh fruit in season.

**Serves 4**

# FISH & SHELLFISH

Freshly caught fish is wholesome, delicious and highly nutritious. It has a high protein content – 15 to 20 per cent, depending on the type of fish – and the protein is of good quality because it contains all of the essential amino-acids. It is also easily digested and is therefore particularly valuable for children, old people and anyone whose appetite is reduced through illness.

The fat contained in fish, unlike fat in meat, is highly unsaturated – a healthy advantage over meat. It is also a useful source of vitamins A and D. The amount of fat in different fish varies enormously. Oily fish, such as herring, mackerel and salmon, contain from 10 to 18 per cent. However white fish, such as cod, plaice (flounder) and sole, contain less than 2 per cent fat and can therefore play an important role in slimming diets – providing a valuable source of protein, vitamins and minerals, with comparatively few calories.

Unfortunately fish has one drawback – it is the most perishable of all fresh foods. Before buying fish, always check carefully to ensure it is absolutely fresh: choose fish with a moist, shiny skin, firm flesh, bright eyes and – most important – no sign of an odour. Although fresh fish can be stored in the refrigerator for a day or two, it is best eaten as soon as possible after purchase.

Care should be taken to avoid overcooking fish, which spoils the flavour and texture. After cooking, fish should be just tender, with creamy, firm flesh. Grilling (broiling) and poaching are the simplest ways to cook fish in order to retain its full flavour. Only a little flavouring is necessary – salt, freshly ground black pepper and a sprinkling of lemon juice. Poaching should be carried out in the minimum quantity of liquid; use a mixture of dry white wine and water, add a bouquet garni and simmer very gently until just tender.

Another delicious way to serve whole fish or fillets is to coat them with wholewheat breadcrumbs and then to quickly grill (broil) or fry in a little vegetable oil. A tasty way of cooking oily fish, such as mackerel, is to bake them, stuffed with onion slices, garlic cloves, herbs, lemon juice and seasoning.

Fish is very versatile and, with the addition of vegetables and herbs, can quickly be turned into a range of delicious dishes – soups, casseroles, pies, mousses and pâtés; it is also excellent served cold in salads.

Both fish and shellfish are ideal to serve as a first course for a three-course meal – providing a tasty, nourishing appetizer which is not so filling that it will detract from the main course. Unless you intend to serve a cold fish salad the following day, only cook as much fish as you intend to serve, because it does not reheat successfully.

Some people – men in particular – do not believe that fish can provide a substantial meal unless it is cooked in batter and eaten with plenty of chips! This is simply not true. Served with wholesome accompaniments – such as wholewheat bread, brown rice, or pulses (legumes) – and tasty vegetables – like mushrooms, tomatoes and spinach – fish becomes a substantial, satisfying meal.

*Spiced fish casserole (page 74); Sailor's mussels (page 66); Baked trout (page 70)*

# Fish Chowder

| Metric/Imperial | American |
|---|---|
| 750 g / 1½ lb cod or haddock fillets | 1½ lb cod or haddock fillets |
| 1.75 litres / 3 pints water | 7½ cups water |
| freshly ground black pepper | freshly ground black pepper |
| 1 onion, peeled and sliced | 1 onion, peeled and sliced |
| 2 potatoes, peeled and sliced | 2 potatoes, peeled and sliced |
| 3 tomatoes, sliced | 3 tomatoes, sliced |
| 2 teaspoons yeast extract | 2 teaspoons Brewer's yeast |
| 1 teaspoon chopped thyme | 1 teaspoon chopped thyme |
| 2 teaspoons chopped parsley | 2 teaspoons chopped parsley |
| 2 teaspoons tomato purée | 2 teaspoons tomato paste |
| salt | salt |
| 2 teaspoons Worcestershire sauce | 2 teaspoons Worcestershire sauce |
| juice of 1 lemon | juice of 1 lemon |

Put the fish in a pan with the water and a pinch of pepper. Bring to the boil, then lower the heat and poach gently for 15 minutes or until the fish is tender. Drain off the water and reserve. Cut the fish into 2.5 cm / 1 inch cubes, discarding the skin and any bones.

Put the fish and the reserved water in the rinsed-out pan with the remaining ingredients, except the Worcestershire sauce and lemon juice. Bring to the boil, then lower the heat, cover and simmer for 45 minutes.

Stir in the Worcestershire sauce and lemon juice, then serve very hot with wholewheat bread or crackers.

**Serves 4**

# Soft Roes on Toast

| Metric/Imperial | American |
|---|---|
| 450 g / 1 lb soft roes, washed | 1 lb soft roes, washed |
| salt | salt |
| 2 tablespoons mushroom ketchup | 4 tablespoons minced cooked mushrooms |
| 1 tablespoon Worcestershire sauce | 1 tablespoon Worcestershire sauce |
| ½ teaspoon anchovy essence (optional) | freshly ground black pepper |
| freshly ground black pepper | 4 slices wholewheat bread |
| 4 slices wholemeal bread | juice of 1 lemon |
| juice of 1 lemon | pinch of cayenne pepper |
| pinch of cayenne pepper | |

Poach the roes in salted water to cover for 15 minutes, then drain very thoroughly.

Mix together the mushroom ketchup (mushrooms), Worcestershire sauce and anchovy essence if using. Add salt and pepper to taste, then add the roes and mix well.

Toast the bread lightly on both sides. Pile the roes on the toast and grill (broil) under medium heat for 3 minutes.

Arrange on individual warmed serving plates, then sprinkle with the lemon juice and cayenne pepper. Serve hot.

**Serves 4**

# Sailors' Mussels

| Metric/Imperial | American |
|---|---|
| 48 mussels | 48 mussels or clams |
| 6 shallots, peeled and chopped | 6 shallots, peeled and chopped |
| 300 ml / ½ pint dry cider | 1¼ cups hard cider |
| 2 teaspoons flour | 2 teaspoons flour |
| 15 g / ½ oz vegetable margarine | 1 tablespoon vegetable margarine |
| 2 tablespoons chopped parsley | 2 tablespoons chopped parsley |
| salt | salt |
| freshly ground black pepper | freshly ground black pepper |

Wash the mussels (or clams) and scrub them very thoroughly. Discard any which are open. Put them in a heavy pan with the shallots and cider. Cover and cook over high heat for 5 minutes until all the mussels (or clams) have opened; discard any which are still closed.

Lift out the mussels (or clams) and discard the top shell from each one. Divide them equally between 4 individual soup bowls and keep hot.

Work the flour and margarine together to form a ball. Drop the ball into the cooking liquid and simmer until the sauce has thickened slightly, stirring constantly. Stir in the parsley, then add salt and pepper to taste. Pour the sauce over the mussels and serve immediately.

**Serves 4**

Put the gelatine and water in a small cup. Stand the cup in a pan of hot water and stir until the gelatine is syrupy.

Put the cottage cheese in a bowl, add salt and pepper to taste, then stir in the crabmeat, cream and lemon juice. Mix very thoroughly, then stir in the gelatine.

Spoon the mixture into a serving bowl, then chill in the refrigerator for 2 hours. Garnish with watercress sprigs just before serving.

**Serves 4**

# Prawn (Shrimp), Apple and Celery Cocktail

| Metric/Imperial | American |
|---|---|
| 1 lettuce, shredded | 1 head of lettuce, shredded |
| salt | salt |
| 2 celery sticks, finely chopped | 2 celery stalks, finely chopped |
| 1 dessert apple, peeled, cored and chopped | 1 dessert apple, peeled, cored and chopped |
| 225 g / 8 oz peeled prawns | 1 cup shelled shrimp |
| juice of 1 lemon | juice of 1 lemon |
| freshly ground black pepper | freshly ground black pepper |
| pinch of paprika to garnish | pinch of paprika to garnish |

Divide the lettuce equally between 4 glasses and sprinkle lightly with salt. Put the remaining ingredients, except the paprika, in a bowl and mix well.

Divide the mixture equally between the glasses, sprinkle with paprika and serve chilled.

**Serves 4**

# Crab and Cottage Cheese Mousse

| Metric/Imperial | American |
|---|---|
| 15 g / ½ oz gelatine | 2 envelopes gelatin |
| 150 ml / ¼ pint water | ⅔ cup water |
| 450 g / 1 lb cottage cheese, sieved | 2 cups cottage cheese, sieved |
| salt | salt |
| freshly ground black pepper | freshly ground black pepper |
| 225 g / 8 oz crabmeat | 1 cup crabmeat |
| 3 tablespoons single cream | 3 tablespoons light cream |
| 2 teaspoons lemon juice | 2 teaspoons lemon juice |
| watercress sprigs to garnish | watercress sprigs to garnish |

# Baked Crab

*The crabmeat may be fresh, canned or frozen provided it is thawed. The dish is best made with a mixture of about one-third dark meat and two-thirds white meat.*

| Metric/Imperial | American |
|---|---|
| 2 tablespoons oil | 2 tablespoons oil |
| 1 onion, peeled and finely chopped | 1 onion, peeled and finely chopped |
| 1 garlic clove, peeled and crushed | 1 garlic clove, peeled and crushed |
| 2 green peppers, cored, seeded and finely chopped | 2 green peppers, cored, seeded and finely chopped |
| 2 tomatoes, skinned, seeded and chopped | 2 tomatoes, skinned, seeded and chopped |
| 2 tablespoons chopped parsley | 2 tablespoons chopped parsley |
| 450 g / 1 lb crabmeat | 2 cups crabmeat |
| salt | salt |
| freshly ground white pepper | freshly ground white pepper |
| 2 eggs, lightly beaten | 2 eggs, lightly beaten |
| 2 tablespoons wholemeal breadcrumbs | 2 tablespoons wholewheat breadcrumbs |

Heat the oil in a pan, add the onion and fry gently for 5 minutes until soft and golden, stirring occasionally. Add the garlic, green peppers, tomatoes and parsley and continue cooking gently for 15 minutes, stirring occasionally.

Add the crabmeat to the pan with salt and pepper to taste. Then add the eggs and cook until just set, stirring constantly.

Spread the crab mixture in a greased shallow baking dish and sprinkle the breadcrumbs on top. Bake in a preheated moderately hot oven (190°C / 375°F, Gas Mark 5) for 10 minutes or until the crumbs are crisp and brown. Serve hot.

**Serves 4**

# Prawn (Shrimp) Quiches

**Metric/Imperial**

wholewheat pastry made
with 225 g / 8 oz flour
(see page 227)
25 g / 1 oz vegetable
margarine
1 small onion, peeled and
chopped
2 eggs, beaten
100 g / 4 oz cottage cheese,
sieved
2 tablespoons single cream
2 teaspoons chopped
parsley
salt
freshly ground white pepper
100 g / 4 oz peeled prawns
chopped parsley to garnish

**American**

wholewheat dough made
with 2 cups flour (see
(see page 227)
2 tablespoons vegetable
margarine
1 small onion, peeled and
chopped
2 eggs, beaten
½ cup cottage cheese,
sieved
2 tablespoons light cream
2 teaspoons chopped
parsley
salt
freshly ground white pepper
½ cup shelled shrimp
chopped parsley to garnish

Roll out the pastry dough on a lightly floured surface and use to line 4 individual quiche dishes. Prick the bases lightly with a fork, cover with kitchen foil, then weigh down with baking beans or rice.

Bake in a preheated moderately hot oven (200°C / 400°F, Gas Mark 6) for 10 minutes, then remove the beans or rice and the foil.

Meanwhile, melt the margarine in a pan, add the onion and fry gently for 3 minutes, stirring occasionally.

Put the eggs, cottage cheese, cream, parsley and salt and pepper to taste in a bowl and beat well to mix. Stir in the onion and prawns (shrimp). Divide the mixture equally between the flan cases.

Bake in a preheated moderate oven (180°C / 350°F, Gas Mark 4) for 20 minutes. Garnish with parsley and serve hot.
**Serves 4**

*RIGHT: Spiced herrings; Swedish pickled shrimp*
*BELOW: Prawn (shrimp) quiches*

# Swedish Pickled Shrimp

| Metric/Imperial | American |
|---|---|
| 450 g / 1 lb peeled shrimps | 2 cups shelled shrimp |
| 6 black peppercorns, crushed | 6 black peppercorns, crushed |
| ½ teaspoon chopped thyme | ½ teaspoon chopped thyme |
| 1 bay leaf | 1 bay leaf |
| 150 ml / ¼ pint tarragon vinegar | ⅔ cup tarragon vinegar |
| 1 lettuce | 1 head of lettuce |
| dill leaves to garnish | dill leaves to garnish |

The shrimps may be fresh, or thawed frozen ones which have been well drained.

Put the shrimps in a bowl and sprinkle with the crushed peppercorns and the thyme. Put the bay leaf on top and pour on the vinegar. Chill in the refrigerator for 2 hours.

Arrange a bed of lettuce leaves in 4 individual serving bowls. Drain the shrimps and arrange a mound of them on each bed of lettuce. Sprinkle with dill leaves. Serve with thinly sliced brown bread or crispbread, and butter.

**Serves 4**

# Spiced Herrings

| Metric/Imperial | American |
|---|---|
| 4 herrings | 4 herrings |
| 2 onions, peeled and chopped | 2 onions, peeled and chopped |
| 2 tablespoons whole pickling spice | 2 tablespoons whole pickling spice |
| salt | salt |
| freshly ground black pepper | freshly ground black pepper |
| 450 ml / ¾ pint dry cider | 2 cups hard cider |

Split the fish down the back, open out and clean. Reserve the roes. Wash the herrings well and dry them on kitchen paper towels. Mash the roes with a fork and mix with one quarter of the onion. Stuff the fish with this mixture and arrange them head to tail in a baking dish.

Sprinkle the remaining onion, the pickling spice and salt and pepper to taste, over the fish. Pour on the cider. Cover and bake in a preheated moderate oven (170°C/325°F, Gas Mark 3) for 1¼ hours. Leave the fish to cool in the cooking liquid, then chill in the refrigerator overnight. Serve cold with salad.

**Serves 4**

# Trout in Yogurt Sauce

| Metric/Imperial | American |
|---|---|
| 150 ml / ¼ pint wine vinegar | ⅔ cup wine vinegar |
| 150 ml / ¼ pint water | ⅔ cup water |
| 1 small onion, peeled and sliced | 1 small onion, peeled and sliced |
| 1 bay leaf | 1 bay leaf |
| 1 parsley sprig | 1 parsley sprig |
| 1 thyme sprig | 1 thyme sprig |
| salt | salt |
| freshly ground white pepper | freshly ground white pepper |
| 4 × 225 g / 8 oz trout, cleaned, washed and dried | 4 × ½ lb trout, cleaned, washed and dried |
| SAUCE: | SAUCE: |
| 150 ml / ¼ pint natural yogurt | ⅔ cup unflavored yogurt |
| 3 tablespoons grated horseradish | 3 tablespoons grated horseradish |
| juice of ½ lemon | juice of ½ lemon |
| 1 tablespoon tarragon vinegar | 1 tablespoon tarragon vinegar |
| 1 teaspoon snipped chives | 1 teaspoon snipped chives |
| pinch of cayenne pepper | pinch of cayenne pepper |

Put the vinegar, water, onion, bay leaf, parsley and thyme in a small pan with salt and pepper to taste. Bring to the boil, then lower the heat and simmer for 30 minutes.

Put the trout in a separate pan, then strain the vinegar liquid over the trout. Simmer very gently for 20 minutes, then drain well and place on a warmed serving dish. Keep hot.

To make the sauce: put all the ingredients in a heatproof bowl and stand over a pan of gently simmering water. Stir until the sauce is thick and creamy, then pour over the fish and serve immediately. This dish can alternatively be served cold.

**Serves 4**

# Baked Trout

| Metric/Imperial | American |
|---|---|
| 2 tablespoons oil | 2 tablespoons oil |
| 2 garlic cloves, peeled and crushed | 2 garlic cloves, peeled and crushed |
| 2 onions, peeled and finely chopped | 2 onions, peeled and finely chopped |
| 100 g / 4 oz mushrooms, chopped | 1 cup chopped mushrooms |
| 2 tablespoons capers | 2 tablespoons capers |
| 2 tablespoons wholemeal flour | 2 tablespoons wholewheat flour |
| 25 g / 1 oz ground almonds | ¼ cup ground almonds |
| 4 × 225 g / 8 oz trout, cleaned, washed and dried | 4 × ½ lb trout, cleaned, washed and dried |
| 2 tablespoons chopped parsley | 2 tablespoons chopped parsley |
| pinch of chopped marjoram | pinch of chopped marjoram |
| 1 teaspoon salt | 1 teaspoon salt |
| ½ teaspoon freshly ground black pepper | ½ teaspoon freshly ground black pepper |
| 150 ml / ¼ pint chicken stock | ⅔ cup chicken stock |
| toasted flaked almonds to garnish | toasted sliced almonds to garnish |

Heat the oil in a large, shallow flameproof casserole or heavy-based pan. Add the garlic and onions and fry gently for 5 minutes until the onions are soft and golden, stirring occasionally. Stir in the mushrooms, capers, flour and ground almonds and fry gently for a further 3 minutes.

Put the trout on top of the onion mixture, then sprinkle with the parsley, marjoram, salt and pepper. Pour on the stock.

Bake in a preheated moderately hot oven (200°C / 400°F, Gas Mark 6) for 25 minutes, basting twice. Sprinkle with almonds and serve immediately.

**Serves 4**

# Summer Fish Salad

| Metric/Imperial | American |
|---|---|
| 450 g / 1 lb haddock or cod fillets | 1 lb haddock or cod fillets |
| 1 onion, peeled | 1 onion, peeled |
| 450 ml / ¾ pint water | 2 cups water |
| 1 teaspoon salt | 1 teaspoon salt |
| 4 tablespoons mayonnaise | ¼ cup mayonnaise |
| 1 teaspoon chopped parsley | 1 teaspoon chopped parsley |
| 1 teaspoon grated onion | 1 teaspoon grated onion |
| 1 teaspoon Worcestershire sauce | 1 teaspoon Worcestershire sauce |
| ¼ teaspoon freshly ground black pepper | ¼ teaspoon freshly ground black pepper |
| 2 celery sticks, finely chopped | 2 celery stalks, finely chopped |
| 1 dessert apple, peeled, cored and diced | 1 dessert apple, peeled, cored and diced |
| ½ cucumber, peeled and diced | ½ cucumber, peeled and diced |
| TO GARNISH: | TO GARNISH: |
| 1 lettuce, shredded | 1 head of lettuce, shredded |
| 1 hard-boiled egg, shelled and finely chopped | 1 hard-cooked egg, shelled and finely chopped |

Put the fish in a pan with the onion, water and salt. Bring to the boil, then lower the heat and poach gently for 25 minutes or until the fish is tender. Drain off the water, then flake the fish into a serving bowl, discarding the skin and any bones. Leave the fish to cool.

Mix together the mayonnaise, parsley, onion, Worcestershire sauce and pepper. Add the celery, apple, cucumber and mayonnaise mixture to the fish and fold gently to mix.

Arrange a border of shredded lettuce around the edge of the bowl and sprinkle the chopped egg in the middle.

**Serves 4**

# Cod Kebabs

| Metric/Imperial | American |
|---|---|
| 450 g / 1 lb cod fillet, skinned and cut into 5 cm / 2 inch squares | 450 g / 1 lb cod fillet, skinned and cut into 5 cm / 2 inch squares |
| 1 green pepper, cored and seeded | 1 green pepper, cored and seeded |
| 2 tablespoons lemon juice | 4 tablespoons corn oil |
| 4 tablespoons corn oil | 1 teaspoon chopped parsley |
| 1 teaspoon chopped parsley | 1 teaspoon chopped marjoram (optional) |
| 1 teaspoon chopped marjoram (optional) | 1 garlic clove, peeled and crushed |
| 1 garlic clove, peeled and crushed | 4 lean bacon slices, derinded |
| 4 lean rashers bacon, derinded | 1 green pepper, cored, seeded and sliced |
| 1 green pepper, cored, seeded and sliced | 4 small tomatoes |
| 4 small tomatoes | |

Place the fish in a shallow dish and sprinkle liberally with salt and pepper. Mix together the lemon juice, oil, parsley, marjoram and garlic and pour over the fish. Cover and leave to marinate in a cool place for about 4 hours.

Cut the bacon and green pepper into 5 cm / 2 inch squares. Drain the fish, reserving the marinade. Thread alternate pieces of fish, bacon and green pepper onto 4 kebab skewers. Press the pieces together firmly and place a whole tomato on one end of each skewer.

Place on a grill (broiler) rack and baste with the marinade. Cook under a preheated moderate grill (broiler) for 8 to 10 minutes until the fish is tender and the green pepper is softened. Turn the skewers and brush with the oil mixture frequently during cooking.

Serve the kebabs hot, with a crisp green salad and brown rice or wholewheat bread.

**Serves 4**

# Seafood Salad with Dill

| Metric/Imperial | American |
|---|---|
| 450 g / 1 lb smoked haddock fillets | 1 lb smoked haddock fillets |
| 600 ml / 1 pint water | 2¹/₂ cups water |
| 1 bay leaf | 1 bay leaf |
| 1 small onion, peeled and sliced | 1 small onion, peeled and sliced |
| 1 small carrot, peeled and sliced | 1 small carrot, peeled and sliced |
| 4 black peppercorns | 4 black peppercorns |
| 225 g / 8 oz peeled prawns | 1 cup shelled shrimp |
| 120 ml / 4 fl oz oil | ¹/₂ cup oil |
| 3 tablespoons wine vinegar | 3 tablespoons wine vinegar |
| freshly ground black pepper | freshly ground black pepper |
| 1 lettuce | 1 head of lettuce |
| 1 bunch watercress, trimmed | 1 bunch watercress, trimmed |
| 1 tablespoon chopped parsley | 1 tablespoon chopped parsley |
| 2 tablespoons chopped dill | 2 tablespoons chopped dill |

Put the fish in a pan with the water, bay leaf, onion, carrot and peppercorns. Bring to the boil, then lower the heat and poach gently for 15 minutes or until the fish is tender. Drain off the water, then flake the fish into a bowl, discarding the skin and any bones.

Add the prawns (shrimp) to the haddock. Mix together the oil, vinegar and black pepper and pour over the fish. Chill in the refrigerator for 2 hours.

Arrange a bed of lettuce leaves in a serving bowl, then arrange the watercress on top. Drain the fish, place in the centre of the bowl and sprinkle generously with parsley and dill.

**Serves 4**

# Seafood Curry

| Metric/Imperial | American |
|---|---|
| 25 g / 1 oz vegetable margarine | 2 tablespoons vegetable margarine |
| 1 small onion, peeled and chopped | 1 small onion, peeled and chopped |
| 1 teaspoon curry powder | 1 teaspoon curry powder |
| 2 teaspoons flour | 2 teaspoons flour |
| 150 ml / ¹/₄ pint natural yogurt | ²/₃ cup unflavored yogurt |
| 1 small dessert apple, cored and chopped | 1 small dessert apple, cored and chopped |
| 225 g / 8 oz peeled prawns | 1 cup shelled shrimp |
| 2 tomatoes, skinned, seeded and chopped | 2 tomatoes, skinned, seeded and chopped |
| salt | salt |
| freshly ground black pepper | freshly ground black pepper |
| lemon wedges to garnish | lemon wedges to garnish |

Melt the margarine in a pan, add the onion and fry gently for 3 minutes until soft and golden, stirring occasionally. Stir in the curry powder and flour and cook for 2 minutes.

Remove from the heat and stir in the yogurt, apple and prawns (shrimp). Return to the heat and cook gently for 5 minutes.

Add the tomatoes to the pan and continue cooking for 3 minutes. Add salt and pepper to taste. Garnish with lemon wedges and serve hot, with brown rice.

**Serves 4**

*ABOVE: Seafood curry*
*RIGHT: Seafood salad with dill; Smoked haddock flan*

# Smoked Haddock Flan

**Metric/Imperial**

wholewheat pastry made
with 175 g / 6 oz flour
(see page 227)
225 g / 8 oz smoked
haddock fillets
150 ml / ¼ pint water
juice of 1 lemon
25 g / 1 oz vegetable
margarine
1 small onion, peeled and
chopped
50 g / 2 oz button
mushrooms, sliced
2 eggs, beaten
3 tablespoons single cream
100 g / 4 oz cottage cheese
1 tablespoon chopped
parsley
salt
freshly ground white pepper
25 g / 1 oz grated Parmesan
cheese
parsley sprig to garnish

**American**

wholewheat dough made
with 1½ cups flour (see
(see page 227)
½ lb smoked haddock fillets
⅔ cup water
juice of 1 lemon
2 tablespoons vegetable
margarine
1 small onion, peeled and
chopped
½ cup sliced button
mushrooms
2 eggs, beaten
3 tablespoons light cream
½ cup cottage cheese
1 tablespoon chopped
parsley
salt
freshly ground white pepper
¼ cup grated Parmesan
cheese
parsley sprig to garnish

Roll out the pastry dough on a lightly floured surface and use to line a 20 cm / 8 inch flan ring placed on a baking sheet. Prick the base lightly with a fork, cover with foil, then weigh down with baking beans or rice.

Bake blind in a preheated moderately hot oven (200°C / 400°F, Gas Mark 6) for 15 minutes, then remove the beans or rice and the foil.

Meanwhile, put the fish in a pan with the water and half the lemon juice and poach gently for 15 minutes until the fish is tender. Drain off the water, then flake the fish into a bowl, discarding the skin and any bones.

Melt the margarine in a pan, add the onion and mushrooms and fry gently for 3 minutes, stirring occasionally. Add to the fish, mix well, then spread the mixture in the flan case.

Put the eggs, cream, cottage cheese, parsley, remaining lemon juice and salt and pepper to taste in a bowl. Beat well, then pour over the fish. Sprinkle with the Parmesan cheese.

Bake in a preheated moderately hot oven (190°C / 375°F, Gas Mark 5) for 40 minutes and serve hot.
**Serves 4**

# Spiced Fish Casserole

| Metric/Imperial | American |
|---|---|
| 3 large tomatoes, skinned and sliced | 3 large tomatoes, skinned and sliced |
| 2 celery sticks, finely chopped | 2 celery stalks, finely chopped |
| 1 garlic clove, peeled and crushed | 1 garlic clove, peeled and crushed |
| 50 g / 2 oz mushrooms, sliced | ½ cup sliced mushrooms |
| salt | salt |
| freshly ground black pepper | freshly ground black pepper |
| pinch of grated nutmeg | pinch of grated nutmeg |
| 1 teaspoon chopped parsley | 1 teaspoon chopped parsley |
| 1 teaspoon chopped basil | 1 teaspoon chopped basil |
| 1 bay leaf | 1 bay leaf |
| 1 onion, peeled and sliced | 1 onion, peeled and sliced |
| 1 carrot, peeled and sliced | 1 carrot, peeled and sliced |
| 750 g / 1½ lb cod fillets | 1½ lb cod fillets |
| 3 tablespoons wine vinegar | 3 tablespoons wine vinegar |
| 150 ml / ¼ pint water | ⅔ cup water |

Arrange half the tomato slices in a baking dish and cover with the celery, garlic and mushrooms. Season well with salt and pepper, then sprinkle with the nutmeg and parsley. Add the basil and the bay leaf and top with the onion and carrot.

Arrange the fish on top of this mixture, then cover with the remaining tomato slices. Pour on the vinegar and water. Cover and bake in a preheated moderate oven (180°C / 350°F, Gas Mark 4) for 40 minutes. Serve hot.

**Serves 4**

# Smoked Haddock and Cheese Bake

| Metric/Imperial | American |
|---|---|
| 450 g / 1 lb smoked haddock fillets | 1 lb smoked haddock fillets |
| 25 g / 1 oz grated Parmesan cheese | ¼ cup grated Parmesan cheese |
| salt | salt |
| freshly ground white pepper | freshly ground white pepper |
| 150 ml / ¼ pint natural yogurt | ⅔ cup unflavored yogurt |
| 300 ml / ½ pint milk | 1¼ cups milk |
| 2 eggs, beaten | 2 eggs, beaten |
| 1 tablespoon chopped parsley | 1 tablespoon chopped parsley |

Put the fish in a pan with enough water to just cover. Bring to the boil, then lower the heat and poach gently for 15 minutes or until the fish is tender. Drain off the water, then place the fish in a baking dish.

Sprinkle the cheese and salt and pepper to taste over the fish. Put the remaining ingredients in a bowl, mix well, then pour over the fish.

Stand the dish in a roasting pan and pour in enough water to come 2.5 cm / 1 inch up the sides of the pan. Bake in a preheated moderate oven (180°C / 350°F, Gas Mark 4) for 40 minutes. Serve hot.

**Serves 4**

# Swedish Baked Fish

**Metric/Imperial**
4 halibut fillets
1 onion, peeled and sliced
4 tablespoons chopped
  parsley
450 ml / ¾ pint tomato
  juice
salt
freshly ground black pepper

**American**
4 halibut fillets
1 onion, peeled and sliced
¼ cup chopped parsley
2 cups tomato juice
salt
freshly ground black pepper

Put the fish in a greased baking dish. Arrange the onion slices on top and sprinkle with half the parsley. Pour on the tomato juice, season well with salt and pepper, then cover with foil.

Bake in a preheated moderately hot oven (200°C / 400°F, Gas Mark 6) for 30 minutes. Sprinkle with the remaining parsley and serve hot.

**Serves 4**

Work the mixture through a sieve (strainer), taste and adjust seasoning, then pour over the fish. Bake in a pre-heated moderate oven (180°C / 350°F, Gas Mark 4) for 45 minutes or until the fish is cooked. Serve hot.

**Serves 4**

# Haddock in Tomato Sauce

**Metric/Imperial**
450 g / 1 lb haddock fillets
1 teaspoon salt
½ teaspoon freshly ground
  black pepper
1 tablespoon oil
1 onion, peeled and finely
  chopped
1 green pepper, cored,
  seeded and finely
  chopped
2 celery sticks, finely
  chopped
1 garlic clove, peeled and
  crushed
1 teaspoon chilli powder
1 bay leaf
1 tablespoon
  Worcestershire saucee
1 × 400 g / 14 oz can
  tomatoes

**American**
1 lb haddock fillets
1 teaspoon salt
½ teaspoon freshly ground
  black pepper
1 tablespoon oil
1 onion, peeled and finely
  chopped
1 green pepper, cored,
  seeded and finely
  chopped
2 celery stalks, finely
  chopped
1 garlic clove, peeled and
  crushed
1 teaspoon chili powder
1 bay leaf
1 tablespoon
  Worcestershire sauce
1 lb can tomatoes

# Fish in a Packet

**Metric/Imperial**
450 g / 1 lb cod fillets
2 tablespoons oil
2 tablespoons lemon juice
salt
freshly ground black pepper
2 tomatoes, sliced
4 fennel sprigs

**American**
1 lb cod fillets
2 tablespoons oil
2 tablespoons lemon juice
salt
freshly ground black pepper
2 tomatoes, sliced
4 fennel sprigs

Cut the fish into 4 pieces. Cut out four 30 cm / 12 inch squares of foil and brush them liberally with oil. Place one piece of fish on each square of foil, then sprinkle with the remaining oil, the lemon juice and salt and pepper to taste. Place 2 tomato slices on each piece of fish, then top each with a fennel sprig.

Fold the foil around each fish to form a parcel, then place the parcels on a baking sheet. Bake in a preheated moderate oven (180°C / 350°F, Gas Mark 4) for 30 minutes.

Unwrap each parcel carefully, lift the fish out onto warmed serving plates, pour over the cooking juices and serve hot.

**Serves 4**

Cut the fish into 4 pieces, then place in a lightly oiled shallow baking dish. Sprinkle with the salt and pepper then chill in the refrigerator for 30 minutes.

Meanwhile, heat the oil in a pan. Add the onion, green pepper, celery and garlic and fry gently for 5 minutes, stirring occasionally. Add the remaining ingredients and continue cooking gently for 10 minutes, stirring well.

# Somerset Fish

| Metric/Imperial | American |
|---|---|
| 4 trout or herring, cleaned, washed and dried | 4 trout or herring cleaned, washed and dried |
| salt | salt |
| freshly ground black pepper | freshly ground black pepper |
| 3 small onions, peeled and cut into rings | 3 small onions, peeled and cut into rings |
| 2 dessert apples, peeled and finely chopped | 1 cup finely chopped dessert apple |
| pinch of cinnamon | pinch of cinnamon |
| juice of 2 oranges | juice of 2 oranges |
| 150 ml / 1/4 pint fish stock | 2/3 cup fish stock |
| 2 bay leaves | 2 bay leaves |
| orange slices to garnish | oranges slices to garnish |

Sprinkle the fish with salt and pepper and put them in a casserole.

Add the onions, apples and cinnamon. Pour in the orange juice and fish stock. Add the bay leaves.

Cook in a preheated moderately hot oven (190°C/ 375°F, Gas Mark 5) for 30 to 35 minutes.

Serve garnished with orange slices.

Somerset Fish could be served cold as part of a buffet, or as a summer supper dish. If you plan to serve it cold, cook it for only 25 to 30 minutes, then allow it to cool in the liquor. It will continue to cook slightly as it cools. Serve with a selection of fresh, crisp salads.

**Serves 4**

# Steamed Trout with Mushrooms and Shrimps

| Metric/Imperial | American |
|---|---|
| 4 trout*, cleaned, washed and dried | 4 trout*, cleaned, washed and dried |
| 1/2 teaspoon salt | 1/2 teaspoon salt |
| freshly ground black pepper | freshly ground black pepper |
| 4 tablespoons lemon juice | 1/4 cup lemon juice |
| sprigs of fresh dill | sprigs of fresh dill |
| 50-75 g / 2-3 oz mushrooms, sliced | 1/2 cup sliced mushrooms |
| TO GARNISH: | TO GARNISH: |
| few peeled prawns | few shelled shrimp |
| lemon quarters | lemon quarters |

Place the fish on a large sheet of foil or greaseproof paper. Sprinkle them with salt, pepper, lemon juice and dill. Fold in the foil or paper, so that none of the juice can escape. Place it between two plates, and stand them on a pan of boiling water. Steam for 10 to 15 minutes, or until cooked. Transfer to a hot serving dish.

Strain the juice from the foil into a small pan. Bring it to the boil. Add the mushrooms and allow to simmer for 4 to 5 minutes.

Pour the mushrooms and juice over the fish, and garnish with prawns (shrimp) and lemon quarters.

NOTE: This same recipe could apply equally well to other fish, such as plaice (flounder), sole, haddock or cod.

**Serves 4**

*BELOW: Somerset fish*

# Cold Jellied Trout

| Metric/Imperial | American |
|---|---|
| 4 large trout, cleaned, washed and dried | 4 large trout, cleaned, washed and dried |
| salt | salt |
| freshly ground black pepper | freshly ground black pepper |
| 450 ml / ¾ pint fish stock | 2 cups fish stock |
| juice of 1 lemon | juice of 1 lemon |
| bouquet garni | bouquet garni |
| 15 g / ½ oz aspic jelly powder | 1 envelope aspic jelly powder |
| TO GARNISH: | TO GARNISH: |
| peeled prawns | shelled shrimp |
| lemon slices | lemon slices |
| asparagus spears | asparagus spears |
| cubes of peeled, seeded tomato | cubes of peeled, seeded tomato |

Slit each trout along the stomach and carefully remove the backbones. Your fishmonger might do this for you if he has time. Leave the heads on. Season them very lightly. Put them in a fish kettle or large pan and add the fish stock and lemon juice. Add the bouquet garni, bring to the boil and simmer very gently for 8 to 10 minutes.

Lift out the fish carefully and drain them well before arranging them on a serving dish. Garnish them with prawns (shrimp), lemon, asparagus and tomato.

Strain the liquid and measure it. If necessary add more water to make up to just over 300 ml / ½ pint (1¼ cups). Soften the aspic jelly powder in a little of the liquid. Heat the rest, then add the softened aspic and stir until totally dissolved. Leave it to cool. When it has stiffened slightly, spoon it over the fish and leave until quite set. Garnish with parsley.

**Serves 4**

*ABOVE: Cold jellied trout*

# Whiting Fillets with Butter Sauce

| Metric/Imperial | American |
|---|---|
| 700 g / 1½ lb whiting fillets | 1½ lb whiting fillets |
| 125 g / 4 oz vegetable margarine | ¼ cup vegetable margarine |
| seasoned flour | seasoned flour |
| 1 egg, beaten | 1 egg, beaten |
| 1 tablespoon lemon juice | 1 tablespoon lemon juice |
| 2 teaspoons chopped parsley | 2 teaspoons chopped parsley |

Melt the margarine in a large frying pan (skillet). Dip the whiting fillets in the seasoned flour, then the egg, shaking off any excess. Add them to the pan, in batches, and fry quickly until they are golden brown on both sides (about 8 to 10 minutes).

Transfer the fillets to a warmed serving dish. Stir the lemon juice into the pan juices and swirl around until blended. Pour the juice over the fillets and garnish with parsley before serving.

**Serves 4**

# Baked Turbot with Yogurt

| Metric/Imperial | American |
|---|---|
| 450 g / 1 lb turbot, cleaned, washed and dried | 1 lb turbot, cleaned, washed and dried |
| 300 ml / ½ pint natural yogurt | 1¼ cups unflavored yogurt |
| 1 tablespoon lemon juice | 1 tablespoon lemon juice |
| 1 tablespoon dry sherry | 1 tablespoon dry sherry |
| 1 blade of mace | 1 blade of mace |
| 1 egg yolk | 1 egg yolk |
| salt and pepper | salt |
| | freshly ground black pepper |

Arrange the turbot in an ovenproof dish. Beat together the yogurt, lemon juice, sherry, mace, egg yolk, salt and pepper. Pour this over the turbot. Cover with foil and bake in a preheated moderately hot oven (190°C / 375°F, Gas Mark 5) for 45 to 50 minutes. Serve immediately.

**Serves 4**

# Lemony Bass

| Metric/Imperial | American |
| --- | --- |
| 25 g / 2 oz vegetable margarine | 4 tablespoons vegetable margarine |
| 450 g / 1 lb carrots, finely chopped | 4 cups finely chopped carrots |
| 2 large onions, peeled and finely chopped | 2 cups finely chopped onions |
| 2 medium leeks, finely chopped | 2 medium leeks, finely chopped |
| salt | salt |
| freshly ground black pepper | freshly ground black pepper |
| sprig of fresh tarragon or fennel | sprig of fresh tarragon or fennel |
| 1 kg / 2 lb bass, cleaned, washed and dried | 2 lb bass, cleaned, washed and dried |
| 150 ml / ¼ pint water | ⅔ cup water |
| 150 ml / ¼ pint lemon juice | ⅔ cup lemon juice |
| lemon slices to garnish | lemon slices to garnish |

Heat half of the margarine in a pan. Add the carrots, onions and leeks. Season with salt and pepper, cover and allow to cook gently for 15 minutes.

Spread this mixture in the bottom of a long roasting pan.

Place the sprig of fresh tarragon or fennel inside the bass. Rub the fish all over with the remaining margarine, and place it on the bed of vegetables in the roasting pan. Pour over the water and lemon juice.

Bake for 30 to 35 minutes in a preheated moderately hot oven (190°C / 375°F, Gas Mark 5).

Carefully transfer the fish to a hot serving dish and surround it with the vegetables.

Strain the cooking liquor into a pan and boil it quickly over a high heat for a few minutes. Pour it over the fish before serving garnished with lemon slices.

**Serves 6-8**

# Foiled Sole

| Metric/Imperial | American |
| --- | --- |
| 1 tablespoon melted vegetable margarine | 1 tablespoon melted vegetable margarine |
| 4 small whole sole, cleaned and skinned | 4 small whole sole, cleaned and skinned |
| salt | salt |
| freshly ground black pepper | freshly ground black pepper |
| 4 small onions, peeled and cut into rings | 4 small onions, peeled and cut into rings |
| 4 tablespoons lemon juice | ¼ cup lemon juice |
| TO GARNISH: | TO GARNISH: |
| lemon slices | lemon slices |
| sprigs of parsley | sprigs of parsley |

Take 4 large sheets of foil and brush each one with melted margarine. Wash the fish and dry them with paper towels. Brush the fish with melted margarine, too, and season each one with salt and pepper.

On each sheet of foil place some onion and sole. Sprinkle each one with lemon juice. Wrap the foil around the fish, to make 4 airtight packages. Put them on flat baking sheets and bake in the centre of a preheated moderately hot oven (200°C / 400°F, Gas Mark 6) for 35 to 40 minutes.

Transfer the fish carefully to a serving dish, pouring over any liquid from the foil. Garnish with lemon slices and parsley.

**Serves 4**

*BELOW: Foiled sole*

*ABOVE: Plaice (flounder) with mushroom sauce in preparation*

# Plaice (Flounder) with Mushroom Sauce

| Metric/Imperial | American |
|---|---|
| 700 g / 1½ lb plaice fillets | 1½ lb flounder fillets |
| 2 tablespoons lemon juice | 2 tablespoons lemon juice |
| salt | salt |
| freshly ground pepper | freshly ground black pepper |
| 15 g / ½ oz vegetable margarine | 1 tablespoon vegetable margarine |
| 225 g / 8 oz mushrooms, sliced | 2 cups sliced mushrooms |
| 6 spring onions, sliced | 6 scallions, sliced |
| 1 egg, beaten | 1 egg, beaten |

Sprinkle the plaice (flounder) fillets with lemon juice, salt and pepper and allow to stand for 15 minutes.

Heat the margarine in a pan. Add the mushrooms and spring onions (scallions) and fry quickly for 4 to 5 minutes.

Transfer the vegetables to a casserole. Arrange the plaice (flounder) fillets on top.

Cover with foil and bake in a preheated moderately hot oven (190°C / 375°F, Gas Mark 5) for 15 to 20 minutes.

Transfer the fish to a warm serving plate.

Work the mushrooms, spring onions (scallions) and cooking liquor to a purée in an electric blender. Add a spoonful of this purée to the beaten egg, whisking all the time. Place this mixture and the rest of the mushroom purée in a pan. Reheat gently, without allowing to boil, and stirring all the time. Check the seasoning before serving this sauce with the fish.

**Serves 4**

# Shrimp and Halibut Salad

| Metric/Imperial | American |
|---|---|
| 300 ml / ½ pint water | 1¼ cups water |
| 2 tablespoons lemon juice | 2 tablespoons lemon juice |
| 1 bay leaf | 1 bay leaf |
| salt | salt |
| freshly ground black pepper | freshly ground black pepper |
| 175 g / 6 oz halibut | 6 oz halibut |
| 225 g / 8 oz peeled shrimp | 1 cup shelled shrimp |
| 1 small green pepper, cored, seeded and diced | 1 small green pepper, cored, seeded and diced |
| 1 small red pepper, cored, seeded and diced | 1 small red pepper, cored, seeded and diced |
| few lettuce leaves, or sprigs of watercress | few lettuce leaves, or sprigs of watercress |
| SAUCE: | SAUCE: |
| ½ teaspoon French mustard | ½ teaspoon French mustard |
| 2 tablespoons vegetable oil | 2 tablespoons vegetable oil |
| 1 tablespoon wine vinegar | 1 tablespoon wine vinegar |
| 2 hard-boiled egg yolks, sieved | 2 hard-cooked egg yolks, strained |
| 2 tablespoons soured cream | 2 tablespoons sour cream |
| black olives to garnish | ripe olives to garnish |

Bring to the boil the water, lemon juice, bay leaf, salt and pepper. Add the piece of halibut and poach it gently until barely cooked. Allow it to cool in the liquid.

When cold, cut the fish into small pieces and mix with the shrimp. Add the green and red pepper. Arrange the fish and pepper on a bed of lettuce or watercress.

Whisk together the mustard, oil, wine vinegar, egg yolks, and cream. Season to taste with salt and pepper.

Pour this sauce over the fish and pepper, and garnish with olives.

**Serves 4**

# Leftover Fish

*Mix flaked cooked fish with sprigs of lightly steamed cauliflower, a few olives and slivers of green pepper and toss in French dressing.

*Cover a layer of flaked cooked fish with a well seasoned spinach purée, top with a little grated Edam cheese and grill (broil) lightly.

*Mash to a purée some flaked cooked fish, anchovy essence, lemon juice, salt and pepper, and use this mixture to stuff hard-boiled (hard-cooked) eggs or tomatoes.

# Sole Véronique

| Metric/Imperial | American |
|---|---|
| the fillets of 2 whole sole | the fillets of 2 whole sole |
| juice of 1 lemon | juice of 1 lemon |
| salt and black pepper | salt and black pepper |
| 25 g / 1 oz vegetable margarine | 2 tablespoons vegetable margarine |
| 225 g / 8 oz green grapes | 2 cups green grapes |
| 100 ml / 4 fl oz white wine | ½ cup white wine |
| 2 egg yolks | 2 egg yolks |
| 150 ml / 5 fl oz single cream or natural yogurt | ⅔ cup light cream or unflavored yogurt |
| COURT BOUILLON: | COURT BOUILLON: |
| the trimmings of the sole, including the head and skin | the trimmings of the sole, including the head and skin |
| 2-3 parsley sprigs | 2-3 parsley sprigs |
| 1 bay leaf | 1 bay leaf |
| 1 small onion, peeled and halved | 1 small onion, peeled and halved |
| salt and pepper | salt and pepper |

To make the **court bouillon**: put the fish trimmings into a saucepan and cover with cold water. Add the remaining ingredients and bring to a gentle boil. Reduce the heat and simmer for 20 minutes.

Meanwhile, wash and pat dry the fish fillets. Sprinkle them with half the lemon juice, then season to taste with salt and pepper. Roll up each fillet, starting from the tail end, and arrange them, in one layer, in a generously greased ovenproof dish.

Halve the grapes and remove the pips (pits). Put about half of them into the centres of the rolls and scatter the remainder over and among the rolls. Pour over the wine. Strain the **bouillon** then add just enough of it to the dish to come up the sides of the fillets; do not cover them with liquid.

Cover with greased foil and bake in a preheated moderately hot oven (190°C / 375°F, Gas Mark 5) for 20 minutes, or until a light white froth can be seen on the fish. Transfer the fish and the grapes to a warmed serving plate. Pour the cooking juices into a small pan and cook until they have reduced by half. Strain the juices and set aside.

In a heatproof bowl, beat together the egg yolks and cream or yogurt. Gradually add 2 teaspoons of the strained cooking juices. Place the bowl over a pan of gently simmering water, taking care not to let it touch the water. Stir until the mixture coats the back of a spoon, with a consistency of light cream. Season to taste and stir in the remaining lemon juice. Pour over the fish and serve immediately.

**Serves 4**

*RIGHT: Shrimp and halibut salad*

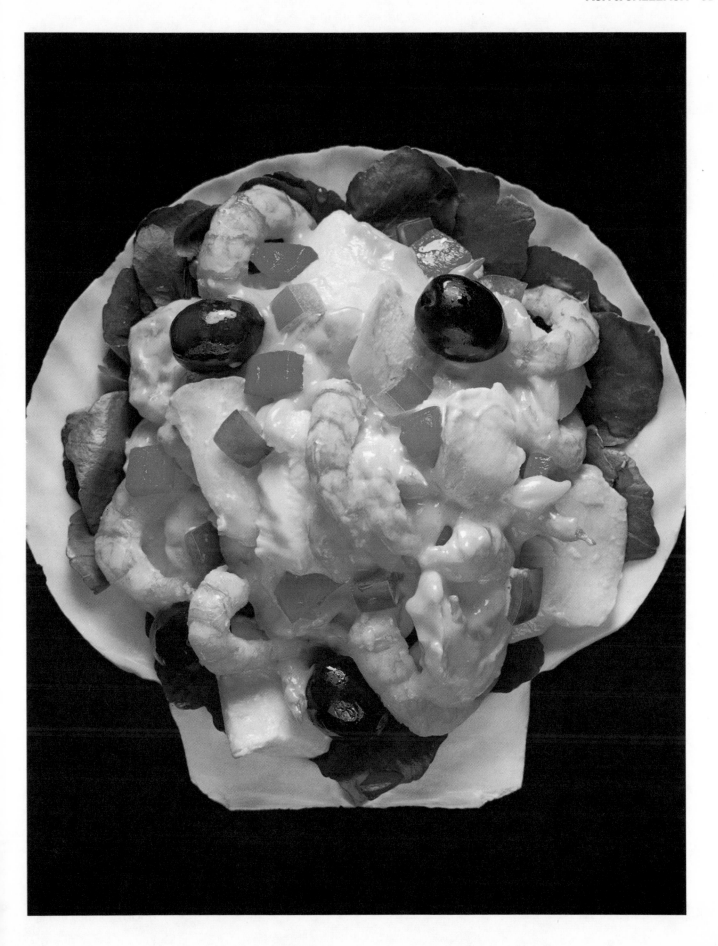

# Soused Herrings

| Metric/Imperial | American |
|---|---|
| 4 herrings, cleaned, washed and dried | 4 herrings, cleaned, washed and dried |
| 1 onion, peeled and sliced | 1 onion, peeled and sliced |
| wine vinegar | wine vinegar |
| 3 bay leaves | 3 bay leaves |
| 2 cloves | 2 cloves |
| 12 allspice | 12 allspice |
| 2 blades of mace | 2 blades of mace |
| 1 teaspoon salt | 1 teaspoon salt |

Remove the backbones from the herrings. Lay them, skin side down, on a working surface and place some onion slices on each. Roll them up, from head to tail, and secure them with toothpicks.

Place them in a casserole. Add enough vinegar and water to cover the fish, in the proportion of 3 parts vinegar to 1 part water. Add the bay leaves, cloves, allspice, mace and salt. Cover and cook in a preheated cool oven (150°C/300°F, Gas Mark 2) for 3 hours, or until the fish is cooked. The liquid must not be allowed to boil.

Transfer the fish to a serving dish and strain the liquor over them. Allow to cool, then chill in the refrigerator.

Serve with a cucumber salad and some sprigs of raw cauliflower blended in a mustardy soured cream.

**Serves 4**

# Lemony Fish

| Metric/Imperial | American |
|---|---|
| 700 g / 1½ lb cod, haddock or turbot fillets, or a combination of the three | 1½ lb cod, haddock or turbot fillets or a combination of the three |
| salt and pepper | salt and pepper |
| 6-8 coriander seeds, crushed | 6-8 coriander seeds, crushed |
| 1 red pepper, cored, seeded and finely chopped | ½ cup finely chopped, cored and seeded red pepper |
| 1 green pepper, cored, seeded and finely chopped | ½ cup finely chopped, cored and seeded green pepper |
| 50 g / 2 oz white grapes, peeled, halved and pipped | ½ cup peeled, halved and seeded white grapes |
| juice of 1 lemon | juice of 1 lemon |
| 300 ml / ½ pint water | 1¼ cups water |

Arrange the fish in a single layer in a shallow casserole. Season with salt, pepper and coriander.

Add the peppers, grapes, lemon juice and water. Cover the dish and bake in a preheated moderate oven (180°C/350°F, Gas Mark 4) for 20 to 30 minutes.

**Serves 4**

# Tuna Provençale

| Metric/Imperial | American |
|---|---|
| 2 × 200 g / 7 oz cans tuna | 2 × 7 oz cans tuna |
| juice of ½ lemon | juice of ½ lemon |
| salt | salt |
| freshly ground black pepper | freshly ground black pepper |
| 4 anchovy fillets | 4 anchovy fillets |
| ½ tablespoon vegetable oil | ½ tablespoon vegetable oil |
| 1 large onion, peeled and chopped | 1 large onion, peeled and chopped |
| 1 garlic clove, crushed | 1 garlic clove, crushed |
| 175 g / 6 oz tomatoes, skinned, seeded and chopped | ¾ cup skinned, seeded and chopped tomatoes |
| bouquet garni | bouquet garni |
| 150 ml / ¼ pint fish stock, or 125 ml / 4 fl oz water and 2 tablespoons lemon juice | ⅔ cup fish stock, or ½ cup water and 2 tablespoons lemon juice |
| finely chopped parsley to garnish | finely chopped parsley to garnish |

Remove the tuna from the cans very carefully, so that it stays in shape. Arrange the pieces side by side in an ovenproof serving dish. Sprinkle them with lemon juice and season lightly with salt and pepper. Arrange the anchovy fillets on top.

Brush a frying pan (skillet) with oil. Heat it and fry the onion and garlic for 5 minutes until soft but not brown. Add the tomatoes, bouquet garni and fish stock, or water and lemon juice. Bring to the boil and cook rapidly, uncovered, until reduced and thickened.

Pour the sauce over the tuna, cover and bake in a preheated moderate oven (180°C/350°F, Gas Mark 4) for 10 to 15 minutes. Discard the bouquet garni. Serve sprinkled with chopped parsley.

**Serves 4**

*RIGHT: Soused herrings*

# Fisherman's Stew

| Metric/Imperial | American |
| --- | --- |
| 700 g-1 kg / 1½-2 lb mixed fresh fish (try to include at least 5 varieties) | 1½-2 lb mixed fresh fish (try to include at least 5 varieties) |
| 1 tablespoon vegetable oil | 1 tablespoon vegetable oil |
| 1 large onion | 1 large onion |
| 1 garlic clove, crushed | 1 garlic clove, crushed |
| 100 g / 4 oz tomatoes, skinned, seeded and chopped | ½ cup skinned, seeded and chopped tomatoes |
| bouquet garni | bouquet garni |
| pinch of saffron | pinch of saffron |
| salt and pepper | salt and pepper |
| pinch of nutmeg | pinch of nutmeg |
| 600 ml / 1 pint boiling water | 2½ cups boiling water |
| 2 tablespoons orange juice | 2 tablespoons orange juice |
| 1 tablespoon grated orange rind | 1 tablespoon grated orange rind |

Clean all the fish, discarding any skin or bones. Cut into pieces. Put the softer, quicker cooking fish on one side.

Heat the oil in a large pan. Add the onion and cook for 5 minutes until soft but not brown. Add the garlic, tomatoes, bouquet garni, saffron, salt, pepper and nutmeg.

Add the boiling water and the firm fleshed fish and bring back to the boil. Cook rapidly, uncovered, for 10 minutes.

Add the softer fish, orange juice and grated orange rind. Continue cooking for a further 5 minutes. Serve very hot.

**Serves 4-6**

# Mackerel en Papillote

| Metric/Imperial | American |
| --- | --- |
| 4 mackerel, cleaned, washed and dried | 4 mackerel, cleaned, washed and dried |
| 50 g / 2 oz vegetable margarine | 4 tablespoons vegetable margarine |
| 1 large onion, peeled and finely chopped | 1 large onion, peeled and finely chopped |
| juice and rind of 1 lemon | juice and rind of 1 lemon |
| 1 teaspoon prepared mustard | 1 teaspoon prepared mustard |
| salt and black pepper | salt and black pepper |
| 3 parsley sprigs, chopped | 3 parsley sprigs, chopped |

Cut the mackerel lengthwise and set aside.

Cream the margarine until it is pale and creamy, then gradually beat in the remaining ingredients until thoroughly blended. Spoon the stuffing mixture into the mackerel.

Cover the mackerel with foil to make a parcel. Bake in a preheated moderate oven (180°C/350°F, Gas Mark 4) for 35 minutes, or until the fish is tender.

**Serves 4**

# Curried Haddock Mousse

| Metric/Imperial | American |
| --- | --- |
| 450 g / 1 lb fresh or smoked haddock | 1 lb fresh or smoked haddock |
| ½ tablespoon vegetable oil | ½ tablespoon vegetable oil |
| 1 medium onion, peeled and finely chopped | 1 medium onion, peeled and finely chopped |
| 2 teaspoons curry powder | 2 teaspoons curry powder |
| 100 g / 4 oz cottage cheese | ½ cup cottage cheese |
| 5 cm / 2 inches cucumber, finely chopped | ½ cup finely chopped cucumber |
| 2 tablespoons finely chopped parsley | 2 tablespoons finely chopped parsley |
| 1 tablespoon lemon juice | 1 tablespoon lemon juice |
| 7 g / ¼ oz gelatine | ½ envelope gelatin |
| 1 egg white | 1 egg white |

Steam the haddock between two plates, over a pan of boiling water, for 10 to 15 minutes. Leave it to cool, then flake it with a fork, discarding any skin or bones.

Brush a frying pan (skillet) with oil and fry the onion and curry powder in this for 5 to 7 minutes. Allow it to cool, then stir it into the cottage cheese. Stir in the fish, cucumber and parsley.

Heat the lemon juice – a metal soup ladle held over the gas flame is a useful utensil for this operation. Dissolve the gelatine in the hot lemon juice, then add it to the fish mixture, blending it in thoroughly.

Whip the egg white until stiff and fold it into the mixture. Transfer the mousse to a mould, previously rinsed out with cold water, and leave in the refrigerator to set. Invert on to a plate before serving with a selection of carefully prepared salads:

*cucumber and beetroot (beet) mixed with a little soured cream;

*peeled and thinly sliced tomatoes, topped with plenty of black pepper, a few onion rings and a spoonful of fresh orange juice;

*a mixed green salad of lettuce, chicory, spinach and watercress in an oil and vinegar dressing;

*cold cooked French beans and leeks, well seasoned and tossed in an oil and lemon dressing.

This mousse would make a perfect first course, prepared in individual cocotte dishes.

**Serves 4**

*RIGHT: Curried haddock mousse*

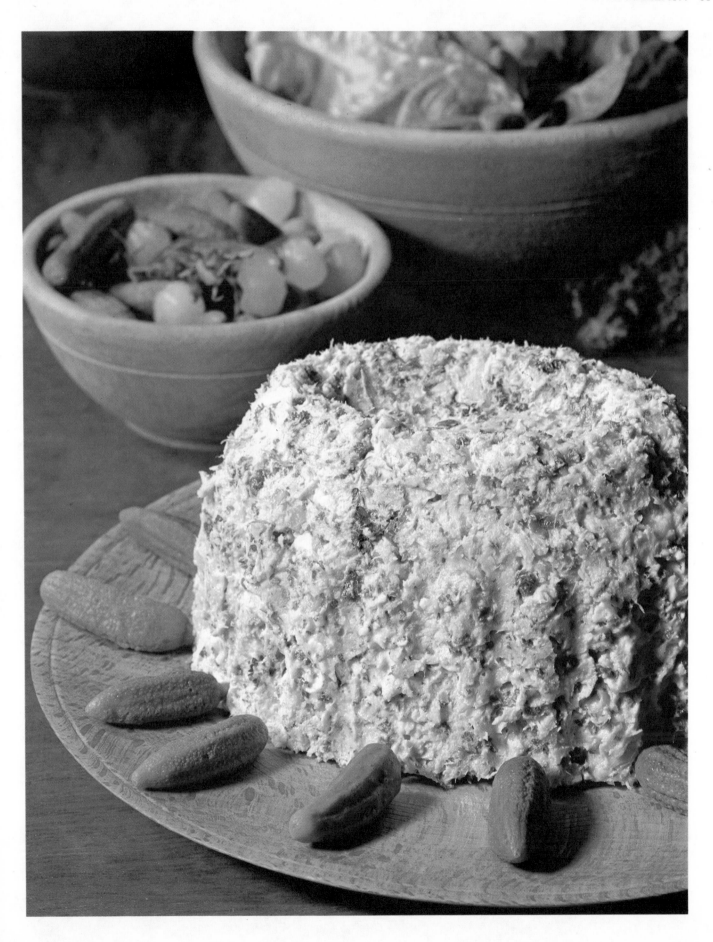

# Scallops with Peppers

| Metric/Imperial | American |
|---|---|
| 450 g / 1 lb scallops | 1 lb scallops |
| 2 spring onions, finely chopped | 2 scallions, finely chopped |
| ½ tablespoon vegetable oil | ½ tablespoon vegetable oil |
| 1 teaspoon salt | 1 teaspoon salt |
| 2 green peppers, cored, seeded and sliced | 2 cups sliced, cored and seeded green pepper |
| 4 tablespoons water | ¼ cup water |

Wash, trim and slice the scallops. Brush a frying pan (skillet) with oil. Heat it and fry the scallops and spring onions (scallions) in this for 3 minutes, stirring all the time. Add the salt and mix well.

Add the peppers and the water and bring to the boil, stirring all the time. Simmer for 2 minutes, then serve immediately.

**Serves 4**

# Summer Fish

| Metric/Imperial | American |
|---|---|
| 4 mackerel, herring or mullet | 4 mackerel, herring or mullet |
| 600 ml / 1 pint dry cider or fish stock | 2½ cups hard cider or fish stock |
| 750 ml / 1¼ pints water | 3 cups water |
| juice of 1 lemon | juice of 1 lemon |
| 2 onions, peeled and sliced | 2 onions, peeled and sliced |
| 1 teaspoon dill seeds | 1 teaspoon dill seeds |
| peel of ½ lemon | peel of ½ lemon |
| 8 whole black peppercorns | 8 whole black peppercorns |
| 2 bay leaves | 2 bay leaves |
| ½ teaspoon salt | ½ teaspoon salt |
| French mustard | French mustard |
| chopped parsley to garnish | chopped parsley to garnish |

Clean the fish, removing the fins and tails.

Put the cider or stock, water, lemon juice, onion, dill seeds, lemon peel, peppercorns, bay leaves and salt in a pan. Bring to the boil and allow to simmer for 10 minutes. Strain this liquid and leave it to cool.

Arrange the fish in a wide pan. Cover them with the cooled liquid. Bring to the boil and simmer very gently for 10 minutes, or until the fish are no longer pink inside.

Carefully lift the fish out of the liquid. Divide each fish into two fillets, discarding all the skin and bones. Arrange the fish fillets on a serving plate.

Strain off 900 ml / 1½ pints (3¾ cups) of the liquid. Stir in French mustard to taste. Pour over fish. Chill before serving.

**Serves 4**

BELOW: Scallops with peppers

# Summer Fish with Orange

| Metric/Imperial | American |
|---|---|
| 4 large fillets of sole, plaice or whiting | 4 large fillets of sole, flounder or whiting |
| salt | salt |
| freshly ground black pepper | freshly ground black pepper |
| 1 tablespoon orange juice | 1 tablespoon orange juice |
| 1 tablespoon grated orange rind | 1 tablespoon grated orange rind |
| 4 thick slices orange, peeled | 4 thick slices orange, peeled |
| SAUCE: | SAUCE: |
| 100 g/4 oz cottage cheese | 1/2 cup cottage cheese |
| 2 hard-boiled egg yolks, sieved | 2 hard-cooked egg yolks, strained |
| salt | salt |
| freshly ground black pepper | freshly ground black pepper |
| 2 tablespoons grated orange rind | 2 tablespoons grated orange rind |
| TO GARNISH: | TO GARNISH: |
| paprika | paprika |
| white grapes, skinned, halved and pipped | white grapes, skinned, halved and seeded |

Sprinkle the fillets lightly with salt, pepper, orange juice and orange rind. Roll them up, from head to tail, and secure each with a toothpick.

Steam them gently between two plates over a pan of boiling water until they are just cooked, but still firm. They will continue to cook a little more as they cool.

When quite cold, carefully transfer each fish fillet to a slice of orange. Arrange on a serving dish.

Rub the cottage cheese through a sieve (strainer). Blend in the egg yolks, salt, pepper and orange rind. Spoon a little of this sauce over each fillet, sprinkle with paprika and garnish with grapes.

**Serves 4**

# Stuffed Cod Fillets

| Metric/Imperial | American |
|---|---|
| 4 cod steaks, each about 100 g/4 oz | 4 cod steaks, each about 1/4 lb |
| salt and pepper | salt and pepper |
| 25 g/1 oz vegetable margarine | 2 tablespoons vegetable margarine |
| 1 small onion | 1 small onion |
| 1 garlic clove, crushed | 1 garlic clove, crushed |
| 100 g/4 oz mushrooms, finely chopped | 1 cup minced mushrooms |
| 25 g/1 oz wholemeal breadcrumbs | 1/2 cup wholewheat breadcrumbs |
| parsley | parsley |
| 2 tablespoons lemon juice | 2 tablespoons lemon juice |
| pinch of cayenne pepper | pinch of cayenne pepper |

Arrange the cod steaks on a piece of foil and season with salt and pepper. Melt the margarine in a shallow flameproof casserole. Add the onion and garlic and fry gently for 5 minutes until soft but not brown. Stir in the mushrooms and cook for about 2 to 3 minutes. Remove from the heat and add the remaining ingredients, seasoning to taste with salt and pepper.

Spread the mixture over the cod steaks, then cover with the foil. Bake in a preheated moderate oven (180°C/350°F, Gas Mark 4) for 30-40 minutes. Serve straight from the dish.
**Serves 4**

# Chinese Braised Fish

| Metric/Imperial | American |
|---|---|
| 1 × 1 kg/2 lb whole fish (bream, bass or snapper are most suitable) | 2 lb whole fish (bream, bass or snapper are most suitable) |
| 1 teaspoon salt | 1 teaspoon salt |
| 4 Chinese dried mushrooms | 4 Chinese dried mushrooms |
| 1 teaspoon vegetable oil | 1 teaspoon vegetable oil |
| 4 spring onions, cut into 1 cm/1/2 inch lengths | 4 scallions, cut into 1/2 inch lengths |
| 6 water chestnuts, sliced | 6 water chestnuts, sliced |
| 1 teaspoon root ginger, finely chopped | 1 teaspoon fresh ginger, finely chopped |
| 2 garlic cloves, crushed | 2 garlic cloves, crushed |
| 300 ml/1/2 pint fish stock or water | 1 1/4 cups fish stock or water |
| 2 tablespoons soy sauce | 2 tablespoons soy sauce |
| 1 tablespoon lemon juice | 1 tablespoon lemon juice |

Clean the fish, leaving on the head and tail. Wipe it inside and out with paper towels. Make two gashes on each side, in the thickest part, with a sharp knife. Sprinkle the fish well with salt.

Soak the mushrooms in warm water for 20 minutes, rinse them, squeeze them dry and remove their stalks, which may be used for flavouring soup. Cut the mushrooms into strips.

Heat the oil in a frying pan (skillet) large enough to take the whole fish. Fry the fish quickly on both sides until golden. Add the mushrooms, spring onions (scallions), water chestnuts, ginger, garlic, stock, soy sauce and lemon juice. Cover the pan, bring to the boil and simmer for about 30 minutes, carefully turning the fish once.

Serve on a large heated plate with the sauce poured over.
**Serves 4**

*Chinese braised fish*

# MEAT & POULTRY

Some people believe that meat and poultry can have no part in a healthy diet, but this is far from true. Meat and poultry are good sources of high-quality protein, iron and B group vitamins. Unfortunately, they also contain a relatively high proportion of saturated fats, as well as a moderate amount of cholesterol.

Man has, of course, evolved as a flesh-eater, and while a number of people prefer not to eat meat for humanitarian or aesthetic reasons, the fact remains that most of us are accustomed to eating meat and consider it to be an essential part of our meals. Both meat and non-meat diets can be healthy. Vegetarians must make sure that they balance their intake of protein foods to obtain sufficient quantities of all of the essential amino-acids. Meat-eaters should try to moderate the amount they consume in order to restrict intake of saturated fats.

Different types of meat vary in their nutrient composition. Offal (variety meats), especially liver and kidney, contain less fat and are therefore particularly valuable for those on slimming diets – providing rich sources of protein, iron, vitamin A and B group vitamins with comparatively few calories. Liver and kidney also have the advantage of being relatively cheap. Many people do not like the strong flavour of liver or kidney, but combined with other ingredients in pâtés, soups and casseroles – for example – their flavour is less distinct and acceptable to most.

The amount of fat varies considerably from one kind of meat to another and also depends on the cut. Pork and ham contain more fat than lamb or beef. Some meat fat is visible and can be trimmed off, but even apparently lean meat has fat distributed throughout the tissue. Grilling (broiling) and roasting are preferred methods of cooking for less lean cuts of meat, because they enable a certain amount of fat to drain away.

Always use as little fat as possible when cooking meat. Minced (ground) beef will brown effectively in its own fat and bacon can be cooked in a frying pan (skillet) without additional fat.

Like carcass meat, chicken is an excellent source of protein. It is also extremely versatile and can be cooked in numerous different ways. Nowadays chickens are mass produced; they are normally fed antibiotics and hormones to aid growth and feed efficiency. Most people agree that there is a consequent lack of flavour, but there is no significant difference between the nutrient composition of broiler chickens and free-range hens. For maximum flavour it is well worth trying to obtain a free-range bird when serving roast poultry.

*Chicken and olive bake (page 92); Chicken bake with yogurt topping (page 93); Chicken and vegetable fricassee (page 92)*

# Chicken and Vegetable Fricassée

**Metric/Imperial**
4 chicken portions
3 onions, peeled and finely chopped
1 garlic clove, peeled and crushed
2 celery sticks, thinly sliced
2 carrots, peeled and thinly sliced
1 bay leaf
150 ml / ¼ pint chicken stock
1 teaspoon chopped thyme
1 teaspoon paprika
salt
freshly ground black pepper
chopped parsley to garnish

**American**
4 chicken portions
3 onions, peeled and finely chopped
1 garlic clove, peeled and crushed
2 celery stalks, thinly sliced
2 carrots, peeled and thinly sliced
1 bay leaf
⅔ cup chicken stock
1 teaspoon chopped thyme
1 teaspoon paprika
salt
freshly ground black pepper
chopped parsley to garnish

Take a piece of fat from the chicken and rub over the base of a heavy pan. Put in the chicken and cook gently over very low heat until golden on all sides. Add the onions and garlic and continue cooking gently for 3 minutes, stirring occasionally.

Add the remaining ingredients, except the parsley, then cover and cook over low heat for 1¼ hours or until the chicken is tender. Taste and adjust the seasoning. Sprinkle with parsley and serve hot.

**Serves 4**

# Chicken Liver Skewers

**Metric/Imperial**
16 mushrooms
4 lean bacon rashers, derinded
225 g / 8 oz chicken livers
salt
freshly ground black pepper
few drops of Tabasco sauce
1 tablespoon oil

**American**
16 mushrooms
4 Canadian bacon slices, derinded
½ lb chicken livers
salt
freshly ground black pepper
few drops of Tabasco sauce
1 tablespoon oil

Wipe the mushrooms but do not wash or peel them. Cut each bacon slice into 3 pieces. Cut each chicken liver in half.

Take 4 kebab skewers, thread 1 mushroom on each. Alternate bacon, chicken livers and mushrooms on each skewer, finishing with a mushroom. Sprinkle with salt, pepper and Tabasco sauce, then brush with oil.

Grill (broil) under medium heat for 6 minutes, turning the skewers frequently until the bacon and livers are completely cooked. Serve hot with salad.

**Serves 4**

# Chicken and Olive Bake

**Metric/Imperial**
4 chicken portions
5 tablespoons cider vinegar
4 tomatoes, skinned and chopped
2 green peppers, cored, seeded and chopped
2 onions, peeled and chopped
1 small garlic clove, peeled and crushed
1 teaspoon chopped marjoram
salt
freshly ground black pepper
1 tablespoon olive oil
2 tablespoons tomato purée
75 g / 3 oz stuffed olives
chopped thyme to garnish

**American**
4 chicken portions
⅓ cup cider vinegar
4 tomatoes, skinned and chopped
2 green peppers, cored, seeded and chopped
2 onions, peeled and chopped
1 small garlic clove, peeled and crushed
1 teaspoon chopped marjoram
salt
freshly ground black pepper
1 tablespoon olive oil
2 tablespoons tomato paste
½ cup stuffed olives
chopped thyme to garnish

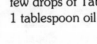

Put the chicken in a shallow dish. Mix together the vinegar, tomatoes, peppers, onions, garlic, marjoram and salt and pepper to taste. Pour over the chicken. Leave to marinate for 2 hours, turning the chicken once.

Heat the oil in a deep frying pan (skillet). Drain the chicken, reserving the marinade. Add the chicken to the pan and fry until browned on all sides. Stir in the reserved marinade with the tomato purée (paste) and the olives. Cover and simmer over low heat for 1 hour. Taste and adjust seasoning, sprinkle with thyme and serve hot.

**Serves 4**

# Herbed Chicken

| Metric/Imperial | American |
|---|---|
| 1 × 1.75 kg / 4 lb roasting chicken | 1 × 4 lb roasting chicken |
| 1 tablespoon oil | 1 tablespoon oil |
| 3 tablespoons lemon juice | 3 tablespoons lemon juice |
| salt | salt |
| freshly ground black pepper | freshly ground black pepper |
| 1 × 400 g / 14 oz can tomatoes | 1 × 1 lb can tomatoes |
| 1 teaspoon chopped marjoram | 1 teaspoon chopped marjoram |
| 1 teaspoon chopped parsley | 1 teaspoon chopped parsley |
| 1 teaspoon snipped chives | 1 teaspoon snipped chives |
| 1 teaspoon chopped thyme | 1 teaspoon chopped thyme |

Put the chicken in a roasting pan, brush with the oil and lemon juice, then sprinkle with salt and pepper.

Roast in a preheated moderately hot oven (190°C / 375°F, Gas Mark 5) for 45 minutes.

Mix together the tomatoes, herbs, and salt and pepper to taste, then pour over the chicken. Reduce the oven temperature to moderate (180°C / 350°F, Gas Mark 4) and continue roasting for 45 minutes, basting the chicken frequently with the tomato mixture. Serve hot with seasonal vegetables or a salad.

**Serves 4 to 6**

# Chicken Bake with Yogurt Topping

| Metric/Imperial | American |
|---|---|
| 15 g / ½ oz vegetable margarine | 1 tablespoon vegetable margarine |
| 1 small onion, peeled and finely chopped | 1 small onion, peeled and finely chopped |
| 2 celery sticks, finely chopped | 2 celery stalks, finely chopped |
| 100 g / 4 oz button mushrooms | 1 cup button mushrooms |
| 350 g / 12 oz cooked chicken, finely chopped | 1½ cups finely chopped cooked chicken |
| 1 tablespoon chopped parsley | 1 tablespoon chopped parsley |
| salt | salt |
| freshly ground white pepper | freshly ground white pepper |
| TOPPING: | TOPPING: |
| 300 ml / ½ pint natural yogurt | 1¼ cups unflavored yogurt |
| 2 egg yolks | 2 egg yolks |
| 1 teaspoon prepared mustard | 1 teaspoon prepared mustard |

Melt the margarine in a pan. Add the onion, celery and mushrooms and fry gently for 5 minutes, stirring frequently. Add the chicken, parsley and salt and pepper to taste, then transfer the mixture to a casserole and press down firmly.

To make the topping: put the yogurt in a bowl with the egg yolks, mustard and salt and pepper to taste. Mix well, then pour over the chicken.

Bake in a preheated moderately hot oven (190°C / 375°F, Gas Mark 5) for 25 minutes. Serve hot.

**Serves 4**

# Lemon Chops

**Metric/Imperial**
4 lamb chops
2 tablespoons corn oil
grated rind of 1 lemon
2 tablespoons lemon juice
2 teaspoons Muscovado sugar
1 teaspoon ground ginger
salt
freshly ground black pepper
parsley sprigs to garnish

**American**
4 lamb chops
2 tablespoons corn oil
grated rind of 1 lemon
2 tablespoons lemon juice
2 teaspoons Barbados sugar
1 teaspoon ground ginger
salt
freshly ground black pepper
parsley sprigs to garnish

Put the chops into a shallow dish. Mix together the oil, lemon rind and juice, sugar and ginger and pour over the chops. Cover and leave to marinate in a cool place for 3 hours, turning the chops occasionally.

Transfer the chops to a grill (broiler) rack and brush with the marinade. Cook under a preheated grill (broiler) for 15 minutes, turning the chops 2 or 3 times and basting them frequently.

Garnish with parsley sprigs and serve immediately accompanied by brown rice and a crisp green salad or vegetables.
**Serves 4**

# Lamb Provençal

**Metric/Imperial**
450 g / 1 lb lean boned leg of lamb
2 tablespoons vegetable oil
1 large onion, sliced
1 garlic clove, crushed
1 × 400 g / 14 oz can tomatoes
1 tablespoon tomato purée
150 ml / 1/4 pint dry white wine
1 rosemary sprig
1 thyme sprig
1 bay leaf
salt
freshly ground black pepper
100 g / 4 oz mushrooms, sliced
1 green pepper, cored, seeded and sliced
chopped parsley to garnish

**American**
1 lb lean boneless leg of lamb
2 tablespoons vegetable oil
1 large onion, sliced
1 garlic clove, crushed
1 lb can tomatoes
1 tablespoon tomato paste
2/3 cup dry white wine
1 rosemary sprig
1 thyme sprig
1 bay leaf
salt
freshly ground black pepper
1 cup sliced mushrooms
1 green pepper, cored, seeded and sliced
chopped parsley to garnish

Trim any excess fat from the lamb and cut into 2.5 cm / 1 inch cubes. Heat the oil in a flameproof casserole or heavy based pan. Add the onion and garlic and sauté until golden.

Add the lamb cubes and cook, stirring frequently, for 5 minutes or until evenly browned. Stir in the tomatoes and their juice, tomato purée (paste) and wine. Add the rosemary, thyme, bay leaf and salt and pepper to taste. Stir well, then cover and simmer for 45 minutes.

Add the sliced mushrooms and green pepper to the casserole. Check the seasoning, cover and continue simmering for a further 20 minutes.

Discard the herbs. Sprinkle with chopped parsley and serve with brown rice.

**Serves 4**

# Lamb Skewers

| **Metric/Imperial** | **American** |
|---|---|
| 450 g / 1 lb boned leg or shoulder of lamb, trimmed of fat and cut into cubes | 1 lb boneless leg or shoulder of lamb trimmed of fat and cut into cubes |
| 3 small onions, peeled | 3 small onions, peeled |
| 1 garlic clove, peeled and crushed | 1 garlic clove, peeled and crushed |
| 1 teaspoon salt | 1 teaspoon salt |
| 1 teaspoon ground ginger | 1 teaspoon ground ginger |
| few drops of Tabasco sauce | few drops of Tabasco sauce |
| ½ teaspoon ground turmeric | ½ teaspoon ground turmeric |
| pinch of ground coriander | pinch of ground coriander |
| juice of 1 large lemon | juice of 1 large lemon |
| 1 large green pepper, cored, seeded and cut into 2.5 cm / 1 inch squares | 1 large green pepper, cored, seeded and cut into 1 inch squares |
| 8 mushrooms | 8 mushrooms |
| 4 small tomatoes | 4 small tomatoes |
| 1 tablespoon oil | 1 tablespoon oil |
| chopped mixed herbs to garnish | chopped mixed herbs to garnish |

Put the lamb in a shallow dish. Grate 1 onion, then mix with the garlic, salt, ginger, Tabasco, turmeric, coriander and lemon juice and pour over the lamb. Leave to marinate for 2 hours, stirring frequently.

Cut the remaining onions into quarters. Thread 4 kebab skewers with the lamb cubes, onion quarters, green pepper and mushrooms, alternating the ingredients until they are all used up. Thread a tomato at the end of each skewer, then brush the meat and vegetables with the oil.

Grill (broil) under high heat for 12 minutes, turning the skewers frequently until the meat is cooked through and no longer pink. Sprinkle with herbs and serve hot on a bed of rice.

**Serves 4**

*LEFT: Lamb provençal*
*ABOVE: Lemon chops; Lamb skewers*

# Lamb in Mint Jelly

| Metric/Imperial | American |
|---|---|
| 450 g / 1 lb cooked lamb, thinly sliced | 1 lb cooked lamb, thinly sliced |
| 1 packet aspic jelly powder, to set 600 ml / 1 pint liquid | 4 teaspoons unflavored gelatin, to set 2½ cups clear chicken stock |
| salt | salt |
| freshly ground white pepper | freshly ground white pepper |
| 2 tablespoons dry sherry | 2 tablespoons dry sherry |
| 2 tablespoons chopped mint | 2 tablespoons chopped mint |

Arrange the lamb slices on a flat serving dish. If using aspic, make up according to packet directions. (If using gelatin, dissolve in a little of the stock, then add the remainder.) Leave in a cool place until the liquid is thick and syrupy. Add salt and pepper to taste and stir in the sherry and mint.

Spoon over the lamb slices very carefully so that the meat is evenly covered. Chill in the refrigerator for 2 hours until set. Serve with salad.

**Serves 4**

# Lamb and Vegetable Casserole

| Metric/Imperial | American |
|---|---|
| 750 g / 1½ lb boned leg or shoulder of lamb, trimmed of fat and cut into cubes | 1½ lb boneless leg or shoulder of lamb trimmed of fat and cut into cubes |
| 2 onions, peeled and chopped | 2 onions, peeled and chopped |
| 1 garlic clove, peeled and crushed | 1 garlic clove, peeled and crushed |
| 2 carrots, peeled and sliced | 2 carrots, peeled and sliced |
| 2 green peppers, cored, seeded and chopped | 2 green peppers, cored, seeded and chopped |
| 300 ml / ½ pint tomato juice | 1¼ cups tomato juice |
| salt | salt |
| freshly ground black pepper | freshly ground black pepper |
| 2 potatoes, peeled and diced | 2 potatoes, peeled and diced |
| 225 g / 8 oz French beans, diced | 1 cup diced green beans |

Take a piece of fat from the lamb and rub over the base of a heavy pan. Add the lamb and cook gently until the meat is browned on all sides.

Add the onions and garlic and continue cooking gently for 5 minutes, stirring occasionally. Add the carrots, peppers, tomato juice and salt and pepper to taste, then cover and simmer for 1 hour.

Add the potatoes and beans to the pan, cover and continue simmering for 30 minutes. Taste and adjust the seasoning, then serve hot with a seasonal green vegetable.

**Serves 4**

# Grilled (Broiled) Liver with Herbs

| Metric/Imperial | American |
|---|---|
| 25 g / 1 oz vegetabble margarine, melted | 2 tablespoons vegetable margarine, melted |
| 450 g / 1 lb lamb's liver, sliced | 1 lb lamb's liver, sliced |
| 1 tablespoon lemon juice | 1 tablespoon lemon juice |
| salt | salt |
| freshly ground black peppper | freshly ground black pepper |
| 2 teaspoons chopped parsley | 2 teaspoons chopped parsley |
| 2 teaspoons chopped thyme | 2 teaspoons chopped thyme |
| 2 teaspoons snipped chives | 2 teaspoons snipped chives |

Brush the grill (broiler) pan with a little of the margarine. Arrange the liver in the pan and brush with the remaining margarine. Grill (broil) under medium heat for 3 minutes on each side; allow 4 minutes on each side if well-done liver is preferred.

Arrange on a warmed serving plate, pour over the lemon juice, then season with salt and pepper to taste. Sprinkle with the herbs and serve immediately.

**Serves 4**

# Italian Supper

| **Metric/Imperial** | **American** |
| --- | --- |
| 450 g / 1 lb lamb's liver, thinly sliced | 1 lb lamb's liver, thinly sliced |
| 2 tablespoons wholemeal flour | 2 tablespoons wholewheat flour |
| salt | salt |
| freshly ground black pepper | freshly ground black pepper |
| 1 tablespoon oil | 1 tablespoon oil |
| 1 tablespoon vegetable margarine | 1 tablespoon vegetable margarine |
| 2 large onions, peeled and sliced | 2 large onions, peeled and sliced |
| 150 ml / ¼ pint beef stock | ⅔ cup beef stock |
| 2 tablespoons tomato purée | 2 tablespoons tomato paste |
| 1 garlic clove, peeled and crushed | 1 garlic clove, peeled and crushed |
| 2 teaspoons chopped basil | 2 teaspoons chopped basil |
| 150 ml / ¼ pint single cream | ⅔ cup light cream |
| chopped parsley to garnish | chopped parsley to garnish |

Coat the liver in the flour, seasoned with salt and pepper. Heat the oil and margarine in a pan. Add the liver and fry gently for 2 minutes on each side. Remove the liver from the pan and keep hot.

Add the onions to the pan and fry gently for 5 minutes until soft and golden. Stir in the stock, tomato purée (paste), garlic and basil. Bring to the boil, then lower the heat and return the liver to the pan. Cover and simmer for 25 minutes.

Remove the liver from the pan, arrange on a warmed serving dish and keep warm.

Stir the cream into the sauce in the pan and heat through gently without boiling. Taste and adjust the seasoning of the sauce, then pour over the liver. Sprinkle with parsley and serve hot.

**Serves 4**

# Baked Liver in Yogurt Sauce

| **Metric/Imperial** | **American** |
| --- | --- |
| 25 g / 1 oz vegetable margarine | 2 tablespoons vegetable margarine |
| 450 g / 1 lb lamb's liver, thinly sliced | 1 lb lamb's liver, thinly sliced |
| 300 ml / ½ pint natural yogurt | 1¼ cups unflavored yogurt |
| 2 teaspoons chopped mixed herbs | 2 teaspoons chopped mixed herbs |
| salt | salt |
| freshly ground white pepper | freshly ground white pepper |
| pinch of paprika to garnish | pinch of paprika to garnish |

Melt the margarine in a flameproof casserole. Add the liver and fry gently until browned on both sides. Drain off any excess fat.

Mix the yogurt with the herbs and salt and pepper to taste, then pour over the liver and bring to the boil.

Cover the casserole, transfer to a preheated moderate oven (170°C / 325°F, Gas Mark 3) and cook for 25 minutes.

Taste and adjust the seasoning, then sprinkle with paprika and serve hot.

**Serves 4**

# Beef Olives

| Metric/Imperial | American |
|---|---|
| 750 g / 1½ lb rump steak | 1½ lb top rump |
| 2 tablespoons corn oil | 2 tablespoons corn oil |
| 1 onion, peeled and chopped | 1 onion, peeled and chopped |
| 2 cloves garlic, peeled and crushed | 2 cloves garlic, peeled and crushed |
| 50 g / 2 oz mushrooms, chopped | ½ cup chopped mushrooms |
| 1 tablespoon chopped parsley | 1 tablespoon chopped parsley |
| 1 teaspoon chopped thyme | 1 teaspoon chopped thyme |
| 1 large slice wholemeal bread, crusts removed | 1 large slice wholewheat bread, crusts removed |
| salt | salt |
| freshly ground black pepper | freshly ground black pepper |
| 150 ml / ¼ pint beef stock | ⅔ cup beef stock |
| 150 ml / ¼ pint dry red wine | ⅔ cup dry red wine |
| parsley sprigs to garnish | parsley sprigs to garnish |

Cut the beef into 4 thin slices. Place between sheets of greaseproof (waxed) paper and beat to flatten. Trim each slice.

# Herb Pâté

| Metric/Imperial | American |
|---|---|
| 450 g / 1 lb pig's liver, coarsely minced | 2 cups coarsely ground pork liver |
| 100 g / 4 oz lean bacon, derinded and coarsely minced | ½ cup coarsely ground Canadian bacon |
| 2 garlic cloves, peeled and crushed | 2 garlic cloves, peeled and crushed |
| 1 egg, beaten | 1 egg, beaten |
| 3 tablespoons beef stock | 3 tablespoons beef stock |
| 1 teaspoon chopped parsley | 1 teaspoon chopped parsley |
| 1 teaspoon chopped thyme | 1 teaspoon chopped thyme |
| 1 teaspoon snipped chives | 1 teaspoon snipped chives |
| salt | salt |
| freshly ground black pepper | freshly ground black pepper |

Heat 1 tablespoon oil in a saucepan and sauté the onion and garlic until softened. Add the mushrooms and herbs and fry, stirring frequently, for 2 minutes.

Place the bread in an electric blender and grind coarsely. Remove the vegetable mixture from the heat and stir in the breadcrumbs. Add salt and pepper to taste and mix well.

Divide the stuffing between the beef slices and spread evenly. Roll up and secure with string. Heat the remaining oil in a flameproof casserole and fry the beef rolls, turning, until evenly browned.

Pour in the stock and wine. Cover and cook in a pre-heated moderate oven (170°C/325°F, Gas Mark 3) for 1½ hours. Serve hot, garnished with parsley sprigs.

**Serves 4**

Put all the ingredients in a bowl and mix well. Press the mixture into a small casserole, then cover with a lid or foil. Stand the casserole in a roasting pan, then pour in enough water to come 2.5 cm / 1 inch up the sides of the pan.

Bake in a preheated moderate oven (180°C / 350°F, Gas Mark 4) for 1½ hours.

Cover the pâté with clean foil, put a heavy weight on top, then leave in the refrigerator for 24 hours. Serve with toast or salad.
**Serves 4**

*Kidney and mushroom supper; Beef olives; Herb pâté*

# Kidney and Mushroom Supper

| Metric/Imperial | American |
|---|---|
| 25 g / 1 oz vegetable margarine | 2 tablespoons vegetable margarine |
| 1 large onion, peeled and finely chopped | 1 large onion, peeled and finely chopped |
| 1 garlic clove, peeled and crushed | 1 garlic clove, peeled and crushed |
| 1 carrot, peeled and grated | 1 carrot, peeled and grated |
| 100 g / 4 oz button mushrooms | 1 cup mushrooms |
| 8 lambs' kidneys, skinned, cores removed and cut in half lengthways | 8 lambs' kidneys, skinned, cores removed and cut in half lengthways |
| 2 tablespoons wholemeal flour | 2 tablespoons wholewheat flour |
| 2 teaspoons tomato purée | 2 teaspoons tomato paste |
| 150 ml / ¼ pint dry red wine | ⅔ cup dry red wine |
| 300 ml / ½ pint beef stock | 1¼ cups beef stock |
| salt | salt |
| freshly ground black pepper | freshly ground black pepper |
| chopped parsley to garnish | chopped parsley to garnish |

Melt the margarine in a heavy pan. Add the onion, garlic, carrot and mushrooms and cook gently for 5 minutes, stirring occasionally.

Add the kidneys and cook gently for a further 5 minutes, turning frequently, until browned on all sides. Remove the kidneys and mushrooms from the pan with a slotted spoon and transfer to a casserole.

Add the flour to the onion mixture and stir well to mix. Add the tomato purée (paste), wine and stock then simmer for 5 minutes, stirring frequently. Add salt and pepper to taste, then pour over the kidneys.

Cover and cook in a preheated moderate oven (180°C / 350°F, Gas Mark 4) for 20 minutes. Taste and adjust the seasoning, sprinkle with parsley and serve hot.
**Serves 4**

# Devilled Kidneys on Toast

**Metric/Imperial**
1 tablespoon mushroom
  ketchup or 2 tablespoons
  finely chopped
  mushrooms
juice of 1 lemon
1 tablespoon
  Worcestershire sauce
150 ml / ¼ pint water
1 teaspoon mustard powder
salt
freshly ground black pepper
8 lambs' kidneys, skinned,
  cores removed and split
  in half lengthways
4 slices wholemeal bread
chopped parsley to garnish

**American**
2 tablespoons minced
  mushrooms
juice of 1 lemon
1 tablespoon
  Worcestershire sauce
⅔ cup water
1 teaspoon mustard powder
salt
freshly ground black pepper
8 lambs' kidneys, skinned,
  cores removed and split
  in half lengthways
4 slices wholewheat bread
chopped parsley to garnish

Mix together the mushroom ketchup or mushrooms, lemon juice, Worcestershire sauce, water, mustard and salt and pepper to taste.

Grill (broil) the kidneys under medium heat for 3 minutes on the cut sides. Pour the devilled mixture into the grill (broiler) pan, then turn the kidneys and grill (broil) the other sides for 2 minutes. Baste and turn the kidneys, then grill (broil) for a further 2 minutes.

Meanwhile, toast the bread lightly on both sides. Arrange on warmed individual serving plates, then place 2 kidneys on each slice of toast. Pour the sauce over the kidneys, garnish with chopped parsley and serve immediately.
**Serves 4**

# Spring Beef Casserole

**Metric/Imperial**
750 g / 1½ lb chuck steak,
  trimmed of fat and cut
  into cubes
300 ml / ½ pint dry red
  wine
1 garlic clove, peeled and
  crushed
2 cloves
1 bay leaf
1 teaspoon salt
¼ teaspoon freshly ground
  black pepper
1 lean bacon rasher,
  derinded and diced
2 celery sticks, chopped
3 parsley sprigs
150 ml / ¼ pint beef stock
6 small pickling onions,
  peeled
4 carrots, peeled and sliced
12 button mushrooms
100 g / 4 oz peas
chopped parsley to garnish

**American**
1½ lb chuck steak, trimmed
  of fat and cut into cubes
1¼ cups dry red wine
1 garlic clove, peeled and
  crushed
2 cloves
1 bay leaf
1 teaspoon salt
¼ teaspoon freshly ground
  black pepper
2 tablespoons diced
  Canadian bacon
2 celery stalks, chopped
3 parsley sprigs
⅔ cup beef stock
6 baby onions, peeled
4 carrots, peeled and sliced
12 button mushrooms
¾ cup peas
chopped parsley to garnish

Put the beef in a shallow dish. Mix together the wine, garlic, cloves, bay leaf, salt and pepper and pour over the beef. Leave to marinate for 2 hours, stirring frequently.

Put the bacon in a heavy pan and heat gently until the fat begins to run. Drain the meat, reserving the marinade. Add the meat to the bacon and fry briskly until browned on all sides.

Transfer the beef and bacon to a casserole. Pour in the reserved marinade, then add the celery, parsley sprigs and stock. Cover and cook in a preheated moderate oven (170°C / 325°F, Gas Mark 3) for 1 hour.

Add the onions and carrots. Cover and continue cooking for 30 minutes or until the beef is tender. Add the mushrooms and peas and cook for a further 15 minutes. Remove the bay leaf and parsley sprigs. Taste and adjust the seasoning, then sprinkle with chopped parsley and serve hot.
**Serves 4**

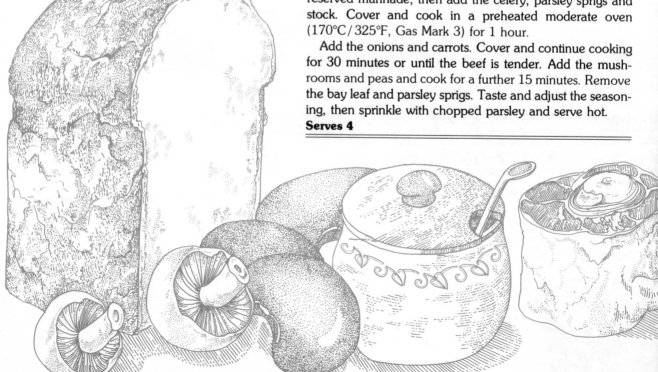

# Oxtail and Kidney Casserole

| Metric/Imperial | American |
|---|---|
| 25 g / 1 oz vegetable margarine | 2 tablespoons vegetable margarine |
| 1 oxtail, trimmed of excess fat and cut into pieces | 1 oxtail, trimmed of excess fat and cut into pieces |
| 100 g / 4 oz ox kidney, skinned, core removed and chopped | ½ cup skinned and chopped beef kidney |
| 1 large onion, peeled and sliced | 1 large onion, peeled and sliced |
| 450 g / 1 lb carrots, peeled and sliced | 3 cups peeled and sliced carrots |
| 1 large potato, peeled and grated | 1 large potato, peeled and grated |
| 1 garlic clove, peeled and crushed | 1 garlic clove, peeled and crushed |
| 2 teaspoons paprika | 2 teaspoons paprika |
| 1 teaspoon caraway seeds | 1 teaspoon caraway seeds |
| 1 tablespoon tomato purée | 1 tablespoon tomato paste |
| salt | salt |
| freshly ground black pepper | freshly ground black pepper |
| 600 ml / 1 pint beef stock | 2½ cups beef stock |

Melt the margarine in a heavy pan. Add the oxtail and fry briskly until browned on all sides. Lower the heat, add the kidney, onion, carrots, potato and garlic and cook gently until the vegetables are lightly coloured, stirring frequently.

Drain off any excess fat, then stir in the remaining ingredients. Bring to the boil, then lower the heat, cover and simmer for 3½ hours or until the oxtail is tender. Taste and adjust the seasoning.

Serve hot with plain boiled potatoes, brown rice or wholewheat bread.

**Serves 4**

# Meat-Stuffed Marrow (Squash)

| Metric/Imperial | American |
|---|---|
| 1 medium marrow | 1 medium summer squash |
| 450 g / 1 lb minced beef | 2 cups ground beef |
| 1 onion, peeled and finely chopped | 1 onion, peeled and finely chopped |
| 1 egg, beaten | 1 egg, beaten |
| 1 teaspoon chopped parsley | 1 teaspoon chopped parsley |
| 1 teaspoon chopped thyme | 1 teaspoon chopped thyme |
| 1 tablespoon tomato purée | 1 tablespoon tomato paste |
| ½ teaspoon Worcestershire sauce | ½ teaspoon Worcestershire sauce |
| 300 ml / ½ pint beef stock | 1¼ cups beef stock |
| salt | salt |
| freshly ground black pepper | freshly ground black pepper |
| 25 g / 1 oz grated Parmesan cheese | ¼ cup grated Parmesan cheese |

Peel the marrow (squash) and cut in half lengthways. Scoop out the seeds and pith with a spoon and discard.

Put the beef in a bowl with the remaining ingredients, except the Parmesan cheese. Mix well, then use to fill the marrow (squash) halves.

Put the stuffed marrows (squash) in a baking dish and cover with foil. Bake in a preheated moderate oven (180°C / 350°F, Gas Mark 4) for 1 hour. Remove the foil, sprinkle the cheese over the meat filling then bake for a further 30 minutes. Serve hot.

**Serves 4**

# Grilled (Broiled) Sweetbreads

| Metric/Imperial | American |
|---|---|
| 2 pairs sweetbreads | 2 pairs sweetbreads |
| 1 tablespoon vinegar | 1 tablespoon vinegar |
| 600 ml / 1 pint water | 2½ cups water |
| 1 teaspoon salt | 1 teaspoon salt |
| 40 g / 1½ oz vegetable margarine, melted | 3 tablespoons vegetable margarine, melted |
| 25 g / 1 oz wholemeal breadcrumbs | ½ cup wholewheat breadcrumbs |
| lemon wedges to garnish | lemon wedges to garnish |

Wash the sweetbreads, put them in a bowl and cover with cold water. Leave to stand for 20 minutes, then drain off the water.

Put the sweetbreads in a pan with the vinegar, water and salt. Bring to the boil, then lower the heat, cover and simmer for 20 minutes.

Drain thoroughly, then transfer to a bowl. Cover with cold water and leave to stand again for 20 minutes. Drain the sweetbreads thoroughly, then pat dry with kitchen paper towels. Remove the membranes and split the sweetbreads in half lengthways.

Brush the grill (broiler) pan with a little of the margarine. Brush the sweetbreads with a little more of the margarine, then roll in the breadcrumbs.

Place the sweetbreads in the pan and coat with the remaining margarine. Grill (broil) under high heat for 3 minutes on each side. Serve with lemon wedges.

**Serves 4**

# Baked Tongue

| Metric/Imperial | American |
|---|---|
| 1 × 1.75 kg / 4 lb pickled ox tongue | 1 × 4 lb pickled ox tongue |
| 3 onions, peeled and sliced | 3 onions, peeled and sliced |
| 2 cloves | 2 cloves |
| 1 bay leaf | 1 bay leaf |
| 1 × 500 g / 1 lb can tomatoes | 1 × 1 lb can tomatoes |
| freshly ground black pepper | freshly ground black pepper |

Put the tongue in a large pan, then add enough cold water to just cover. Bring to the boil, then drain off the water. Cover with fresh cold water and bring to the boil again. Lower the heat, cover and simmer for 2 hours. Drain and reserve 300 ml / ½ pint / 1¼ cups cooking liquid.

Discard the skin, fat and bones and place the tongue in a casserole. Add the remaining ingredients and the reserved cooking liquid.

Bake in a preheated moderate oven (180°C / 350°F, Gas Mark 4) for 1 hour, basting twice.

To serve: do not roll the tongue, but carve across the grain in thick slices and arrange on a flat serving dish. Remove the cloves and bay leaf from the casserole, taste and adjust the seasoning of the sauce, then pour over the tongue and serve hot. The tongue can also be served cold with a selection of salads.

**Serves 4**

*Baked tongue; Grilled (broiled) sweetbreads; Roast veal with orange*

# Roast Veal with Orange

**Metric/Imperial**

1 × 1.75 kg / 4 lb leg of
  veal, boned and rolled
2 garlic cloves, peeled and
  quartered lengthways
salt
freshly ground black pepper
1 rosemary sprig
300 ml / ½ pint water
finely grated rind of
  1 orange
juice of 2 oranges
1 orange, peeled and sliced,
  to garnish

**American**

1 × 4 lb boneless leg of
  veal, rolled
2 garlic cloves, peeled and
  quartered lengthways
salt
freshly ground black pepper
1 rosemary sprig
1¼ cups water
finely grated rind of
  1 orange
juice of 2 oranges
1 orange, peeled and sliced,
  to garnish

Make 8 small slits in the surface of the veal with a sharp, pointed knife. Insert the garlic quarters into the slits. Place the meat in a roasting pan, sprinkle with salt and pepper, then place the rosemary on top.

Pour the water around the meat, then roast in a pre-heated hot oven (220°C / 425°F, Gas Mark 7) for 15 minutes. Lower the heat to moderate (180°C / 350°F, Gas Mark 4) and continue roasting for 1¼ hours.

Sprinkle the orange rind over the meat, then stir the orange juice into the pan juices. Continue cooking for 30 minutes, basting once.

To serve the veal, carve into slices and arrange on a warmed serving dish. Taste and adjust the seasoning of the gravy, then pour a little gravy over the veal and garnish with orange slices. Serve the remaining gravy in a sauceboat. The meat can also be served cold with a selection of salads.

**Serves 4**

# Slimmers' Stroganoff

| Metric/Imperial | American |
|---|---|
| 450 g / 1 lb good quality stewing beef | 1 lb good quality stewing beef |
| 15 g / ½ oz vegetable margarine | 1 tablespoon vegetable margarine |
| 2 medium onions, peeled and finely chopped | 2 medium onions, peeled and finely chopped |
| 100 g / 4 oz mushrooms, sliced | 1 cup sliced mushrooms |
| salt | salt |
| freshly ground black pepper | freshly ground black pepper |
| pinch of nutmeg | pinch of nutmeg |
| ½ teaspoon chopped basil | ½ teaspoon chopped basil |
| 150 ml / ¼ pint beef stock | ⅔ cup beef stock |
| 300 ml / ½ pint natural yogurt | 1¼ cups unflavored yogurt |
| 2 tablespoons soured cream | 2 tablespoons sour cream |
| chopped parsley or chives to garnish | chopped parsley or chives to garnish |

Cut the meat into thin slices and then into strips, like thick matchsticks. Heat the margarine in a pan, add the onions and fry for 5 minutes until soft but not brown. Add the meat and brown over a fairly high heat. When each piece of meat is brown all over, reduce the heat and add the mushrooms, salt, pepper, nutmeg, basil and stock.

Bring to the boil, then cover and simmer for 40 to 45 minutes. Stir in the yogurt and cream.

Check the seasoning and reheat, without allowing it to boil. Sprinkle with parsley or chives before serving.

**Serves 3-4**

# Beef with Celery and Cabbage

| Metric/Imperial | American |
|---|---|
| 450 g / 1 lb rump steak | 1 lb rump steak |
| 1 teaspoon cornflour | 1 teaspoon cornstarch |
| 2 tablespoons corn oil | 2 tablespoons corn oil |
| 2 sticks celery | 2 sticks celery |
| 4 spring onions | 4 scallions |
| 100 g / 4 oz white cabbage, shredded | 1 cup shredded white cabbage |
| 1 tablespoon soy sauce | 1 tablespoon soy sauce |
| pinch of salt and black pepper | pinch of salt and black pepper |

Wipe the meat and cut into paper thin slices. Mix the cornflour (cornstarch) to a smooth paste with about 2 tablespoons water, add to the beef and mix well until the beef is completely coated with the mixture. Heat the oil and fry the meat over a fierce heat, stirring all the time, for 3 minutes. Remove from the pan.

Wash and shred the celery then wash and finely chop the onions (scallions). Add all the vegetables to the remaining fat in the pan and fry gently for 5 minutes, stirring occasionally. Add the meat, soy sauce, salt and pepper, mix well and cook for 2-3 minutes. Serve immediately.

**Serves 3-4**

*LEFT: Slimmers' stroganoff*

# Beef and Tomato Casserole

**Metric/Imperial**
1 tablespoon vegetable oil
0.75 kg/ 1³/₄ lb chuck steak, diced
8 small onions, peeled
8 small carrots, peeled and quartered lengthwise
3 celery sticks, diced
100 g/ 4 oz button mushrooms
4 medium leeks, sliced
225 g/ 8 oz tomatoes, peeled and chopped
1 tablespoon tomato purée
600 ml/ 1 pint beef stock
pinch of cinnamon
bouquet garni
freshly grated nutmeg
salt
freshly ground black pepper
finely chopped parsley to garnish

**American**
1 tablespoon vegetable oil
1³/₄ lb chuck steak, diced
8 small onions, peeled
8 small carrots, peeled and quartered lengthwise
3 celery stalks, diced
1 cup button mushrooms
1½ cups sliced leeks
1 cup peeled and chopped tomatoes
1 tablespoon tomato paste
2½ cups beef stock
pinch of cinnamon
bouquet garni
freshly grated nutmeg
salt
freshly ground black pepper
finely chopped parsley to garnish

Heat the oil in a frying pan (skillet) and fry the meat in this until brown all over. Transfer it to a casserole.

Fry the onions, carrots, celery, mushrooms and leeks in the same pan for 5 minutes, then add them to the meat.

Fry the tomatoes and tomato purée (paste) for 2 minutes, scraping the pan to incorporate any juices from the meat and vegetables. Add the boiling stock, cinnamon, bouquet garni, nutmeg, salt and pepper. Bring back to the boil and pour over the beef and vegetables.

Cover the dish and simmer in a preheated cool oven (150°C/ 300°F, Gas Mark 2) for 2 to 2½ hours.

Discard the bouquet garni and serve the casserole sprinkled with parsley.

**Serves 4**

# Meat Tips

Meat is too expensive to make mistakes with, so be sure that you buy meat which has been properly hung and butchered, and which is the appropriate cut for the recipe which you have chosen. This means patronizing a reliable butcher or supermarket.

Tougher cuts of meat can always be made more tender – and more tasty – by soaking in a marinade for several hours before cooking. Marinades usually contain a little oil, some wine, lemon juice or vinegar, herbs and seasonings.

*RIGHT: Beef and tomato casserole*

# French Country Casserole

| Metric/Imperial | American |
|---|---|
| 15 g/ ½ oz vegetable margarine | 1 tablespoon vegetable margarine |
| 1 tablespoon vegetable oil | 1 tablespoon vegetable oil |
| 12 small onions or shallots | 12 small onions or shallots |
| 2 garlic cloves, chopped | 2 garlic cloves, chopped |
| 1 kg/ 2 lb topside steak, cut into 2.5 cm/ 1 inch cubes | 2 lb top round of beef, cut into 1 inch cubes |
| 225 g/ 8 oz tomatoes, peeled and chopped | 1 cup peeled and chopped tomatoes |
| 1 tablespoon tomato purée | 1 tablespoon tomato paste |
| pinch of cinnamon | pinch of cinnamon |
| salt | salt |
| freshly ground black pepper | freshly ground black pepper |
| 450 ml/ ¾ pint beef stock | 2 cups beef stock |
| 100 g/ 4 oz mushrooms, sliced | 1 cup sliced mushrooms |
| 2 tablespoons lemon juice | 2 tablespoons lemon juice |

Heat the margarine and oil in a flameproof casserole. Fry the peeled onions and garlic until golden all over.

Fry the cubed beef until brown all over. Remove it from the pan and set aside. Fry the tomatoes until they start to soften. Stir in the tomato purée (paste), cinnamon, salt, pepper and stock. Bring to the boil, add the meat, onions and garlic. Return to the boil, cover and cook in a preheated moderate oven (170°C/ 325°F, Gas Mark 3) for 1½ to 2 hours.

Sprinkle the mushrooms with lemon juice, and add them to the casserole 15 minutes before cooking is complete.

**Serves 4**

# Mixed Grill

| Metric/Imperial | American |
|---|---|
| 2 lamb cutlets | 2 small lamb chops |
| 2 sausages | 2 sausages |
| vegetable oil for basting | vegetable oil for basting |
| 2 lamb's kidneys | 2 lamb's kidneys |
| 2 large tomatoes | 2 large tomatoes |
| 15 g/ ½ oz vegetable margarine | 1 tablespoon vegetable margarine |
| 2 rashers smoked bacon | 2 smoked bacon slices |
| 4 large button mushrooms | 4 large button mushrooms |

Trim the lamb chops and arrange them with the sausages, in an oiled grill (broiler) pan. Baste with a little oil and grill (broil) until they are browned, about 5 minutes. Turn the sausages from time to time, but not the cutlets.

Meanwhile, trim the kidneys and open them out. Brush with oil. Halve the tomatoes, season them with salt and pepper and dot with margarine.

Stretch the bacon slices with the back of a knife, then roll them up and arrange on a skewer.

When the cutlets are browned on one side, turn them over and add the kidneys, tomato halves, bacon and mushrooms to the pan. Turn the kidneys, sausages and bacon as necessary, but not the lamb or vegetables.

**Serves 2**

# Pepper Steak

| Metric/Imperial | American |
|---|---|
| 4 steaks, fillet or rump | 4 steaks, fillet or rump |
| ½ tablespoon vegetable oil | ½ tablespoon vegetable oil |
| 3 teaspoons whole black peppercorns | 3 teaspoons whole black peppercorns |

Trim the steaks neatly. Beat them with a steak mallet or rolling pin to tenderize. Paint each one with oil.

Crush the peppercorns coarsely with a rolling pin. Press these into the steaks on both sides and stand for 1 hour.

Preheat the grill (broiler) at its maximum temperature for 5 minutes before grilling (broiling) the steaks for 2 minutes on both sides to seal in the juices. Then reduce the heat and cook according to taste – rare, medium or well done.

**Serves 4**

*ABOVE: French country casserole. RIGHT: Pepper steak*

# Boiled Salt Silverside (Brisket), or Ox (Beef) Tongue

You have to plan ahead when you are cooking salted meat. It must be soaked in cold water for at least 12 hours before cooking; longer still if you know it to be heavily brined or if you wish it to be particularly mild.

When the meat has soaked for the required length of time, throw away the soaking water. Choose a large pan for cooking. This will allow the liquid to surround the meat completely, otherwise it might become dry and cooking might be uneven.

Put the soaked meat in the pan together with whatever chopped or sliced vegetables you choose – celery, onions, carrots, leeks. Cover generously with fresh, cold water, flavoured perhaps with a little lemon or orange juice. Do not add salt, but a few black peppercorns, some slivers of orange or lemon peel and a bouquet garni would make flavourful additions.

Bring to the boil, removing any scum from the surface as it rises. Then simmer gently, allowing 25 to 30 minutes per 450 g / 1 lb, plus an extra 25 to 30 minutes.

Boiled salted beef may be served hot, with its accompanying vegetables. Alternatively, if it is to be served cold, it should be allowed to cool in the liquid, then sliced neatly and served with a selection of salads and sharp tasting pickles.

# Cold Baked Silverside (Brisket) of Beef

| Metric/Imperial | American |
|---|---|
| 1.25-1.5 kg / 2½-3 lb silverside of beef, or top sirloin roast, salted | 2½-3 lb brisket of beef, or top sirloin roast, salted |
| 1 carrot, roughly chopped | ¾ cup roughly chopped carrot |
| 1 onion, roughly chopped | ¾ cup roughly chopped onion |
| 1 garlic clove, crushed | 1 garlic clove, crushed |
| 1 bay leaf | 1 bay leaf |
| 6 black peppercorns | 6 black peppercorns |
| 2 cloves | 2 cloves |
| 125 ml / 4 fl oz brown ale, bottled | ½ cup dark beer, bottled |

Soak the salted beef in cold water for 12 hours. Drain it, and place it in a flameproof casserole with the carrot, onion, garlic, bay leaf, peppercorns, cloves and brown ale (dark beer).

Add sufficient water to cover the beef. Bring to the boil, cover with a lid and cook in a preheated moderately low oven (150°C / 300°F, Gas Mark 2) for 2½ to 3 hours, or until tender. Test by inserting a skewer or fork; it should come out easily if the meat is cooked.

Transfer the cooked beef to a large bowl. Cover it with a plate or board, resting on the meat. Cover with a heavy weight. Leave to stand, overnight if possible.

Serve cold and sliced.

**Serves 10-12**

Instead of preparing several different salads to serve with the Cold Baked Silverside (Brisket), make one large but very varied salad. An Israeli Salad would be suitable, with lettuce, green pepper (cored and seeded), cucumber, tomatoes, spring onions (scallions), and soft-boiled (soft-cooked) eggs, whose yolks mingle with an oil and lemon dressing. Or a Salade Niçoise could be prepared or a mixture of diced cooked French beans, leeks, parsnips, broccoli with some sliced raw mushrooms and onions all blended in a herb and yogurt dressing.

*LEFT: Boiled salt silverside (brisket)*

*RIGHT: Baked silverside (brisket) of beef*

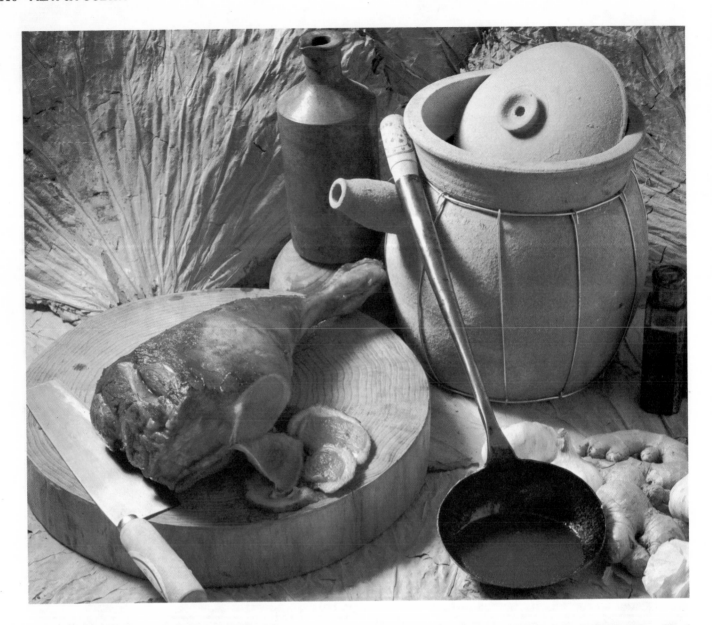

ABOVE: *Spiced simmered leg of lamb*

# Spiced Simmered Leg of Lamb

| Metric/Imperial | American |
|---|---|
| 1.5 kg / 3 lb leg (or shoulder) of lamb | 3 lb leg (or shoulder) of lamb |
| 1 teaspoon salt | 1 teaspoon salt |
| 1 tablespoon soy sauce | 1 tablespoon soy sauce |
| 1 tablespoon lemon juice | 1 tablespoon lemon juice |
| 2 garlic cloves, crushed | 2 garlic cloves, crushed |
| 25 g / 1 oz root ginger, shredded, or 1 teaspoon ground ginger | 1 oz fresh ginger, shredded or 1 teaspoon ground ginger |
| 1 tablespoon vegetable oil | 1 tablespoon vegetable oil |
| 1.2 litres / 2 pints mild stock, vegetable or chicken | 5 cups mild stock, vegetable or chicken |

Wipe the meat and rub salt into the skin. Put it into a pan with enough cold water to cover. Bring to the boil and remove the scum from the surface with a perforated spoon. Cover the pan and allow to simmer for 20 minutes. Drain off the liquid.

Blend together the soy sauce, lemon juice, garlic and ginger. Rub the lamb with this mixture and allow it to stand for at least 10 minutes.

Heat the oil and fry the lamb quickly until brown all over. Add the stock, bring to the boil, cover and simmer for 2½ hours. Transfer the lamb to a serving dish and keep it hot.

Boil the liquid over a high heat until well reduced, and serve this separately.

**Serves 8-10**

# Lamb Shish Kebabs with Herbs

**Metric/Imperial**
SAUCE:
250 ml / 8 fl oz tomato juice
2 teaspoons prepared
   mustard
300 ml / ½ pint natural
   yogurt
pinch of cayenne pepper
2 teaspoons finely chopped
   mint
2 teaspoons snipped chives
   or spring onions
salt
freshly ground black pepper
¼ teaspoon ground
   cinnamon
KEBABS:
450 g / 1 lb lean lamb (from
   the leg), cut into
   2.5 cm / 1 inch cubes
1 green pepper, cored,
   seeded and cut into
   8 pieces
12 button mushrooms
4 small tomatoes, halved
12 pickling onions
1 tablespoon vegetable oil
salt
freshly ground black pepper

**American**
SAUCE:
1 cup tomato juice
2 teaspoons prepared
   mustard
1¼ cups unflavored yogurt
pinch of cayenne pepper
2 teaspoons finely chopped
   mint
2 teaspoons snipped chives
   or scallions
salt
freshly ground black pepper
¼ teaspoon ground
   cinnamon
KEBABS:
1 lb lean lamb (from the
   leg) cut into 1 inch cubes
1 green pepper, cored,
   seeded and cut into
   8 pieces
12 button mushrooms
4 small tomatoes, halved
12 pickling onions
1 tablespoon vegetable oil
salt
freshly ground black pepper

In a shallow dish mix together the tomato juice, mustard, yogurt, cayenne pepper, mint, chives or spring onions (scallions), salt, pepper and cinnamon. Marinade the lamb in this sauce for 3 to 4 hours, turning it occasionally.

Thread the meat, pepper, mushrooms, tomatoes and onions alternately on 4 long metal skewers. Brush the vegetables with oil.

Season the kebabs lightly with salt and pepper. Cook under a hot grill (broiler), or on a barbecue, turning several times and basting with the sauce. Heat the remaining sauce and serve it separately.

**Serves 4**

*ABOVE: Lamb shish kebabs with herbs*

# Lamb Casserole with Orange

| Metric/Imperial | American |
|---|---|
| 1 kg/2 lb lean lamb, from the leg, diced | 2 lb lean lamb, from the leg, diced |
| ½ tablespoon vegetable oil | ½ tablespoon vegetable oil |
| 1 large onion, peeled and chopped | 1 large onion, peeled and chopped |
| 150 ml/¼ pint chicken stock | ⅔ cup chicken stock |
| MARINADE: | MARINADE: |
| 4 tablespoons fresh orange juice | ¼ cup fresh orange juice |
| 2 teaspoons grated orange rind | 2 teaspoons grated orange rind |
| 1 teaspoon ground ginger | 1 teaspoon ground ginger |
| salt and pepper | salt and pepper |

To make the marinade: blend together the orange juice, orange rind, ginger, salt and pepper. Allow the meat to soak in this for at least 2 hours, turning it from time to time. Remove the meat carefully and wipe it with kitchen paper.

Brush a frying pan (skillet) with the oil and when hot, toss the meat in this quickly until brown all over. Transfer it to a casserole.

Fry the chopped onion quickly until golden and add it to the meat.

Pour the marinade into the frying pan (skillet), add the stock and bring to the boil. Pour this over the meat, cover and cook in a preheated moderate oven (170°C/325°F, Gas Mark 3) for 2 to 2½ hours.

**Serves 6-8**

# Lamb Chops in Parcels

| Metric/Imperial | American |
|---|---|
| 4 lamb chops, trimmed | 4 lamb chops, trimmed |
| seasoned flour | seasoned flour |
| 50 g/2 oz vegetable margarine | 4 tablespoons vegetable margarine |
| 2 onions, peeled and sliced | 2 onions, peeled and sliced |
| 1 garlic clove, crushed | 1 garlic clove, crushed |
| 350 g/12 oz tomatoes, peeled, seeded and chopped | 1½ cups tomatoes, peeled, seeded and chopped |
| 1 thyme sprig | 1 thyme sprig |
| 2 tablespoons Worcestershire sauce | 2 tablespoons Worcestershire sauce |
| salt and pepper | salt and pepper |
| chopped parsley | chopped parsley |

Coat the lamb chops in the seasoned flour and set aside.

Melt the margarine in a large frying pan (skillet). Add the chops and fry quickly until they are lightly browned on both sides. Transfer each chop to individual pieces of foil.

Add the onions and garlic to the pan and fry gently for about 5 minutes until they are soft but not brown. Stir in the tomatoes, thyme, Worcestershire sauce and season to taste with salt and pepper. Cook gently for about 5 minutes. Stir in chopped parsley to taste and adjust the seasoning.

Divide the mixture equally between the lamb chops and spoon over the top. Bring the foil up and over to cover the mixture completely and seal to form a parcel. Bake in a preheated hot oven (220°C/425°F, Gas Mark 7) for 15 minutes or until the meat is cooked through and tender.

**Serves 4**

# Minced Veal Escalopes (Scallops)

| Metric/Imperial | American |
|---|---|
| 450 g/1 lb minced veal | 2 cups (firmly packed) ground veal |
| 1 garlic clove, crushed | 1 garlic clove, crushed |
| juice and grated rind of ½ lemon | juice and grated rind of ½ lemon |
| 2 teaspoons salt | 2 teaspoons salt |
| 1 egg, beaten | 1 egg, beaten |
| 3 tablespoons vegetable oil | 3 tablespoons vegetable oil |
| 125 ml/4 fl oz beef stock | ½ cup beef stock |

Blend together the veal, garlic, lemon juice, lemon rind, salt and egg. Form the mixture into 8 balls of equal size. Stand in a cool place for 1 hour, then roll them out to a thickness of 1 cm/½ inch. Heat the oil and when really hot, add the escalopes. Cook for 2 minutes on each side. Add the stock and simmer gently for 10 to 12 minutes.

**Serves 4**

# Piquant Veal Escalopes (Scallops)

| Metric/Imperial | American |
|---|---|
| 4 escalopes of veal | 4 scallops of veal |
| salt and pepper | salt and pepper |
| 1 lemon | 1 lemon |
| 25 g/1 oz margarine | 2 tablespoons margarine |
| 6 spring onions | 6 scallions |
| 2 teaspoons rosemary | 2 teaspoons rosemary |
| ¼ teaspoon Tabasco | ¼ teaspoon Tabasco |

Flatten the escalopes (scallops) with a steak mallet or rolling pin. Cut each one in half. Season with salt, pepper and the juice of ½ lemon. Melt the margarine in a frying pan (skillet). Put in the meat and fry it until golden, turning each piece once. Remove from the pan (skillet) and keep the meat hot.

In the same pan (skillet) fry the chopped white part of the spring onions (scallions) until soft. Replace the veal and add the rosemary and Tabasco. Cook for 2 to 3 minutes.

**Serves 4**

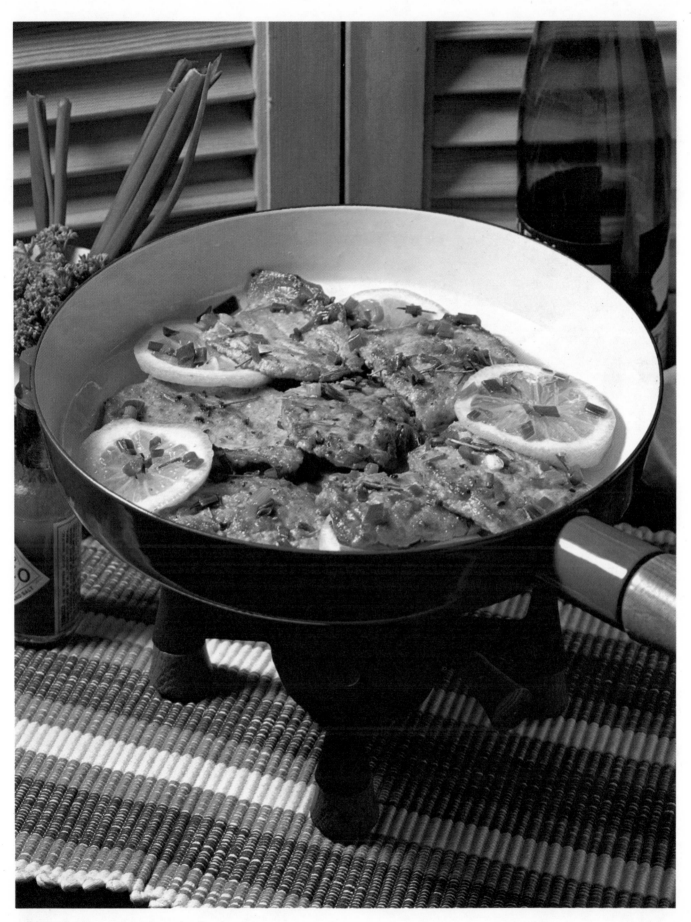

ABOVE: *Piquant veal escalopes (scallops)*

*ABOVE: Chicken with bacon and mushrooms*

# Chicken with Bacon and Mushrooms

| **Metric/Imperial** | **American** |
|---|---|
| 1 × 1.5 kg / 3-3½ lb roasting chicken | 3-3½ lb roasting chicken |
| 15 g / ½ oz margarine | 1 tablespoon margarine |
| 100 g / 4 oz lean bacon, diced | ½ cup diced lean bacon |
| 100 g / 4 oz button mushrooms, halved | 1 cup halved button mushrooms |
| 12 small onions or shallots | 12 small onions or shallots |
| 300 ml / ½ pint chicken stock | 1¼ cups chicken stock |
| juice of ½ lemon | juice of ½ lemon |
| bouquet garni | bouquet garni |

Cut the chicken into four portions. Melt the margarine in a frying pan (skillet) and fry the chicken pieces until lightly browned all over. Transfer them to a casserole.

Fry the bacon, mushrooms and onions for 4 to 5 minutes, then add them to the chicken.

Pour the stock and lemon juice into the frying pan (skillet) and bring to the boil, stirring well. When boiling, pour this over the chicken. Add the bouquet garni. Cover, and cook in a preheated moderate oven (170°C / 325°F, Gas Mark 3) for 1 hour.

**Serves 4**

# Chicken with Grapes

| **Metric/Imperial** | **American** |
|---|---|
| 4 tablespoons dry white wine | ¼ cup dry white wine |
| 2 tablespoons vegetable oil | 2 tablespoons vegetable oil |
| juice of ½ lemon | juice of ½ lemon |
| 225 g / 8 oz grapes, peeled, halved and pipped | 2 cups peeled, halved and seeded grapes |
| 1 cooked chicken (approximately 1.5 kg / 3 lb) | 1 cooked chicken (approximately 3 lb) |
| 1 lettuce, washed and shredded | 1 head lettuce, washed and shredded |

Boil the wine in a small pan until reduced by half. Add the oil, lemon juice and grapes. Mix well and allow to cool.

Cut the chicken into neat pieces, discarding any skin or bones. Toss together the chicken, lettuce and grape dressing before serving.

**Serves 4**

# Chicken with Peppers

**Metric/Imperial**

1 tablespoon vegetable oil
1 large onion
1 green pepper, cored, seeded and cut into rings
2 red peppers, cored, seeded and cut into rings
1 teaspoon salt
4 tablespoons fresh orange juice
450 g / 1 lb cooked chicken, cut into 2.5 cm / 1 inch pieces
pinch of ground cinnamon

**American**

1 tablespoon vegetable oil
1 large onion
1 green pepper, cored, seeded and cut into rings
2 red peppers, cored, seeded and cut into rings
1 teaspoon salt
¼ cup fresh orange juice
2 cups roast chicken, cut into 1 inch pieces
pinch of ground cinnamon

Brush a frying pan (skillet) with the oil. Heat it and add the onion. Cook gently for 5 minutes until soft but not brown. Add the peppers and salt and fry for 1 minute.

Pour in the orange juice, bring to the boil, cover and allow to simmer for 2 minutes.

Stir in the chicken and cinnamon and simmer for a further 5 minutes, or until thoroughly heated. Check the seasoning before serving.

**Serves 4**

*BELOW: Chicken with peppers*

*ABOVE: Chicken and peach salad*

# Chicken and Peach Salad

| **Metric/Imperial** | **American** |
|---|---|
| 1 small or ½ large cold roast chicken | 1 small or ½ large cold roast chicken |
| 1 lettuce | 1 head of lettuce |
| 1 head of chicory | 1 head of Belgian endive |
| few sprigs watercress | few sprigs watercress |
| 1 ripe pear, peeled, cored and cut into 8 pieces | 1 ripe pear, peeled, cored and cut into 8 pieces |
| 2 ripe peaches, peeled, stoned and sliced, or 1 × 450 g/1 lb can sliced peaches, drained | 2 ripe peaches, peeled, pitted and sliced, or 1 × 1 lb can sliced peaches |
| 3 tablespoons lemon juice | 3 tablespoons lemon juice |
| 12 black grapes, halved and pipped | 12 purple grapes, halved and seeded |
| slice of lemon to garnish | slice of lemon to garnish |
| SAUCE: | SAUCE: |
| 225 g/8 oz cottage cheese | 1 cup cottage cheese |
| 2 tablespoons lemon juice | 2 tablespoons lemon juice |
| salt | salt |
| freshly ground black pepper | freshly ground black pepper |
| pinch of paprika | pinch of paprika |

Cut the chicken into smallish pieces, removing the bones. Wash the lettuce, chicory (Belgian endive) and watercress. Tear them into bite-size pieces and arrange them on a serving plate.

Toss each piece of pear and peach in lemon juice, to prevent browning. Arrange them, with the chicken and grapes on the plate. Top with a slice of lemon.

To make the sauce: blend together the cottage cheese, lemon juice, salt, black pepper and paprika. Serve this sauce separately.

**Serves 4**

# Coq à l'Orange

**Metric/Imperial**

1 × 1 kg / 2 lb roasting chicken, cut into neat joints
15 g / ½ oz vegetable margarine
½ tablespoon vegetable oil
2 rashers bacon, rinded and chopped
4 small pickling onions
175 ml / 6 fl oz fresh orange juice
150 ml / 5 fl oz chicken stock
1 garlic clove, crushed (optional)
bouquet garni
salt
freshly ground black pepper
TO GARNISH:
finely chopped parsley
grated orange rind

**American**

1 × 2 lb roasting chicken, cut into neat joints
1 tablespoon vegetable margarine
½ tablespoon vegetable oil
2 slices bacon, rinded and chopped
4 small pickling onions
¾ cup fresh orange juice
⅔ cup chicken stock
1 garlic clove, crushed (optional)
bouquet garni
salt
freshly ground black pepper
TO GARNISH:
finely chopped parsley
grated orange rind

Wipe the chicken pieces with a damp cloth. Heat the margarine and oil together in a flameproof casserole. Add the chicken joints and cook them quickly until browned all over. Remove the chicken from the casserole.

In the same margarine and oil fry the bacon and onions until lightly browned. Return the chicken to the casserole. Add the orange juice, stock, garlic, bouquet garni, salt and pepper. Bring to the boil, cover and cook gently in a preheated moderate oven (170°C / 325°F, Gas Mark 3) or simmer gently on top of the stove for 1 hour.

Remove the bouquet garni and serve sprinkled with parsley and orange rind.

**Serves 4**

# Spanish Chicken

**Metric/Imperial**

4 joints roasting chicken
salt
freshly ground black pepper
15 g / ½ oz vegetable margarine
½ tablespoon vegetable oil
2 large onions, peeled and sliced
2 garlic cloves, crushed (optional)
450 g / 1 lb tomatoes, blanched, peeled and chopped
300 ml / ½ pint chicken stock
100 g / 4 oz button mushrooms
chopped parsley to garnish

**American**

4 joints roasting chicken
salt
freshly ground black pepper
1 tablespoon vegetable margarine
½ tablespoon vegetable oil
2 large onions, peeled and sliced
2 garlic cloves, crushed (optional)
2 cups blanched, peeled and chopped tomatoes
1¼ cups chicken stock
1 cup button mushrooms
chopped parsley to garnish

Wash and dry the chicken. Season it well with salt and pepper. Heat the margarine and oil in a frying pan (skillet). Add the chicken joints and cook them quickly until golden all over. Transfer them to a casserole.

Fry the onions and garlic for 5 minutes, then add the tomatoes and stock. Bring to the boil. Add the mushrooms and more seasoning if required. Add this mixture to the chicken.

Cover the casserole and cook in a preheated moderate oven (170°C / 325°F, Gas Mark 3) for 1 hour. Serve sprinkled with parsley.

**Serves 4**

*BELOW: Spanish chicken*

# Devilled Chicken Legs

**Metric/Imperial**
4 chicken legs
225 g / 8 oz mushrooms
parsley to garnish
SAUCE:
1 1/2 tablespoons vegetable
  oil
1/2 tablespoon Worcester-
  shire sauce
1/2 tablespoon tarragon
  vinegar
1/2 tablespoon finely
  chopped onion
1/2 teaspoon French
  mustard
salt
freshly ground black pepper

**American**
4 chicken legs
2 cups mushrooms
parsley to garnish
SAUCE:
1 1/2 tablespoons vegetable
  oil
1/2 tablespoon
  Worcestershire sauce
1/2 tablespoon tarragon
  vinegar
1/2 tablespoon finely
  chopped onion
1/2 teaspoon French
  mustard
salt
freshly ground black pepper

To make the sauce: mix together the oil, Worcestershire sauce, vinegar, onion, mustard, salt and pepper. Score the chicken legs with the point of a sharp knife and brush them liberally with the sauce.

Place them in a grill pan (broiling pan) under a hot grill (broiler) for 8 to 10 minutes, basting frequently. Then turn the chicken legs over, brush them with more sauce and continue grilling (broiling) for a further 8 to 10 minutes, or until cooked.

Brush the mushrooms with any remaining sauce and add them to the grill pan (broiling pan) for the last 5 minutes of the cooking time.

Serve very hot, garnished with parsley.
**Serves 4**

*BELOW: Devilled chicken legs*

# Roast Turkey

With smaller birds on the market now, turkeys no longer need to be reserved for a large houseful of guests. Remember, too, that turkeys carry a considerable weight of bone, so allow at least 350 g/12 oz per person.

The greatest problem with a turkey is to keep it moist during its lengthy cooking time. A good rich stuffing will help, both inside the skin of the neck and right inside the bird, and you should cover the breast with fat or fat bacon. Frequent basting, too, is essential, unless the bird is wrapped in foil.

Add the weight of the stuffing to the weight of the bird before you calculate cooking times. Choose the *Quick Roasting Method* for prime birds; the *Slower Roasting Method* for frozen or poorer quality birds.

Always allow frozen poultry to thaw completely in the refrigerator before cooking and remember that a large turkey could take up to 48 hours to thaw.

## Quick Roasting Method

Place the turkey in a preheated hot oven (220-230°C/425-450°F, Gas Mark 7-8). Reduce the temperature after 30 minutes, to 190-200°C/375-400°F, Gas Mark 5-6.

## Cooking times

Turkeys up to 5.5 kg/12 lb – 15 minutes per 450 g/1 lb plus an extra 15 minutes
5.5-9.5 kg/12-21 lb – 27 minutes per 450 g/1 lb plus an extra 27 minutes
9.5 kg/21 lb and over – allow 10 minutes for each additional 450 g/1 lb

If the bird is exceptionally broad-breasted, be a little generous with the cooking time.

## Slower Roasting Method

Place the turkey in a preheated moderate oven (180-190°C/350-375°F, Gas Mark 4-5).

## Cooking times

Turkeys up to 5.5 kg/12 lb – 25 minutes per 450 g/1 lb plus an extra 25 minutes
5.5-9.5 kg/12-21 lb – 47 minutes per 450 g/1 lb plus an extra 47 minutes
9.5 kg/21 lb and over – allow 10 minutes for each additional 450 g/1 lb

If the bird is exceptionally broad-breasted, allow an extra 5 minutes per 450 g/1 lb.

If you are using a covered roasting pan or foil, allow an extra 15-20 minutes, but not if using cooking film or roasting bags.

Thirty minutes before cooking is complete, remove the lid of the roasting pan, or open the foil, so that the skin may become crisp and brown.

*ABOVE: Roast turkey*

## Accompaniments

Boil the meat juices rapidly for a few minutes to produce a rich but non-fattening gravy, and serve your roast turkey with braised celery, roast onions, a fresh tomato salad and cranberry sauce.

# Turkey Leftovers

*Serve shredded cold roast turkey in a yogurt and herb dressing – natural (unflavored) yogurt, blended with chopped celery leaves, snipped chives, grated horseradish, lemon juice, paprika, parsley, salt and garlic.
*Mince (grind) cold cooked turkey together with some cold boiled or steamed leeks to make a Turkey and Leek Pâté.
*Shred cold roast turkey, boiled ham and roast beef, and serve them on a bed of spinach and watercress, with a well flavoured oil and vinegar dressing.
*Mince (grind) some cold roast turkey, season it well with herbs and minced (ground) onion, moisten it with a little stock and use it as a stuffing for a joint of lamb or veal.

# Boiled Ham or Bacon Joints

Joints of ham or bacon should be soaked in cold water for at least 12 hours before cooking, then drain off the soaking water.

Stud the meat with cloves and place it in a very large saucepan together with sliced onions, carrots and celery.

Cover with plenty of fresh cold water, mixed with dry (hard) cider or fresh orange juice. Add a bouquet garni, some whole black peppercorns and slivers of orange peel.

Bring to the boil, reduce heat, cover and simmer gently, allowing 20 minutes per 450 g/1 lb plus an extra 20 minutes for tender cuts; 35 minutes per 450 g/1 lb plus an extra 35 minutes for less tender cuts. Add some sliced cooking (baking) apple just 10 to 15 minutes before cooking is complete.

Serve the ham hot, as it is; or, remove its skin and spread it with a mixture of prepared mustard and crumbled rolls, and bake in a hot oven until crisp. Or, allow the ham to cool in the liquid and serve it cold, thinly sliced with salad.

# Gammon (Ham) Steaks with Orange Sauce

| Metric/Imperial | American |
|---|---|
| 150 ml / ¼ pint dry cider | ⅔ cup hard cider |
| 150 ml / ¼ pint orange juice | ⅔ cup orange juice |
| 2 tablespoons marmalade | 2 tablespoons marmalade |
| 4 gammon steaks | 4 smoked ham slices |
| 1 tablespoon caraway seeds | 1 tablespoon caraway seeds |
| orange slices to garnish | orange slices to garnish |

Boil together the cider, orange juice and marmalade over a high heat until well reduced and slightly thickened.

Sprinkle the gammon (ham) steaks with caraway seeds and grill (broil) them for 5 minutes on each side under a preheated grill (broiler).

Pour the orange sauce over the gammon (ham) steaks and garnish with orange slices before serving.

**Serves 4**

# Pork Chops with Lemon and Ginger

| Metric/Imperial | American |
|---|---|
| 2 tablespoons vegetable oil | 2 tablespoons vegetable oil |
| grated rind of 2 lemons | grated rind of 2 lemons |
| 4 tablespoons lemon juice | ¼ cup lemon juice |
| 2 tablespoons clear honey | 2 tablespoons clear honey |
| 2 teaspoons ground ginger | 2 teaspoons ground ginger |
| salt | salt |
| freshly ground black pepper | freshly ground black pepper |
| 4 pork chops | 4 pork chops |
| TO GARNISH: | TO GARNISH: |
| lemon | lemon |
| parsley | parsley |

Mix together the oil, lemon rind, lemon juice, honey, ginger, salt and pepper. Place the chops in a single layer in a shallow dish. Pour the marinade over them and leave for at least 3 hours, turning the chops occasionally.

Drain the chops and grill (broil) them under a preheated hot grill (broiler) for 15 minutes, turning once during cooking and basting with the marinade.

Garnish with lemon and parsley if wished.

**Serves 4**

# Pork Chops with Piquant Sauce

| Metric/Imperial | American |
|---|---|
| 4 pork chops | 4 pork chops |
| 40 g / 1½ oz vegetable margarine | 3 tablespoons vegetable margarine |
| 1 large onion, peeled and finely chopped | 1 large onion, peeled and finely chopped |
| 1 garlic clove, crushed | 1 garlic clove, crushed |
| 50 g / 2 oz tomato purée | 4 tablespoons tomato paste |
| 4 tablespoons water | 4 tablespoons water |
| 2 tablespoons caster sugar | 2 tablespoons superfine sugar |
| 3 tablespoons wine vinegar | 3 tablespoons wine vinegar |
| ½ tablespoon salt | ½ tablespoon salt |
| pinch of cayenne pepper | pinch of cayenne pepper |
| 2 tablespoons prepared mustard | 2 tablespoons prepared mustard |
| pinch of dried mixed herbs | pinch of dried mixed herbs |

Melt the margarine in a large pan and brown the pork chops on both sides. Set the chops aside and keep them warm. Add the onion to the pan and fry for 5 minutes until soft but not brown. Stir in all the remaining ingredients, and return the chops to the pan. Cover and simmer the mixture for 25 to 30 minutes or until the chops are cooked through.

**Serves 4**

ABOVE: *Ham and chicken mould*

# Ham and Chicken Mould

**Metric/Imperial**
20 g / ¾ oz gelatine
700 ml / 1⅛ pints rich
  chicken stock
2 hard-boiled eggs
few cooked peas
275 g / 10 oz cooked
  chicken, diced
225 g / 8 oz cooked lean
  ham, diced
1 × 450 g / 1 lb can
  asparagus tips, drained

**American**
1½ envelopes unflavored
  gelatin
2¾ cups rich chicken stock
2 hard-cooked eggs
few cooked peas
1¼ cups diced cooked
  chicken
1 cup diced cooked lean
  ham
1 × 1 lb can asparagus tips,
  drained

Dissolve the gelatine in the stock, according to the directions on the packet. Allow it to cool slightly.

Rinse out a 1.2 litre / 2 pint (5 cup) mould with cold water. Pour a little gelatine into the mould and leave it to set.

Shell and slice the eggs and arrange them in a neat design on the gelatine. Spoon a very little more of the gelatine mixture over the egg and put into refrigerator until set.

Cover with a layer of peas and neatly diced chicken and ham. Cover with more gelatine and allow to set again.

Continue like this, using the very well drained asparagus for the final layer. Cover with the remaining gelatine and chill until firmly set.

Dip the mould in warm water for a few seconds, then invert it on to a serving dish. Serve with salad.

**Serves 4**

*ABOVE: Chinese kidneys*

# Chinese Kidneys

**Metric/Imperial**

4 lamb's kidneys, skinned, cores removed and sliced
2 tablespoons lemon juice
1 small cauliflower, broken into small florets
2 tablespoons vegetable oil
4 spring onions, cut into 2.5 cm / 1 inch lengths
1 tablespoon soy sauce
2 tablespoons water
1 teaspoon salt

**American**

4 lamb kidneys, skinned, cores removed and sliced
2 tablespoons lemon juice
4 cups cauliflower florets
2 tablespoons vegetable oil
4 scallions, cut into 1 inch lengths
1 tablespoon soy sauce
2 tablespoons water
1 teaspoon salt

Soak the kidneys in lemon juice for 10 minutes. Drain them, reserving the juice.

Cook the cauliflower in boiling salted water for 3 minutes, then drain it well.

Heat the oil in a frying pan (skillet). Fry the drained kidneys, cauliflower and spring onions (scallions) for 2 minutes.

Mix together the soy sauce, water, salt and the lemon juice in which the kidneys were soaked. Add to the pan and cook gently for 3 minutes, stirring all the time. Serve immediately.

**Serves 4**

# Liver and Leeks

| Metric/Imperial | American |
|---|---|
| 450 g / 1 lb lamb's liver | 1 lb lamb liver |
| 2 tablespoons lemon juice | 2 tablespoons lemon juice |
| 2 tablespoons soy sauce | 2 tablespoons soy sauce |
| 2 leeks, cut into 2.5 cm / 1 inch pieces | 1 cup leeks, cut into 1 inch pieces |
| 1 tablespoon vegetable oil | 1 tablespoon vegetable oil |
| 2 spring onions, chopped | 2 scallions, chopped |
| salt | salt |

Wash the liver and cut it into strips, 5 × 1 cm / 2 × 1 inch. Cover with boiling water for only 1 minute. Drain it well.

Mix together the lemon juice and soy sauce. Pour this over the liver and toss well.

Cook the leeks in boiling salted water for 4 to 5 minutes, then drain them well.

Heat the oil and fry the liver over a fierce heat for 1 minute, stirring all the time. Add the spring onions (scallions) and drained leeks and a pinch of salt. Heat quickly, stirring, for 1 minute. Serve immediately.

**Serves 4**

*BELOW: Liver and leeks*

# SALADS

Salads are a perfect example of a healthfood because they can comprise such a wide variety of wholesome foods – the essence of a healthy diet. Salads are also very versatile as they can be served as a light vegetable accompaniment to a meal, a starter, main course or as a meal on their own.

Salads have always had a healthy image, although often in the sense that if something is boring and unappetizing it must be good for you, but with a little imagination salads can be a long way from the traditional lettuce leaves, cucumber and tomato.

Salads are especially good for you if the vegetable ingredients are raw, as raw food provides more roughage and none of the nutrients are lost during cooking. Raw vegetables also add a fresh taste and texture to a salad. This is particularly true of root vegetables such as carrots and celeriac; cauliflower, fennel and peppers are also good. One of the most delicious raw vegetables in a salad is the mushroom – especially if marinated in a tasty dressing beforehand. Other vegetables, although they can be eaten raw, are more appetizing if they are very lightly cooked – courgettes (zucchini), leeks, beans and peas, for example. Simply blanch them in boiling water and remove when they are still crisp and slightly crunchy, then rinse in cold water.

Always leave the skins on salad ingredients if possible, especially tomatoes, cucumbers, mushrooms, potatoes and carrots. Not only do they look more attractive, but the nutrients are more concentrated just beneath the skin and they also provide valuable roughage.

The most common salad ingredient is lettuce, but there are many other varieties of leaves which can be substituted and usually have a stronger, more interesting flavour; for example, endive, chicory, spinach, cabbage, Chinese cabbage (bok choy), celtuce and watercress. Many of these are available in winter when lettuce is unavailable, too expensive or of poor quality. Fresh herbs are also a useful addition to salads, especially parsley, thyme, chives and mint.

Salad leaves must be really fresh and crisp and, to retain their vitamin C, should be prepared just before serving. If you have to prepare them in advance, the best way to keep them crisp is to wash and dry them, then store in a covered container or polythene (plastic) bag in the bottom of the refrigerator. Always tear salad leaves with your hands – cutting them breaks the cells and releases an enzyme which then destroys the vitamin C.

Many people do not think of having salads in the winter, but there are lots of ingredients available to make them interesting. Shredded red or white cabbage is always good as a base for a winter salad. Root vegetables, such as carrots, celeriac and beetroot (beet) can be shredded or grated into a salad. Cauliflower florets, celery, fennel, onions and peppers all add to a colourful, tasty salad. And have you ever tried thinly sliced Brussels sprouts?

A wide variety of fruits can also be added to salads to delicious account – oranges, apples, pears, peaches, grapes, bananas, even strawberries, as well as dried fruits. Nuts, sesame and sunflower seeds, bean sprouts, olives and pickled vegetables, cheese and crisply cooked bacon – the possibilities are numerous and the results all tasty and attractive.

More substantial salads can be made using pasta, rice, potatoes and pulses (legumes), all of which must be cooked and cooled before adding to a salad. For main course salads and some starters, add cooked meat, fish, eggs and cheese.

A dressing either makes or breaks a salad, both from a flavour and health point of view – many dressings are too rich and undo all the goodness that the salad is doing. The most common dressing is vinaigrette. For health purposes, use a polyunsaturated oil for vinaigrettes such as sunflower or corn, although a little olive oil can be substituted to give a better flavour if liked. The proportion of vinegar to oil is a matter of taste, but for a healthy dressing use as little oil as possible. Many flavourings can be added to the basic dressing, such as lemon or orange rind and juice, herbs, garlic, mustard and seasoning.

A much simpler and healthier dressing can be made by adding flavourings to fresh lemon, orange or tomato juice. For a creamy dressing that isn't rich, add herbs and seasoning to yogurt. Avoid using cream, soured cream and bottled manufactured dressings.

Delicate salad leaves must be dressed just before serving to prevent them from wilting, but some firmer foods often improve if they are marinated in the dressing for a few hours or even overnight.

# Minted Melon and Strawberry Cocktail

*If obtainable, Cantaloup melons make an attractive variation. Cut them in half, discard the seeds and scoop out the flesh in balls. Serve the salad in the melon shells.*

| Metric/Imperial | American |
|---|---|
| 1 small Honeydew or Ogen melon | 1 small Honeydew or Ogen melon |
| 100 g / 4 oz strawberries, hulled and sliced | 1 cup hulled and sliced strawberries |
| 5 cm / 2 inch piece cucumber, sliced and quartered | 2 inch piece cucumber, sliced and quartered |
| finely grated rind and juice of 1 large orange | finely grated rind and juice of 1 large orange |
| 2 tablespoons chopped mint | 2 tablespoons chopped mint |
| 15 g / ¹/₂ oz split blanched pistachio nuts or toasted almonds | 2 tablespoons split blanched pistachio nuts or toasted almonds |
| ¹/₂ small lettuce, shredded | ¹/₂ small head of lettuce, shredded |
| 4-6 mint sprigs to garnish | 4-6 mint sprigs to garnish |

Cut the melon in half, then remove the seeds and discard them. Cut the flesh into 1 cm / ¹/₂ inch cubes or scoop into balls. Reserve the shells. Place in a bowl with the strawberries and cucumber.

Mix the orange rind and juice with the mint and nuts, then pour on to the salad. Fold gently to mix.

Spoon the salad back into the melon shells, pouring in any orange juice from the bowl. Serve chilled, garnished with sprigs of mint.
**Serves 2**

# Avocado, Grapefruit and Sesame Salad

| Metric/Imperial | American |
|---|---|
| 2 large avocado pears | 2 large avocado pears |
| juice of 1 small lemon | juice of 1 small lemon |
| 2 grapefruit, peel and pith removed and divided into segments | 2 grapefruit, peel and pith removed and divided into segments |
| 1 tablespoon chopped mint | 1 tablespoon chopped mint |
| 1 small lettuce | 1 small head of lettuce |
| 2 tablespoons toasted sesame seeds | 2 tablespoons toasted sesame seeds |

Peel the avocados, cut in half lengthways, then remove the stones (seeds). Slice the pulp, place in a bowl, then sprinkle with the lemon juice. Fold in the grapefruit and mint.

Arrange the lettuce leaves in individual serving bowls. Divide the salad between them, then sprinkle with the sesame seeds. Garnish with mint sprigs and serve immediately.
**Serves 4**

*ABOVE: Minted melon and strawberry cocktail*
*RIGHT: Stuffed tomato salad; Marinated mushrooms with prawns (shrimp); Avocado, grapefruit and sesame salad*

# Stuffed Tomato Salad

| Metric/Imperial | American |
|---|---|
| 4 large or 6 medium tomatoes | 4 large or 6 medium tomatoes |
| 1 dessert apple | 1 dessert apple |
| finely grated rind of 1 orange | finely grated rind of 1 orange |
| juice of ½ orange | juice of ½ orange |
| 225 g / 8 oz cottage cheese | 1 cup cottage cheese |
| 2 tablespoons sultanas | 2 tablespoons seedless white raisins |
| 2 tablespoons chopped walnuts | 2 tablespoons chopped walnuts |
| 1 tablespoon snipped chives or finely chopped spring onions | 1 tablespoon snipped chives or finely chopped scallions |
| salt | salt |
| freshly ground black pepper | freshly ground black pepper |
| 1 small lettuce | 1 small head of lettuce |

Cut the tops off the tomatoes and set aside. Scoop out the centres of the tomatoes, then turn them upside down and leave to drain.

Meanwhile, chop the apple and discard the core. Put the apple in a bowl, sprinkle with the orange rind and juice, then add the remaining ingredients, except the lettuce. Fold gently to mix.

Divide the mixture equally between the tomato cups. Arrange the lettuce leaves on individual serving plates. Place a tomato on each plate and top with the reserved lids. Serve cold, accompanied by crusty wholewheat bread, or serve with Brown rice salad (see page 135)

**Serves 4 to 6**

# Marinated Mushrooms with Prawns (Shrimp)

| Metric/Imperial | American |
|---|---|
| 2 shallots or spring onions, trimmed and sliced | 2 shallots or scallions, trimmed and sliced |
| 1 garlic clove, peeled and crushed (optional) | 1 garlic clove, peeled and crushed (optional) |
| finely grated rind and juice of 1 lemon | finely grated rind and juice of 1 lemon |
| 5 tablespoons oil | ⅓ cup oil |
| 2 tablespoons thyme leaves | 2 tablespoons thyme leaves |
| 2 tablespoons chopped parsley | 2 tablespoons chopped parsley |
| salt | salt |
| freshly ground black pepper | freshly ground black pepper |
| 225 g / 8 oz mushrooms, sliced | 2 cups sliced mushrooms |
| 100 g / 4 oz peeled prawns | ½ cup shelled shrimp |
| pinch of paprika | pinch of paprika |
| TO GARNISH: | TO GARNISH: |
| 4 lemon slices | 4 lemon slices |
| 4 unshelled prawns | 4 unshelled shrimp |

Put the shallots or spring onions (scallions) in a bowl with the garlic if using, the lemon rind and juice, oil, herbs and salt and pepper to taste. Beat well to mix.

Add the mushrooms and toss in the dressing until thoroughly coated. Cover and leave to marinate for 2 hours.

Divide the mushrooms between 4 individual serving plates. Top with the prawns (shrimp) and sprinkle with paprika. Garnish each with a lemon slice and a prawn (shrimp).

**Serves 4**

# Danish Herring Salad

| Metric/Imperial | American |
|---|---|
| 225 g / 8 oz beetroot, cooked and diced | 1 1/3 cups cooked and diced beets |
| 2 dessert apples, cored and thinly sliced | 2 dessert apples, cored and thinly sliced |
| 1 onion, peeled and thinly sliced | 1 onion, peeled and thinly sliced |
| finely grated rind and juice of 1/2 lemon | finely grated rind and juice of 1 lemon |
| 150 ml / 1/4 pint natural yogurt | 2/3 cup unflavored yogurt |
| salt | salt |
| freshly ground white pepper | freshly ground white pepper |
| 4 pickled herrings or rollmops | 4 pickled herrings |
| parsley sprigs to garnish | parsley sprigs to garnish |

Put the beetroot (beets), apples and onion in a bowl. Stir the lemon rind and juice into the yogurt, then add salt and pepper to taste.

Add the yogurt to the beetroot (beet) mixture and stir well until the salad is pale pink in colour. Spoon into a shallow serving dish, arrange the herrings or rollmops on top, then garnish with parsley sprigs. Serve cold.

**Serves 4**

# Mexican Bean Salad

| Metric/Imperial | American |
|---|---|
| 225 g / 8 oz dried red kidney beans | 3/4 cup dried red kidney beans |
| 900 ml / 1 1/2 pints water | 3 3/4 cups water |
| 1 small cauliflower, divided into florets | 1 small cauliflower, divided into florets |
| 1 small green pepper, cored, seeded and cut into strips | 1 small green pepper, cored, seeded and cut into strips |
| 2 celery sticks, sliced | 2 celery stalks, sliced |
| 1 tablespoon grated onion | 1 tablespoon grated onion |
| 2 tablespoons chopped parsley | 2 tablespoons chopped parsley |
| Tabasco sauce to taste | Tabasco sauce to taste |
| 150 ml / 1/4 pint vinaigrette dressing (see page 132) | 2/3 cup French dressing (see page 132) |

Put the beans in a bowl, pour on the water and leave to soak overnight. Alternatively, pour on boiling water and leave to soak for at least 2 hours.

Transfer the beans and soaking water to a pan and bring to the boil. Boil for 10 minutes, then lower the heat and simmer for about 1 1/2 hours until the beans are tender. Drain and cool.

parsley and stir well.

Add Tabasco to taste to the vinaigrette dressing – it should be quite hot. Mix well, then pour over the salad. Leave to marinate for a few hours until the flavour of the dressing penetrates the salad ingredients. Serve cold.

**Serves 4**

# Potato and Courgette (Zucchini) Salad

| Metric/Imperial | American |
|---|---|
| 450 g / 1 lb new potatoes, scrubbed | 1 lb new potatoes, scrubbed |
| salt | salt |
| 225 g / 8 oz courgettes, sliced | 1 1/2 cups sliced zucchini |
| 4 tablespoons oil | 1/4 cup oil |
| finely grated rind and juice of 1 small orange | finely grated rind and juice of 1 small orange |
| 1 tablespoon wine vinegar | 1 tablespoon wine vinegar |
| 1 tablespoon chopped parsley | 1 tablespoon chopped parsley |
| 1 tablespoon snipped chives or finely chopped spring onions | 1 tablespoon snipped chives or finely chopped scallions |
| freshly ground black pepper | freshly ground black pepper |
| TO GARNISH: | TO GARNISH: |
| 50 g / 2 oz bacon, crisply grilled and crumbled, or chopped parsley and snipped chives | 3 bacon slices, crisply broiled and crumbled, or chopped parsley and snipped chives |

Cook the potatoes in boiling salted water until they are just tender but not broken up. Remove from the water and leave to drain. Add the courgettes (zucchini) to the boiling water, simmer for about 3 minutes until just tender, then drain.

Put the oil in a bowl with the orange rind and juice, vinegar, parsley and chives or spring onions (scallions). Add salt and pepper to taste and beat well.

Cut the larger potatoes into halves or quarters and leave the small ones whole. Put the potatoes and courgettes (zucchini) in a salad bowl, pour on the orange dressing and toss lightly to mix. The potatoes will absorb the flavour better if they are still warm.

Sprinkle the bacon or herbs over the salad just before serving. Serve cold.

**Serves 4**

# Tomato Ring Salad

*This is a perfect way to use tomatoes that are too soft for an ordinary salad.*

| Metric/Imperial | American |
|---|---|
| 750 g / 1½ lb tomatoes, roughly chopped | 3 cups roughly chopped tomatoes |
| 1 onion, peeled and chopped | 1 onion, peeled and chopped |
| 150 ml / ¼ pint stock or water | ⅔ cup stock or water |
| finely grated rind and juice of 1 orange or lemon | finely grated rind and juice of 1 orange or lemon |
| 1 small bunch herbs (basil, oregano, parsley, mint, as available) | 1 small bunch herbs (basil, oregano, parsley, mint, as available) |
| 1 bay leaf | 1 bay leaf |
| 1 garlic clove, peeled and crushed (optional) | 1 garlic clove, peeled and crushed (optional) |
| salt | salt |
| freshly ground black pepper | freshly ground black pepper |
| 25 g / ½ oz gelatine | 2 envelopes gelatin |
| 2 tablespoons water | 2 tablespoons water |
| 1 teaspoon Worcestershire sauce | 1 teaspoon Worcestershire sauce |
| TO GARNISH: | TO GARNISH: |
| 1 bunch watercress, or 1 box mustard and cress | 1 bunch watercress, or 1 box mustard and cress |
| 4 hard-boiled eggs, shelled and cut into wedges | 4 hard-cooked eggs, shelled and cut into wedges |

Put the tomatoes and onion in a pan. Pour in the stock or water then add the orange or lemon rind and juice, herbs, garlic if using and salt and pepper to taste.

Bring to the boil, then lower the heat, cover and simmer for 20 minutes until the tomatoes are reduced to a pulp. Rub through a sieve (strainer) to make a purée.

Spriinkle the gelatine over the water in a small cup. Stand the cup in a pan of hot water and stir until the gelatine has dissolved. Stir the gelatine into the purée, then add the Worcestershire sauce and salt and pepper to taste.

Pour into a 600-900 ml / 1-1½ pint / 2½-3¾ cup ring mould, then chill in the refrigerator until set.

Unmould just before serving and garnish with the cress and egg slices.
**Serves 4**

# Christmas Salad

*This winter salad of vegetables, dried fruit and nuts makes an excellent healthy meal at Christmas time.*

| Metric/Imperial | American |
|---|---|
| 175 g / 6 oz red or white cabbage, shredded | 2¼ cups shredded red or white cabbage |
| 2 large carrots, peeled and grated | 2 large carrots, peeled and grated |
| 2 dessert apples, cored and chopped | 2 dessert apples, cored and chopped |
| 2 celery sticks, chopped | 2 celery stalks, chopped |
| 100 g / 4 oz dates, stoned and chopped | ½ cup pitted and chopped dates |
| 50 g / 2 oz sultanas | ⅓ cup seedless white raisins |
| 100 g / 4 oz shelled nuts (Brazils, walnuts, almonds, hazelnuts), chopped if large | 1 cup shelled nuts (Brazils, walnuts, almonds, filberts), chopped if large |
| 2 tangerines or oranges, peel and pith removed and divided into segments | 2 tangerines or oranges, peel and pith removed and divided into segments |
| 100 g / 4 oz Stilton cheese, diced | ⅔ cup diced Stilton cheese |
| 150 ml / ¼ pint salad dressing (yogurt, fruit juice or vinaigrette – see page 132) | ⅔ cup salad dressing (yogurt, fruit juice or French dressing – see page 132) |
| salt | salt |
| freshly ground black pepper | freshly ground black pepper |

Put all the ingredients in a bowl, toss well to mix, then taste and adjust the seasoning. Serve cold.

If not to be used immediately, store in an airtight container in the refrigerator. The salad will keep fresh for several days.

**Serves 4 as a main course, 8 as an accompaniment to cold meats**

# Pasta and Fish Salad

*This salad may be made with any shape of pasta – noodles, spaghetti, shells, etc.*

| Metric/Imperial | American |
|---|---|
| 225 g / 8 oz spinach pasta | ½ lb spinach pasta |
| salt | salt |
| 100 g / 4 oz cooked shelled mussels | ½ cup cooked shelled mussels or clams |
| 100 g / 4 oz peeled prawns, cooked | ½ cup shelled shrimp, cooked |
| 1 × 50 g / 2 oz can anchovies, drained | 1 × 2 oz can anchovies, drained |
| 50 g / 2 oz button mushrooms, sliced | ½ cup sliced button mushrooms |
| 2 tomatoes, cut into wedges | 2 tomatoes, cut into wedges |
| 150 ml / ¼ pint vinaigrette dressing (see page 132) | ⅔ cup French dressing (see page 132) |
| TO GARNISH: | TO GARNISH: |
| 2 tablespoons chopped parsley | 2 tablespoons chopped parsley |
| 2 tablespoons grated Parmesan cheese | 2 tablespoons grated Parmesan cheese |

Cook the pasta in plenty of boiling salted water for 10 to 15 minutes until 'al dente'. Drain in a colander and rinse under cold running water. Drain thoroughly.

Put the cooked pasta in a bowl, then add the fish, mushrooms and tomatoes. Pour on the dressing and mix gently. Sprinkle with parsley and Parmesan just before serving.

**Serves 4**

# Chicken Salad Véronique

| Metric/Imperial | American |
|---|---|
| 1 × 1.5 kg / 3 lb chicken, with giblets | 1 × 3 lb chicken, with giblets |
| 300 ml / ½ pint water | 1¼ cups water |
| 1 small onion, peeled and chopped | 1 small onion, peeled and chopped |
| finely grated rind and juice of ½ lemon | finely grated rind and juice of ½ lemon |
| 1 slice fresh root ginger, peeled and chopped | 1 slice fresh ginger root, peeled and chopped |
| few thyme or parsley sprigs | few thyme or parsley sprigs |
| 1 bay leaf | 1 bay leaf |
| salt | salt |
| freshly ground white pepper | freshly ground white pepper |
| 150 ml / ¼ pint natural yogurt | ⅔ cup unflavored yogurt |
| 1 head curly endive, separated into leaves | 1 head chicory, separated into leaves |
| 100 g / 4 oz green grapes, halved and seeded | 1 cup halved and seeded white grapes |
| 50 g / 2 oz flaked almonds | ½ cup flaked almonds |

Put the chicken in a large pan with the giblets and the water. Add the onion, lemon rind and juice, ginger, herbs and salt and pepper to taste. Bring to the boil, then lower the heat, cover and simmer for 45 minutes or until tender.

Remove the chicken from the cooking liquid, discard the skin and bones and cut the chicken flesh into neat pieces.

Boil the cooking liquid rapidly until reduced to 150 ml / ¼ pint / ⅔ cup. Strain, leave to cool, then skim off the fat. Stir into the yogurt, add salt and pepper to taste and mix well.

Arrange the endive (chicory) on a serving dish. Top with the chicken and grapes. Pour over the yogurt sauce and scatter the almonds over the top. Serve cold.

**Serves 4 to 6**

# Beef and Orange Salad

| Metric/Imperial | American |
|---|---|
| 450 g / 1 lb lean beef (boned sirloin or topside, rump or fillet steak) | 1 lb lean beef (boned sirloin or top round, rump or filet steak) |
| finely grated rind and juice of 1 large orange | finely grated rind and juice of 1 large orange |
| 1 tablespoon wine vinegar | 1 tablespoon wine vinegar |
| 1 bay leaf | 1 bay leaf |
| salt | salt |
| freshly ground black pepper | freshly ground black pepper |
| 200 ml / ⅓ pint water or stock | ¾ cup stock or water |
| 100 g / 4 oz mushrooms, sliced | 1 cup sliced mushrooms |
| 1 lettuce | 1 head of lettuce |
| 1 large carrot, peeled and grated | 1 large carrot, peeled and grated |
| 50 g / 2 oz bean sprouts | 1 cup bean sprouts |

Put the beef in a pan with the orange rind and juice, vinegar, bay leaf and salt and pepper to taste. Pour on the water or stock and bring to the boil.

Lower the heat, cover and simmer for 5 minutes for rare beef, 10 minutes for well done beef. Add the mushrooms and simmer for a further 2 minutes.

Remove the beef and mushrooms from the pan and leave to cool. Boil the cooking liquid until reduced to 150 ml / ¼ pint / ⅔ cup. Leave to cool, then taste and adjust the seasoning.

Cut the beef into strips, then place in a bowl with the mushrooms. Pour over the reduced cooking liquid and leave to marinate for at least 1 hour, turning occasionally.

Arrange the lettuce leaves on a serving dish. Pile the beef mixture in the centre, then strain over the marinade. Mix together the carrot and bean sprouts and arrange around the beef. Serve cold.

**Serves 4**

*Pasta and fish salad; Beef and orange salad; Tomato ring salad (page 129); Chicken salad Véronique*

# Cheese and Bread Salad

*This is a good way to use up stale bread – simply soak cubes of bread in vinaigrette dressing and combine with the other ingredients for a delicious salad.*

| Metric/Imperial | American |
|---|---|
| 150 ml / ¼ pint vinaigrette dressing (see opposite) | ⅔ cup French dressing (see opposite) |
| 2 slices or crusts wholemeal bread, diced | 2 slices or crusts wholewheat bread, diced |
| 100 g / 4 oz Cheddar or Edam cheese, diced | ½ cup diced Cheddar or Edam cheese |
| 100 g / 4 oz Mozzarella cheese, diced | ½ cup diced Mozzarella cheese |
| 4 tomatoes, sliced | 4 tomatoes, sliced |
| 10 cm / 4 inch piece cucumber sliced | 4 inch piece cucumber, sliced |
| 1 × 50 g / 2 oz can anchovy fillets, drained (optional) | 1 × 2 oz can anchovy fillets, drained (optional) |
| 8 olives, halved and stoned | 8 olives, halved and pitted |
| 1 lettuce | 1 head of lettuce |

Pour the dressing into a bowl. Add the bread and toss to coat thoroughly. Add the remaining ingredients, except the lettuce, and fold gently to mix.

Line a serving dish or bowl with lettuce leaves, then pile the salad in the centre. Pour over any remaining dressing. Serve cold.
**Serves 4**

# Lemon Yogurt Dressing

*Yogurt flavoured with lemon and herbs makes a refreshing oil-free salad dressing.*

| Metric/Imperial | American |
|---|---|
| 150 ml / ¼ pint natural yogurt | ⅔ cup unflavored yogurt |
| finely grated rind and juice of ½ lemon | finely grated rind and juice of ½ lemon |
| 1 tablespoon chopped parsley | 1 tablespoon chopped parsley |
| 1 tablespoon snipped chives | 1 tablespoon snipped chives |
| 1 tablespoon chopped thyme, mint, watercress or sorrel | 1 tablespoon chopped thyme, mint, watercress or sorrel |
| salt | salt |
| freshly ground white pepper | freshly ground white pepper |

Put all the ingredients in a bowl and beat well. Taste and adjust the seasoning, then pour over the salad just before serving.
**Makes 150 ml / ¼ pint / ⅔ cup dressing**

# Vinaigrette (French) Dressing

*Use a polyunsaturated oil such as corn, sunflower or safflower. For a stronger flavour, substitute a small quantity of this with olive oil.*

| Metric/Imperial | American |
|---|---|
| 150 ml / ¼ pint oil | ⅔ cup oil |
| 5 tablespoons vinegar or lemon juice | ⅓ cup vinegar or lemon juice |
| 1 garlic clove, peeled (optional) | 1 clove garlic, peeled (optional) |
| 1 sprig herbs (optional) | 1 sprig herbs (optional) |
| mustardd | mustard |
| salt | salt |
| freshly ground black pepper | freshly ground black pepper |

Put all the ingredients in a screw-topped jar, adding mustard, salt and pepper to taste. Shake well.

Store in the refrigerator and use as required, adding dressing just before serving when possible.
**Makes approximately 150 ml / ¼ pint / ⅔ cup dressing**

# Piquant Tomato Dressing

*This tangy tomato juice dressing is a good alternative to vinaigrette when a strong-flavoured dressing is called for.*

| Metric/Imperial | American |
|---|---|
| 6 tablespoons tomato juice | 6 tablespoons tomato juice |
| 2 tablespoons lemon juice | 2 tablespoons lemon juice |
| 1-2 teaspoons Worcestershire sauce | 1-2 teaspoons Worcestershire sauce |
| 1 tablespoon chopped herbs (parsley, chives or mint) | 1 tablespoon chopped herbs (parsley, chives or mint) |
| salt | salt |
| freshly ground black pepper | freshly ground black pepper |

Put all the ingredients in a bowl and beat well. Taste and adjust the seasoning, then pour over the salad just before serving.

**Makes approximately 120 ml / 4 fl oz / ½ cup dressing**

# Minted Fruit Juice Dressing

*Freshly-squeezed orange or grapefruit juice makes an excellent salad dressing for slimmers, as it does not need the addition of oil. However, an equal quantity of oil may be added if liked.*

| Metric/Imperial | American |
|---|---|
| 150 ml / ¼ pint fresh orange or grapefruit juice | ⅔ cup fresh orange or grapefruit juice |
| 1-2 teaspoons chopped mint | 1-2 teaspoons chopped mint |
| salt | salt |
| freshly ground black pepper | freshly ground black pepper |

Put all the ingredients in a bowl and beat well. Taste and adjust the seasoning, then pour over the salad just before serving.

**Makes 150 ml / ¼ pint / ⅔ cup dressing**

# Ginger Yogurt Salad Dressing

| Metric/Imperial | American |
|---|---|
| 150 ml / ¼ pint natural yogurt | ⅔ cup unflavored yogurt |
| 25 g / 1 oz stem ginger, finely chopped | 3 tablespoons finely chopped preserved ginger |
| ¼ teaspoon ground ginger | ¼ teaspoon ground ginger |

Put all the ingredients in a bowl and beat with a fork until well mixed. Chill in the refrigerator for 1 hour.

Serve with a cucumber salad, citrus fruit salad or melon balls.

**Serves 4**

# Cucumber and Tomato Raita

*This Indian salad in a yogurt and mint dressing is very refreshing. It is especially good when served with hot, spicy foods.*

| Metric/Imperial | American |
|---|---|
| 1 small or ½ large cucumber, sliced | 1 small or ½ large cucumber, sliced |
| ½ teaspoon salt | ½ teaspoon salt |
| 4 tomatoes, thinly sliced | 4 tomatoes, thinly sliced |
| 300 ml / ½ pint natural yogurt | 1¼ cups unflavored yogurt |
| 2 tablespoons chopped mint | 2 tablespoons chopped mint |
| freshly ground white pepper | freshly ground white pepper |
| mint sprig to garnish | mint sprig to garnish |

Put the cucumber in a sieve (strainer), sprinkle with the salt and leave to drain for 30 minutes to extract the water.

Arrange the cucumber and tomatoes in a serving dish. Mix the yogurt with the chopped mint and pepper to taste, then pour over the salad. Garnish with mint. Serve chilled.

**Serves 4**

# Italian Salad

| Metric/Imperial | American |
|---|---|
| ½ head curly endive, separated into leaves | ½ head chicory, separated into leaves |
| 1 head chicory, sliced into rings | 1 head Belgian endive, sliced into rings |
| 1 bulb fennel, sliced into rings | 1 bulb fennel, sliced into rings |
| 1 small head radiccio, separated into leaves (optional) | 1 small head red chicory, separated into leaves (optional) |
| 8 radishes, sliced if large | 8 radishes, sliced if large |
| 4 tablespoons vinaigrette dressing (see page 132) | ¼ cup French dressing (see page 132) |
| salt | salt |
| freshly ground black pepper | freshly ground black pepper |

Put all the ingrediennts in a salad bowl, toss well, then taste and adjust the seasoning. Serve cold.

**Serves 4**

*RIGHT: Orange and watercress salad; Brown rice salad*
*BELOW: Cucumber and tomato raita; Italian salad*

# Brown Rice Salad

| Metric/Imperial | American |
|---|---|
| 100 g / 4 oz brown rice | ¹/₂ cup brown rice |
| salt | salt |
| 100 g / 4 oz shelled peas or sliced beans | ³/₄ cup shelled peas, or ¹/₂ cup sliced green beans |
| 100 g / 4 oz sweetcorn kernels | ³/₄ cup kernel corn |
| 150 ml / ¹/₄ pint vinaigrette dressing (see page 132) | ²/₃ cup French dressing (see page 132) |
| 1 red pepper, cored, seeded and diced | 1 red pepper, cored, seeded and diced |
| 50 g / 2 oz salted peanuts | ¹/₂ cup salted peanuts |
| 1 small onion, peeled and grated | 1 small onion, peeled and grated |
| freshly ground black pepper | freshly ground black pepper |

Cook the rice in boiling salted water for 30 minutes or until tender. Add the peas or beans and corn and simmer for a further few minutes until just tender. Drain thoroughly.

Transfer to a bowl and add half of the dressing while the rice and vegetables are still hot. Toss well to mix, then leave to cool.

Add the remaining ingredients and dressing and mix well. Taste and adjust the seasoning just before serving. Serve cold.

**Serves 4**

# Orange and Watercress Salad

*This is an excellent salad to serve with duck.*

| Metric/Imperial | American |
|---|---|
| 1 large bunch watercress, trimmed | 1 large bunch watercress, trimmed |
| 3 oranges, peel and pith removed and thinly sliced into rounds | 3 oranges, peel and pith removed and thinly sliced into rounds |
| 1 onion, peeled and thinly sliced into rings | 1 onion, peeled and thinly sliced into rings |
| 1 small green pepper, cored, seeded and thinly sliced into rings | 1 small green pepper, cored, seeded and thinly sliced into rings |
| 6 tablespoons vinaigrette dressing (see page 132) | 6 tablespoons French dressing (see page 132) |
| black olives to garnish | ripe olives to garnish |

Put the watercress in a salad bowl. Arrange the orange slices on top with the onion and pepper rings. Pour on the dressing and garnish with the olives. Serve cold.

**Serves 4**

# Raw Mushrooms with Lemon Dressing

| Metric/Imperial | American |
|---|---|
| 1 garlic clove | 1 garlic clove |
| DRESSING: | 3 cups sliced button |
| ½ teaspoon finely grated | mushrooms |
| lemon rind | finely chopped parsley to |
| 2 tablespoons vegetable oil | garnish |
| 2 tablespoons lemon juice | DRESSING: |
| pinch of grated nutmeg | ½ teaspoon finely grated |
| salt | lemon peel |
| freshly ground black pepper | 2 tablespoons vegetable oil |
| 350 g / 12 oz button | 2 tablespoons lemon juice |
| mushrooms, sliced | pinch of grated nutmeg |
| finely chopped parsley to | salt |
| garnish | freshly ground black pepper |

Cut the garlic in half and rub the cut surface round the inside of your chosen salad bowl to give just a suspicion of the flavour without drowning the delicate taste of the raw mushrooms. The garlic may then be used for some other purpose.

Make the dressing in the same bowl. Mix together the lemon rind, oil, lemon juice, nutmeg, salt and pepper. When well blended, toss the mushrooms in this until each slice glistens with dressing.

Cover and leave to stand at room temperature for 15 minutes. Sprinkle with parsley.

**Serves 4**

# American Salad

| Metric/Imperial | American |
|---|---|
| 100 g / 4 oz cooked French | ½ cup sliced cooked French |
| beans, sliced | beans |
| 100 g / 4 oz mushrooms, | 1 cup sliced raw |
| sliced | mushrooms |
| 50 g / 2 oz cooked or | ¼ cup cooked or canned |
| canned sweetcorn | corn kernels |
| 2 large tomatoes, peeled | ¾ cup peeled and sliced |
| and sliced | tomato |
| ½ red or green pepper, | ½ red or green pepper, |
| cored, seeded and sliced | cored, seeded and sliced |
| 1 small onion, cut into rings | 1 small onion, cut into rings |
| DRESSING: | ripe olives to garnish |
| 3 tablespoons vegetable oil | DRESSING: |
| 1 tablespoon cider vinegar | 3 tablespoons vegetable oil |
| salt | 1 tablespoon hard cider |
| freshly ground black pepper | vinegar |
| ½ teaspoon dry mustard | salt |
| black olives to garnish | freshly ground black pepper |
| | ½ teaspoon dry mustard |

Arrange the French beans, mushrooms, corn, tomatoes, pepper and onion in a salad bowl.

Whisk together the oil, vinegar, salt, pepper and mustard, or shake them together in a screw-topped jar.

Pour this dressing over the vegetables, toss well and garnish with olives.

**Serves 4**

# Pepper and Olive Salad

| Metric/Imperial | American |
|---|---|
| 2 red peppers, cored and | 2 red peppers, cored and |
| cut into thin rings | cut into thin rings |
| 2 green peppers, cored and | 2 green peppers, cored and |
| cut into thin rings | cut into thin rings |
| 25 g / 1 oz green olives, | ¼ cup pitted green olives |
| stoned | ¼ cup pitted ripe olives |
| 25 g / 1 oz black olives, | DRESSING: |
| stoned | 3 tablespoons olive oil |
| DRESSING: | 1 tablespoon wine vinegar |
| 3 tablespoons olive oil | salt |
| 1 tablespoon wine vinegar | freshly ground black pepper |
| salt | |
| freshly ground black pepper | |

Put the peppers in a heatproof bowl, pour boiling water over them and allow to stand for 2 minutes. Rinse them well under cold running water, and discard any seeds.

Mix together the olives and peppers.

Whisk together the oil, vinegar, salt and pepper. Pour this over the peppers and olives and toss well before serving.

**Serves 4**

# Salade Niçoise

| Metric/Imperial | American |
|---|---|
| 1 small lettuce | 1 small head of lettuce |
| 2 hard-boiled eggs, sliced | 2 hard-cooked eggs, sliced |
| 2 small tomatoes, quartered | 2 small tomatoes, quartered |
| 8 anchovy fillets, drained | 8 anchovy fillets, drained |
| 8 black olives | 8 ripe olives |
| 8 capers | 8 capers |
| ½ red pepper, sliced | ½ red pepper, sliced |
| DRESSING: | DRESSING: |
| 3 tablespoons olive oil | 3 tablespoons olive oil |
| 1 tablespoon tarragon | 1 tablespoon tarragon |
| vinegar | vinegar |
| 2 garlic cloves, crushed | 2 garlic cloves, crushed |
| salt and black pepper | salt and black pepper |
| 2 tablespoons basil | 2 tablespoons basil |

Arrange the lettuce leaves, eggs, tomatoes, anchovies, olives, capers and pepper slices in a large salad bowl.

Beat together the oil, vinegar, garlic, salt and pepper, then pour over the salad. Toss carefully to coat all the lettuce. Just before serving, sprinkle over the basil.

**Serves 4**

*ABOVE: Italian cauliflower salad*

# Italian Cauliflower Salad

**Metric/Imperial**
1 medium cauliflower,
  divided into florets
DRESSING:
1 small onion, grated
3 tablespoons vegetable oil
1 tablespoon wine vinegar
½ tablespoon lemon juice
salt
freshly ground black pepper

**American**
1 medium cauliflower,
  divided into florets
DRESSING:
1 small onion, grated
3 tablespoons vegetable oil
1 tablespoon wine vinegar
½ tablespoon lemon juice
salt
freshly ground black pepper

TO GARNISH:
anchovy fillets, cut into
  small pieces
black olives, halved and
  stoned

TO GARNISH:
anchovy fillets, cut into
  small pieces
ripe olives, halved and
  pitted

Wash the cauliflower florets well, then either boil them gently in salted water, or steam them until they are still slightly crisp. Drain them well.

To make the dressing: in a salad bowl mix together the onion, oil, wine vinegar, lemon juice, salt and pepper. Add the warm cauliflower florets and toss well.

Allow to cool, then chill well before serving garnished with olives and anchovy fillets.

**Serves 4**

# Tomato Salad

| Metric/Imperial | American |
|---|---|
| 450 g / 1 lb tomatoes, peeled and sliced | 2 cups peeled and sliced tomatoes |
| 3 tablespoons fresh orange juice | 3 tablespoons fresh orange juice |
| 1/2 teaspoon salt | 1/2 teaspoon salt |
| freshly ground black pepper | freshly ground black pepper |
| 1 teaspoon finely chopped parsley | 1 teaspoon finely chopped parsley |
| 1 tablespoon chopped onion (optional) | 1 tablespoon chopped onion (optional) |

Arrange the tomatoes in a shallow serving dish. Sprinkle them with the orange juice, salt, pepper, parsley and onion (if liked).

Chill for at least 15 minutes before serving.

**Serves 4**

# Tuna Fish Salad Hors d'Oeuvre

| Metric/Imperial | American |
|---|---|
| 1 × 200 g / 7 oz can of tuna fish in oil | 7 oz can of tuna fish in oil |
| pepper | pepper |
| 3 tablespoons drained capers | 3 tablespoons drained capers |
| 3 tomatoes, thinly sliced | 3 tomatoes, thinly sliced |
| 2 spring onions, thinly sliced | 2 scallions, thinly sliced |
| 1/2 teaspoon lemon juice | 1/2 teaspoon lemon juice |

Drain the tuna from its oil, reserving 1 tablespoon. Shred the tuna with a fork then arrange it in the centre of a serving plate.

Mix the pepper and capers together, then sprinkle over the tuna. Arrange the tomato and spring onion (scallion) slices over the fish. Mix the lemon juice with the reserved oil and sprinkle over the salad. Serve chilled.

**Serves 4**

# Greek Salata

| Metric/Imperial | American |
|---|---|
| 1/4 small red cabbage, shredded | 1 1/2 cups shredded red cabbage |
| 100 g / 4 oz pickled beetroot, cut into strips | 2/3 cup thinly sliced pickled beet |
| 50 g / 2 oz cooked sliced French beans | 1/4 cup sliced cooked French beans |
| 1 tablespoon chopped oregano or marjoram | 1 tablespoon chopped oregano or marjoram |
| salt | salt |
| freshly ground black pepper | freshly ground black pepper |
| DRESSING: | DRESSING: |
| 3 tablespoons olive oil | 3 tablespoons olive oil |
| 1 tablespoon wine vinegar | 1 tablespoon wine vinegar |
| 1 teaspoon coriander seeds, crushed | 1 teaspoon coriander seeds, crushed |
| salt | salt |
| freshly ground black pepper | freshly ground black pepper |
| TO GARNISH: | TO GARNISH: |
| 4 black olives, stoned and chopped | 4 ripe olives, pitted and chopped |
| 1 tablespoon capers | 1 tablespoon capers |

Mix together the red cabbage, beetroot (beet), French beans and oregano or marjoram in a salad bowl. Season with salt and pepper.

Whisk together the oil, wine vinegar, coriander, salt and pepper, or shake them in a screw-topped jar. Pour this dressing over the vegetables and toss well.

Garnish with olives and capers, and chill the salad for 30 minutes before serving.

**Serves 4**

# Cucumber Salad with Yogurt

| Metric/Imperial | American |
|---|---|
| 1 cucumber, peeled and very thinly sliced | 1 cucumber, peeled and very thinly sliced |
| 2 teaspoons salt | 2 teaspoons salt |
| 1 garlic clove, crushed | 1 garlic clove, crushed |
| 1 tablespoon wine vinegar | 1 tablespoon wine vinegar |
| 125 ml / 4 fl oz natural yogurt | 1/2 cup unflavored yogurt |
| 1 tablespoon vegetable oil | 1 tablespoon vegetable oil |
| 1 tablespoon chopped dill, chives or parsley | 1 tablespoon chopped dill, chives or parsley |

Put the cucumber in a colander. Sprinkle it with half of the salt, cover with a saucer then a heavy weight, and allow it to drain for 1 hour.

Blend together the garlic and vinegar. Add the remaining salt and mix to a smooth paste. Stir this into the yogurt. Blend in the oil, dill, chives or parsley.

Pour this yogurt dressing over the well drained cucumber. Toss well and chill before serving.

**Serves 4**

*RIGHT: Tomato salad*

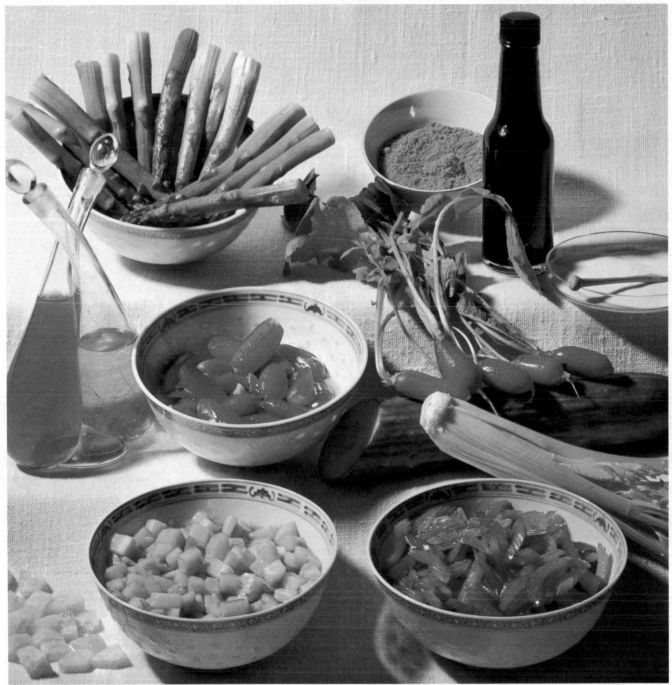

*ABOVE: Salad quartet*

# Orange and Watercress Salad

**Metric/Imperial**
2 bunches watercress
2 large oranges, peel and
   pith removed
DRESSING:
¼ teaspoon salt
freshly ground black pepper
3 tablespoons vegetable oil

**American**
2 bunches watercress
2 large oranges, peel and
   pith removed
DRESSING:
¼ teaspoon salt
freshly ground black pepper
3 tablespoons vegetable oil

1 tablespoon wine vinegar    1 tablespoon wine vinegar

Wash the watercress, drain it well and tear it into bite size sprigs.

Cut the oranges into thin rounds. Mix them with the watercress in a salad bowl.

Whisk together the salt, pepper, oil and vinegar, or shake them together in a screw-topped jar.

Pour this dressing over the watercress and oranges, and toss well before serving.
**Serves 4**

# Salad Quartet

| Metric/Imperial | American |
|---|---|
| 1 head of celery | 1 head of celery |
| 1 teaspoon sesame oil | 1 teaspoon sesame oil |
| 1 tablespoon soy sauce | 1 tablespoon soy sauce |
| ½ teaspoon salt | ½ teaspoon salt |
| | |
| 20 radishes | 20 radishes |
| 1 tablespoon vegetable oil | 1 tablespoon vegetable oil |
| ½ tablespoon wine vinegar | ½ tablespoon wine vinegar |
| | |
| ½ cucumber | ½ cucumber |
| pinch of ground ginger | pinch of ground ginger |
| ½ teaspoon salt | ½ teaspoon salt |
| 3 tablespoons vegetable oil | 3 tablespoons vegetable oil |
| 1 tablespoon lemon juice | 1 tablespoon lemon juice |
| | |
| 12 fresh or canned asparagus spears | 2 tablespoons lemon juice |
| 2 tablespoons lemon juice | 12 fresh or canned asparagus spears |

Wash the celery and cut it into 2.5 cm / 1 inch lengths. Pour boiling water over them, allow to stand for 1 minute, then drain and chill. Mix together the oil, soy sauce and salt and pour it over the celery, tossing well.

Trim the radishes, and soak them in the oil and vinegar.

Peel, seed and finely chop the cucumber. Blend together the ginger, salt, oil and lemon juice. Toss the cucumber in this dressing.

Pour the lemon juice over the asparagus.

Serve well chilled.

**Serves 4**

# Hawaiian Salad

| Metric/Imperial | American |
|---|---|
| 1 small lettuce | 1 small head of lettuce |
| 1-2 heads of chicory | 1-2 heads of Belgian endive |
| 225 g / 8 oz cottage cheese | 1 cup cottage cheese |
| 4 fresh pineapple rings, peeled and halved | 4 fresh pineapple rings, peeled and halved |
| 2 large oranges, peel and pith removed and divided into segments | 2 large oranges, peel and pith removed and divided into segments |
| 5 cm / 2 inches cucumber, thinly sliced | 2 inches cucumber, thinly sliced |
| apple slices to garnish | apple slices to garnish |
| DRESSING: | DRESSING: |
| 3 tablespoons vegetable oil | 3 tablespoons vegetable oil |
| 1 tablespoon lemon juice | 1 tablespoon lemon juice |
| salt | salt |
| freshly ground black pepper | freshly ground black pepper |
| pinch of ground ginger | pinch of ground ginger |
| ½ teaspoon dry mustard | ½ teaspoon dry mustard |

Wash the lettuce and shake the leaves dry. Line a serving plate with them. Separate and wash the chicory (Belgian endive) leaves and arrange them at each end of the plate.

Spoon the cottage cheese into the centre, and surround it with borders of pineapple, orange and cucumber.

Whisk together the oil, lemon juice, salt, pepper, ginger and mustard. Dip the apple slices into this dressing to prevent browning and arrange them on top of the cottage cheese.

Serve the remaining dressing separately.

**Serves 4**

*BELOW: Hawaiian salad*

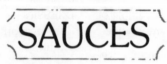

# SAUCES

Sauces and dressings can improve all salad type dishes. Here are some special, healthy recipes, especially suitable for lettuce, artichokes, tomatoes, hard-boiled (hard-cooked) eggs and asparagus. They are all easy to prepare and guaranteed non-fattening.

## Herb Sauce

**Metric/Imperial**
150 ml / ¼ pint natural yogurt
2 teaspoons mild mustard
½ teaspoon of each of the following herbs, finely chopped: tarragon, chives, parsley and chervil

**American**
⅔ cup unflavored yogurt
2 teaspoons mild mustard
½ teaspoon of each of the following herbs, finely chopped: tarragon, chives, parsley and chervil

Mix the yogurt and chopped herbs together, then season the mixture to taste. Beat in the mustard until the mixture is smooth and well combined.

Chill for at least an hour before serving.

**Serves 4**

## Lemon Sauce

*This dressing goes particularly well with vegetable hors d'oeuvre dishes, particularly asparagus.*

**Metric/Imperial**
150 ml / ¼ pint natural yogurt
1 tablespoon lemon juice
1 teaspoon mustard
1 teaspoon chopped parsley

**American**
⅔ cup unflavored yogurt
1 tablespoon lemon juice
1 teaspoon mustard
1 teaspoon chopped parsley

Mix all the ingredients together very carefully. Put the sauce into the refrigerator and chill for at least an hour before serving.

**Serves 4**

# Tomato Vinaigrette Dressing

*This dressing goes well with most salads but tastes particularly good with avocados.*

| Metric/Imperial | American |
|---|---|
| 1 × 175 g / 6 oz can tomato sauce | 6 oz can tomato sauce |
| 1 tablespoon wine vinegar | 1 tablespoon wine vinegar |
| 2 tablespoons lemon juice | 2 tablespoons lemon juice |
| 2 tablespoons chopped parsley | 2 tablespoons chopped parsley |
| salt and black pepper | salt and black pepper |

Put all the ingredients into a small bowl and beat until they are thoroughly blended. Chill until ready to use.
**Serves 4**

# Yogurt Dressing

*Use this dressing for new potato, green bean or mixed salad.*

| Metric/Imperial | American |
|---|---|
| 450 ml / ¾ pint natural yogurt | 2 cups unflavored yogurt |
| 1 small bunch of chives | 1 small bunch of chives |
| 1 onion, peeled | 1 onion, peeled |
| 1 teaspoon brandy | 1 teaspoon brandy |
| salt and black pepper | salt and black pepper |
| curry powder or paprika | curry powder or paprika |

Beat the yogurt until it is light and creamy.

Mince or finely chop the chives and onion and stir into the yogurt. Stir in the brandy and season to taste. Chill until ready to use.
**Serves 4**

# Ketchup Dressing

*This dressing goes particularly well with green salads.*

| Metric/Imperial | American |
|---|---|
| 1 tablespoon lemon juice | 1 tablespoon lemon juice |
| 3 tablespoons tomato ketchup | 3 tablespoons tomato ketchup |
| 1 tablespoon olive oil | 1 tablespoon olive oil |
| salt and black pepper | salt and black pepper |

Put all the ingredients into a small bowl and beat until well blended. Chill until ready to use.
**Serves 4**

# Golden Dressing

*Use this dressing on cos (Romaine) lettuce or any mixed green salad.*

| Metric/Imperial | American |
|---|---|
| the yolks of 2 hard-boiled eggs | the yolks of 2 hard-cooked eggs |
| 1 teaspoon prepared mustard | 1 teaspoon prepared mustard |
| 1 teaspoon lemon juice | 1 teaspoon lemon juice |
| 100 g / 4 oz cream cheese | ½ cup cream cheese |
| salt and black pepper | salt and black pepper |
| chopped mixed herbs | chopped mixed herbs |

Mash the egg yolks through a sieve (strainer) and incorporate them, little by little, with all the other ingredients until thoroughly blended.
**Serves 4**

# Mayonnaise

| Metric/Imperial | American |
|---|---|
| 2 hard-boiled egg yolks | 2 hard-cooked egg yolks |
| 2 raw egg yolks | 2 raw egg yolks |
| 150 ml / ¼ pint natural yogurt | ⅔ cup unflavored yogurt |
| 1 teaspoon mild mustard | 1 teaspoon mild mustard |
| pinch of salt | pinch of salt |
| pinch of freshly ground black pepper | pinch of freshly ground black pepper |
| 1 teaspoon lemon juice | 1 teaspoon lemon juice |
| 1 teaspoon snipped chives | 1 teaspoon snipped chives |

Mash the hard-boiled (hard-cooked) eggs then pass through a strainer until they are smooth. Gently beat in the raw yolks until the mixture is smooth. Gradually add the other ingredients until they are all incorporated and the mixture has a creamy consistency. Chill the dressing until ready to use.
**Serves 4**

# VEGETABLES

Our food would certainly be dull without the abundance of vegetables available. They add colour, texture and flavour to the diet, and provide us with roughage, minerals and vitamins.

Most vegetables contain only a small amount of protein, but pulses (legumes) are an exception, being rich in protein, vitamins and minerals. Vegetable protein is not as complete as animal protein because it lacks a few of the essential amino-acids, and strict vegetarians who do not include any dairy foods in their diet must have a very carefully balanced diet to ensure good health. Also, pulses (legumes) have to be reconstituted with water, which dilutes the nutrients.

Soya beans have a particularly high protein content and are often used in vegetarian diets in place of meat. A cheap source of protein, they have always been used extensively in the Far East where they are manufactured into a wide range of health foods. Because of their high protein content, soya beans are often processed to simulate meat, but it seems more appropriate to use them in the many traditional bean recipes available from all over the world – or substitute them for some or all of the meat in such recipes as moussaka, curry or stews. Pulses (legumes) do not contain any vitamin C or A and therefore must be used with, and not instead of, fresh vegetables.

Raw vegetables are the healthiest because no loss of minerals, vitamins or roughage can occur during cooking. However, to most of us a diet of raw vegetables would prove unacceptable so we must prepare and cook them so as to retain as much of the goodness as possible.

When preparing vegetables, throw away as little as possible. So often the tastiest and most nutritious parts are trimmed away, usually because we have been taught that it is not 'nice and proper' to serve them. The most obvious example of this is peeling potatoes and other root vegetables. The nutrients are usually most concentrated just below the skin and peeling removes a high proportion of the goodness. Instead they should be well washed.

Many other vegetables are also often trimmed unnecessarily. For example, don't trim the green parts of leeks as they are sweeter and more delicious than the rest – just remove the roots and damaged tops. Most of the green leaves surrounding a cauliflower can be used too, providing a contrast in colour as well as being economical. The stalks from green leaves, such as spinach, can be chopped up and cooked with the leaves or kept whole and cooked separately and served as a starter, like asparagus. The stems and skins of mushrooms contain most of the flavour, so don't trim them away – just wash thoroughly and trim the tops of the stalks if necessary. Don't skin tomatoes unless they are to be cooked in a casserole or soup. Very young peas and beans can be eaten in their pods, particularly mange-tout (snow peas) and broad (lima) beans – just top and tail and cook like green beans.

Vegetables should be cooked in as little fast boiling water as possible until they are only just tender and still retain their crispness and bright colour. Apart from being much better for you, they are more appetizing and much tastier cooked this way. Always add the vegetables to boiling water – this destroys the enzyme present which destroys vitamin C. Also cover the pan so that they will cook more quickly, allowing the vegetables at the top to cook in the steam. An even better way is to steam them over boiling water so that they don't come into contact with the water. *Never* add bicarbonate of soda (baking soda); although it helps vegetables to retain a good colour, it destroys vitamin C.

Use the water in which vegetables are cooked for sauces, soups, stews, etc. Alternatively, reduce the cooking water by boiling to concentrate the flavour and use it as a glaze for the vegetables. Serve vegetables as soon as possible after cooking, as keeping them also reduces vitamin C content.

Another good way of cooking vegetables is stir-frying in the Chinese style. The vegetables are cooked quickly in a little oil over a high heat, stirring all the time until they are just tender and still crisp. This is ideal for cooking a mixture of vegetables together – start with those that take longest to cook, then add the remaining vegetables in stages, ending with those that just need heating through.

Vegetables are incredibly versatile and, with a little imagination, can be prepared and cooked in many different ways to produce delicious soups, mousses, soufflés, quiches, pâtês, casseroles, pies, pasta and rice dishes, or simply enjoyed – raw or cooked – on their own.

# Beetroot (Beet) and Orange Soup

| Metric/Imperial | American |
|---|---|
| 450 g / 1 lb raw beetroot, peeled and diced | 2²/₃ cups peeled and diced raw beets |
| 1 large onion, peeled and chopped | 1 large onion, peeled and chopped |
| finely grated rind and juice of 3 oranges | finely grated rind and juice of 3 oranges |
| 1 bay leaf | 1 bay leaf |
| 1.2 litres / 2 pints stock | 5 cups stock |
| salt | salt |
| freshly ground black pepper | freshly ground black pepper |
| 150 ml / ¼ pint natural yogurt | ²/₃ cup unflavored yogurt |
| 1 orange, sliced, to garnish | 1 orange, sliced, to garnish |

Put the beetroot (beets) in a pan with the onion, orange rind and juice, bay leaf, stock and salt and pepper to taste.

Bring to the boil, then lower the heat, cover and simmer for 1 hour until the beetroot (beet) is tender.

Work the soup to a purée through a sieve (strainer) or in an electric blender. Return to the rinsed-out pan, then bring to the boil, stirring occasionally.

Taste and adjust seasoning, stir in the yogurt and serve hot or chilled, garnished with orange slices.

**Serves 4 to 6**

# Minestrone (Mixed Vegetable Soup)

| Metric/Imperial | American |
|---|---|
| 1 onion, peeled and sliced | 1 onion, peeled and sliced |
| 1 garlic clove, peeled and crushed (optional) | 1 garlic clove, peeled and crushed (optional) |
| 1 carrot, peeled and diced | 1 carrot, peeled and diced |
| 1 turnip, peeled and diced | 1 turnip, peeled and diced |
| 1 leek, trimmed and sliced | 1 leek, trimmed and sliced |
| 1 celery stick, sliced | 1 celery stalk, sliced |
| 225 g / 8 oz tomatoes, skinned and roughly chopped | 1 cup skinned and chopped tomatoes |
| 50 g / 2 oz broken pasta or long-grain rice | ½ cup broken pasta or long-grain rice |
| 1.2 litres / 2 pints stock | 5 cups stock |
| salt | salt |
| freshly ground black pepper | freshly ground black pepper |
| ¼ small cabbage, shredded | ¼ small cabbage, shredded |
| 100 g / 4 oz runner beans, sliced | ½ cup sliced string beans |
| grated Parmesan cheese to serve | grated Parmesan cheese to serve |

*Beetroot (beet) and orange soup; Minestrone (Mixed vegetable soup); Chilled pea soup*

Put the onion, garlic, carrot, turnip, leek, celery, tomatoes and pasta or rice in a large pan. Stir in the stock and add salt and pepper to taste.

Bring to the boil, then lower the heat, cover and simmer for 30 minutes until the vegetables are tender.

Add the cabbage and beans and cook for a further 5 to 10 minutes until tender. Taste and adjust seasoning, then serve hot with Parmesan cheese handed separately.

**Serves 6**

# Chilled Pea Soup

| Metric/Imperial | American |
|---|---|
| 350 g / 12 oz shelled peas (about 750 g / 1¹/₂ lb fresh peas in the pod) | 2¹/₄ cups shelled peas (about 1¹/₂ lb fresh peas in the shell) |
| 1 onion, peeled and chopped | 1 onion, peeled and chopped |
| 1 large mint sprig | 1 large mint sprig |
| finely grated rind and juice of ¹/₂ lemon | finely grated rind and juice of ¹/₂ lemon |
| 900 ml / 1¹/₂ pints stock | 3³/₄ cups stock |
| salt | salt |
| freshly ground black pepper | freshly ground black pepper |
| 150 ml / ¹/₄ pint natural yogurt or milk | ²/₃ cup unflavored yogurt or milk |
| 1 tablespoon chopped mint to garnish | 1 tablespoon chopped mint to garnish |

Put the peas in a pan with the onion, mint, lemon rind and juice, stock and salt and pepper to taste.

Bring to the boil, then lower the heat, cover and simmer for 30 minutes until the peas are soft. Work the soup to a purée through a sieve (strainer) or in an electric blender. Leave to cool.

Stir in the yogurt or milk, taste and adjust seasoning, then chill in the refrigerator.

Sprinkle with chopped mint and serve chilled.

**Serves 4 to 6**

# Guacamole

*This Mexican avocado pâté makes an interesting starter or a party dip. In Mexico they serve it very hot and fiery and usually add chilli peppers. If the guacamole is not to be used immediately, reserve the avocado stones (seeds), bury them in the mixture and cover the dish – this helps to prevent the avocados from browning.*

| Metric/Imperial | American |
|---|---|
| 2 large very ripe avocado pears | 2 large very ripe avocado pears |
| juice of 1 lemon | juice of 1 lemon |
| 4 tomatoes, skinned, seeded and chopped | 4 tomatoes, skinned, seeded and chopped |
| 1 small onion, peeled and grated | 1 small onion, peeled and grated |
| 1 garlic clove, peeled and crushed | 1 garlic clove, peeled and crushed |
| ¼ teaspoon Tabasco sauce | ¼ teaspoon Tabasco sauce |
| salt | salt |
| freshly ground black pepper | freshly ground black pepper |
| 1 small lettuce to serve (optional) | 1 small head of lettuce to serve (optional) |

Cut the avocados in half and remove the stones (seeds). Scoop out the pulp into a bowl and immediately pour over the lemon juice to prevent browning.

Mash the avocados well, then add the remaining ingredients, except the lettuce, and beat well until smooth. Alternatively, put all the ingredients in an electric blender and work to a smooth purée.

Transfer to a serving bowl, or serve on individual plates, lined with lettuce leaves. Serve immediately with toasted wholewheat bread.

**Serves 4 to 6**

# Jerusalem Cocottes

*Eggs are baked in a nest of creamed artichokes for this delicious starter.*

| Metric/Imperial | American |
|---|---|
| 450 g / 1 lb Jerusalem artichokes, scrubbed | 1 lb Jerusalem artichokes, scrubbed |
| salt | salt |
| 150 ml / ¼ pint natural yogurt | ⅔ cup unflavored yogurt |
| freshly ground white pepper | freshly ground white pepper |
| 4 eggs | 4 eggs |
| chopped parsley to garnish | chopped parsley to garnish |

Cook the artichokes in boiling salted water for about 20 minutes until tender. Peel off the skins and mash the artichokes well. Stir in the yogurt with salt and pepper to taste. Alternatively, work the ingredients to a smooth purée in an electric blender.

Spread the mixture in 4 individual ovenproof dishes or in one large baking dish. Make 4 hollows for the eggs and crack 1 egg into each hollow.

Bake in a preheated moderate oven (180°C / 350°F, Gas Mark 4) for 10 to 15 minutes until the eggs are just set. Garnish with parsley and serve hot.

**Serves 4**

# Tomato Tart

| Metric/Imperial | American |
|---|---|
| wholewheat pastry made with 175 g / 6 oz flour (see page 227) | wholewheat dough made with 1½ cups flour (see page 227) |
| 750 g / 1½ lb tomatoes | 1½ lb tomatoes |
| 1 onion, peeled and chopped | 1 onion, peeled and chopped |
| 1 garlic clove, peeled and chopped (optional) | 1 garlic clove, peeled and chopped (optional) |
| 4 thyme sprigs | 4 thyme sprigs |
| salt | salt |
| freshly ground black pepper | freshly ground black pepper |

Roll out the pastry dough on a lightly floured surface and use to line a 20 cm / 8 inch flan dish or flan ring placed on a baking sheet. Prick the base lightly with a fork, cover with foil, then weigh down with baking beans or rice.

Bake in a preheated moderately hot oven (200°C / 400°F, Gas Mark 6) for 15 minutes. Remove the beans or rice and the foil, return the flan case to the oven and bake for a further 5 minutes.

Meanwhile, make the filling: skin 450 g / 1 lb of the tomatoes, then chop them roughly. Put the tomatoes in a pan with the onion, garlic if using, thyme and salt and pepper to taste. Cover and simmer gently until the tomatoes are reduced to a pulp. Discard the thyme sprigs.

Spread the tomato mixture in the flan case. Slice the remaining tomatoes and arrange overlapping around the edge of the tart.

Return to the oven and bake for a further 15 minutes. Serve hot or cold.

**Serves 4 to 6**

# Mushrooms à la Grècque

| Metric/Imperial | American |
|---|---|
| 2 tablespoons oil | 2 tablespoons oil |
| 1 large onion, peeled and sliced | 1 large onion, peeled and sliced |
| 1 large carrot, peeled and sliced | 1 large carrot, peeled and sliced |
| 1 celery stick, sliced | 1 celery stalk, sliced |
| 1 large garlic clove, peeled and crushed | 1 large garlic clove, peeled and crushed |
| 150 ml / ¼ pint dry white wine | ⅔ cup dry white wine |
| 3 tomatoes, skinned, quartered and seeded | 3 tomatoes, skinned, quartered and seeded |
| 3 tablespoons chopped parsley | 3 tablespoons chopped parsley |
| 1 tablespoon thyme leaves | 1 tablespoon thyme leaves |
| 1 bay leaf | 1 bay leaf |
| salt | salt |
| freshly ground black pepper | freshly ground black pepper |
| 450 g / 1 lb button mushrooms | 4 cups button mushrooms |

Heat the oil in a large pan. Add the onion, carrot and celery and fry gently for 3 minutes, stirring occasionally. Add the garlic and fry for a further 1 minute.

Stir in the wine, tomatoes, 1 tablespoon parsley, thyme, bay leaf and salt and pepper to taste. Bring to the boil, then lower the heat and add the mushrooms. Simmer gently for 10 minutes.

Leave to cool, then pour into a serving dish and chill in the refrigerator. Sprinkle with the remaining parsley and serve chilled.

**Serves 4**

# Courgette (Zucchini) Quiche

| Metric/Imperial | American |
|---|---|
| wholewheat pastry made with 175 g / 6 oz flour (see page 227) | wholewheat dough made with 1½ cups flour (see page 227) |
| 2 tablespoons oil | 2 tablespoons oil |
| 2 onions, peeled and sliced | 2 onions, peeled and sliced |
| 450 g / 1 lb courgettes, sliced | 1 lb zucchini, sliced |
| salt | salt |
| freshly ground black pepper | freshly ground black pepper |
| 2 eggs, beaten with 150 ml / ¼ pint milk | 2 eggs, beaten with ⅔ cup milk |
| 2 tablespoons grated Parmesan cheese | 2 tablespoons grated Parmesan cheese |

Roll out the pastry dough on a lightly floured surface and use to line a 20 cm / 8 inch flan dish or flan ring, placed on a baking sheet. Prick the base lightly with a fork, cover with foil, then weigh down with baking beans or rice.

Bake in a preheated moderately hot oven (200°C / 400°F, Gas Mark 6) for 15 minutes. Remove the beans or rice and the foil, return the flan case to the oven and bake for a further 5 minutes.

Meanwhile, make the filling: heat the oil in a frying pan (skillet). Add the onions and courgettes (zucchini) and fry gently for about 10 minutes until lightly browned, stirring occasionally.

Remove the onions and courgettes (zucchini) from the pan with a slotted spoon, then place in the flan case. Add salt and pepper to taste to the egg and milk mixture, then pour into the flan case. Sprinkle with the Parmesan cheese.

Bake in a preheated moderately hot oven (190°C / 375°F, Gas Mark 5) for 25 to 30 minutes until the filling is set and lightly browned on top. Serve hot or cold.

**Serves 4 to 6**

# Italian Bean Soup

**Metric/Imperial**

225 g / 8 oz dried white
  beans (haricot, butter
  beans, etc)
600 ml / 1 pint water
1 large onion, peeled and
  chopped
1 garlic clove, peeled and
  crushed (optional)
1 celery stick, sliced
1 large carrot, peeled and
  sliced
4 tomatoes, skinned and
  chopped
finely grated rind and juice
  of ½ lemon
1 bay leaf
salt
freshly ground black pepper
2 tablespoons chopped
  parsley (optional)

**American**

1 cup dried white beans
  (navy, lima, etc)
2½ cups water
1 large onion, peeled and
  chopped
1 garlic clove, peeled and
  crushed (optional)
1 celery stalk, sliced
1 large carrot, peeled and
  sliced
4 tomatoes, skinned and
  chopped
finely grated rind and juice
  of ½ lemon
1 bay leaf
salt
freshly ground black pepper
2 tablespoons chopped
  parsley (optional)

Put the beans in a large bowl, cover with the water, then
leave to soak overnight. Alternatively, pour over boiling
water and soak for several hours. Drain the beans, reserving
the water. Make up to 1.2 litres / 2 pints / 5 cups with stock
or more water.

Place the beans and liquid in a large pan, then add all the
remaining ingredients, except the parsley. Bring to the boil,
then lower the heat, cover and simmer for 1 to 1½ hours
until the beans are tender, adding more water if necessary.
Discard the bay leaf.

Transfer about half the beans and some of the liquid into
an electric blender. Work to a smooth purée.

Return the purée to the soup and bring to the boil, stirring
constantly. Taste and adjust the seasoning, and add more
liquid if the soup is too thick. Sprinkle with parsley if liked,
and serve hot.

**Serves 4 to 6**

*ABOVE: Mediterranean lentil stew; Italian bean soup*
*RIGHT: Black eye fish hors d'oeuvre*

# Black Eye Fish Hors D'Oeuvre

**Metric/Imperial**
100 g / 4 oz black eye peas
600 ml / 1 pint water
225 g / 8 oz white fish fillets (cod, haddock, etc), cooked, skinned and flaked
1 × 100 g / 4 oz can tuna fish, drained and flaked
100 g / 4 oz peeled prawns
1 small onion, peeled and grated
150 ml / ¼ pint vinaigrette dressing (see page 132)
finely grated rind and juice of ½ lemon
dash of Tabasco sauce
2 teaspoons tomato purée
2 tablespoons chopped parsley
salt
freshly ground black pepper
TO GARNISH:
few unshelled prawns
parsley sprigs

**American**
½ cup black eye peas
2½ cups water
½ lb white fish fillets (cod, haddock, etc), cooked, skinned and flaked
1 × 4 oz can tuna fish, drained and flaked
½ cup shelled shrimp
1 small onion, peeled and grated
⅔ cup French dressing (see page 132)
finely grated rind and juice of ½ lemon
dash of Tabasco sauce
2 teaspoons tomato paste
2 tablespoons chopped parsley
salt
freshly ground black pepper
TO GARNISH:
few unshelled shrimp
parsley sprigs

Put the peas in a large bowl, cover with the water, then leave to soak overnight. Alternatively, pour over boiling water and soak for several hours.

Transfer the peas and water to a pan and bring to the boil. Lower the heat, cover and simmer for 1 to 1½ hours until the beans are tender, adding more water if necessary.

Drain the peas and place in a bowl. Add the flaked fish and prawns (shrimp) and fold lightly to mix.

Mix together the remaining ingredients, then fold in the salad. Leave to marinate for at least 1 hour.

Turn into a serving dish, garnish with the prawns (shrimp) and parsley, and serve cold.
**Serves 6 as a starter, 4 as a main course**

# Mediterranean Lentil Stew

*Lentils do not need soaking before cooking, and mixed with vegetables they make a delicious stew in which most of the liquid has been absorbed to give a moist sauce.*

**Metric/Imperial**
2 tablespoons oil
2 onions, peeled and chopped
1 garlic clove, peeled and crushed
2 celery sticks, sliced
4 small courgettes, sliced
4 tomatoes, skinned and quartered
900 ml / 1½ pints water or stock
¼ teaspoon ground coriander
salt
freshly ground black pepper
225 g / 8 oz brown lentils
2 tablespoons chopped parsley (optional)

**American**
2 tablespoons oil
2 onions, peeled and chopped
1 garlic clove, peeled and crushed
2 celery stalks, sliced
4 small zucchini, sliced
4 tomatoes, skinned and quartered
3¾ cups water or stock
¼ teaspoon ground coriander
salt
freshly ground black pepper
1 cup brown lentils
2 tablespoons chopped parsley (optional)

Heat the oil in a large pan. Add the onions, garlic, celery and courgettes (zucchini) and fry gently for 10 minutes until lightly browned, stirring frequently.

Add the tomatoes, water or stock, coriander and salt and pepper to taste. Bring to the boil. Add the lentils, then cover and simmer for 1 to 1½ hours until the lentils are tender.

Alternatively, transfer the ingredients to a casserole, cover and bake in a preheated moderate oven (180°C / 350°F, Gas Mark 4) for 1½ hours to 2 hours.

Sprinkle with the chopped parsley, if liked, and serve hot.
**Serves 4**

# Haricot (Navy) Bean Paprika

**Metric/Imperial**
350 g / 12 oz haricot beans, soaked overnight
salt
2 tablespoons oil
1 large onion, peeled and sliced
1 clove garlic, peeled and crushed
1 tablespoon paprika
2 tablespoons tomato purée
50 g / 2 oz canned pimento, sliced
1 × 450 g / 1 lb can tomatoes
150 ml / ¼ pint water
4 tablespoons soured cream

**American**
1½ cups navy beans, soaked overnight
salt
2 tablespoons oil
1 large onion, peeled and sliced
1 clove garlic, peeled and crushed
1 tablespoon paprika
2 tablespoons tomato paste
½ cup sliced canned pimento
1 lb can tomatoes
⅔ cup water
4 tablespoons sour cream

Drain the haricot (navy) beans, and cook in boiling salted water for 45 minutes or until almost tender; drain.

Meanwhile, heat the oil in a large pan and sauté the onion and garlic until soft. Stir in the paprika and cook, stirring, for 2 to 3 minutes.

Add the beans, tomato purée (paste), pimento, tomatoes and water. Bring to the boil, cover and simmer gently for about 10 minutes.

Stir in the soured cream just before serving.

**Serves 4**

# Southern Baked Beans

**Metric/Imperial**
225 g / 8 oz haricot beans
600 ml / 1 pint water
1 large onion, peeled and chopped
2 celery sticks, sliced
1 red pepper, cored, seeded and sliced
4 tomatoes, skinned and chopped
1 tablespoon molasses or honey
1 tablespoon tomato purée
2 tablespoons vinegar
2 teaspoons Worcestershire sauce
2 teaspoons mustard powder
salt
freshly ground black pepper
100 g / 4 oz salami, thickly sliced and skinned

**American**
1 cup navy beans
2½ cups water
1 large onion, peeled and chopped
2 celery stalks, sliced
1 red pepper, cored, seeded and sliced
4 tomatoes, skinned and chopped
1 tablespoon molasses or honey
1 tablespoon tomato paste
2 tablespoons vinegar
2 teaspoons Worcestershire sauce
2 teaspoons mustard powder
salt
freshly ground black pepper
¼ lb salami, thickly sliced and skinned

Put the beans in a large bowl, cover with the water, then leave to soak overnight. Alternatively, pour over boiling water and soak for several hours.

Drain the beans, reserving the water. Make up to 600 ml / 1 pint / 2½ cups with more water.

Place the beans and liquid in a large pan, then bring to the boil. Lower the heat, cover and simmer for 1 to 1½ hours until the beans are tender, adding more water if necessary. Drain and reserve 300 ml / ½ pint / 1¼ cups cooking liquid.

Put the beans in layers in a casserole dish with the onion, celery, red pepper and tomatoes.

Mix the reserved cooking liquid with the remaining ingredients, except the salami. Pour over the beans.

Cover and bake in a preheated moderate oven (180°C / 350°F, Gas Mark 4) for 1 hour. Arrange the salami on top and bake for a further 30 minutes until the beans are tender and well-flavoured with the salami. Serve hot.

**Serves 4 to 6**

# Lentil Patties

| Metric/Imperial | American |
|---|---|
| 2 tablespoons oil | 2 tablespoons oil |
| 1 clove garlic, peeled and crushed | 1 clove garlic, peeled and crushed |
| 1 onion, peeled and finely chopped | 1 onion, peeled and finely chopped |
| 1 celery stick, chopped | 1 celery stalk, chopped |
| 1 carrot, peeled and chopped | 1 carrot, peeled and chopped |
| 225 g / 8 oz brown lentils | 1 cup brown lentils |
| 450 ml / ¾ pint water | 2 cups water |
| salt | salt |
| freshly ground black pepper | freshly ground black pepper |
| 4 tablespoons wholemeal flour | 4 tablespoons wholewheat flour |
| ½ teaspoon ground ginger | ½ teaspoon ground ginger |
| ½ teaspoon ground cumin | ½ teaspoon ground cumin |
| 1 teaspoon curry powder | 1 teaspoon curry powder |
| 1 tablespoon mango chutney, chopped | 1 tablespoon mango chutney, chopped |
| oil for shallow frying | oil for shallow frying |
| DRESSING: | DRESSING: |
| 150 ml / ¼ pint natural yogurt | ⅔ cup unflavored yogurt |
| 1 clove garlic, peeled and crushed | 1 clove garlic, peeled and crushed |
| 1 tablespoon chopped parsley | 1 tablespoon chopped parsley |

Heat the oil in a large pan. Add the garlic, onion, celery and carrot and sauté until the vegetables begin to soften.

Add the lentils, water, salt and pepper. Bring to the boil, then lower the heat, cover and simmer for about 1 hour until the lentils are soft and all the liquid is absorbed.

Add 2 tablespoons flour, the spices and chutney to the pan and mix well. Continue to cook gently for 2 to 3 minutes, stirring constantly. Adjust the seasoning, if necessary. Turn the mixture onto a plate and leave until cool enough to handle.

Divide the mixture into 18 equal pieces and form each one into a patty, about 1 cm / ½ inch thick. Coat with the remaining flour. Heat a little oil in a frying pan (skillet) and fry the lentil patties, a few at a time, until crisp and golden brown, turning once.

Mix together the yogurt, garlic and parsley for the dressing. Serve the patties on a bed of rice, topped with the yogurt dressing.

**Serves 6**

# Butter (Lima) Bean, Herb and Tomato Soufflé

*The puréed butter (lima) beans form the sauce for this simple soufflé.*

| Metric/Imperial | American |
|---|---|
| 100 g / 4 oz butter beans | ½ cup lima beans |
| 600 ml / 1 pint water | 2½ cups water |
| 150 ml / ¼ pint milk | ⅔ cup milk |
| 1 large onion, peeled and grated | 1 large onion, peeled and grated |
| 4 tomatoes, skinned and chopped | 4 tomatoes, skinned and chopped |
| 1 tablespoon chopped parsley | 1 tablespoon chopped parsley |
| 1 tablespoon chopped thyme | 1 tablespoon chopped thyme |
| 1 teaspoon chopped sage | 1 teaspoon chopped sage |
| salt | salt |
| freshly ground white pepper | freshly ground white pepper |
| 4 eggs, separated | 4 eggs, separated |

Put the beans in a large bowl, cover with the water, then leave to soak overnight. Alternatively, pour over boiling water and soak for several hours.

Transfer the beans and water to a pan, then bring to the boil. Lower the heat, cover and simmer for about 1½ hours until the beans are soft, adding more water if necessary.

Drain the beans, return to the rinsed-out pan and mash well. Add the milk and onion and bring to the boil, stirring constantly. Simmer for 1 minute.

Remove the pan from the heat, then stir in the tomatoes, herbs and salt and pepper to taste. Stir in the egg yolks and leave to cool slightly.

Beat the egg whites until just stiff, then fold into the bean sauce. Pour the mixture into a 1.5 litre / 2½ pint / 6¼ cup soufflé dish. Bake in a preheated moderate oven (180°C / 350°F, Gas Mark 4) for 1 hour until the soufflé has risen and is lightly browned on top. Serve immediately.

**Serves 4 to 6**

# Chick Pea (Garbanzos) Salad

*This Middle Eastern dish makes an unusual start to a meal. Serve with pitta bread.*

**Metric/Imperial**
175 g / 6 oz chick peas
600 ml / 1 pint water
1 large garlic clove, peeled and crushed
juice of 1 lemon
4 tablespoons tahini (sesame seed paste), or sesame seeds
150 ml / ¼ pint natural yogurt
salt
freshly ground white pepper
TO GARNISH:
1 small lettuce
2 tomatoes, sliced
12 black olives
2 tablespoons chopped parsley

**American**
1 cup garbanzos
2½ cups water
1 large garlic clove, peeled and crushed
juice of 1 lemon
¼ cup tahini (sesame seed paste), or sesame seeds
⅔ cup unflavored yogurt
salt
freshly ground white pepper
TO GARNISH:
1 small head of lettuce
2 tomatoes, sliced
12 ripe olives
2 tablespoons chopped parsley

Put the chick peas (garbanzos) in a large bowl, cover with the water, then leave to soak overnight. Alternatively, pour over boiling water and soak for several hours.

Transfer the chick peas (garbanzos) and water to a pan and bring to the boil. Lower the heat, cover and simmer for about 1 hour until they are soft, adding more water if necessary.

Drain the chick peas (garbanzos), then mash them to a purée. Stir in the garlic, lemon juice, tahini or sesame seeds, yogurt and salt and pepper to taste.

Beat to a smooth, creamy paste, adding a little water if too thick. Alternatively, work all the ingredients to a smooth purée in an electric blender, adding more water as necessary to blend.

To serve: arrange the lettuce leaves on individual serving plates, then divide the purée equally between them, piling it up in the centre. Garnish with tomato slices, olives and parsley and serve cold.

**Serves 6 as a starter, 4 as a main course**

# Soya Bean Moussaka

*This Greek dish is traditionally made with minced (ground) lamb or beef, but soya beans are substituted in this recipe to make a cheap and tasty dish. Omit the bacon for a vegetarian dish.*

| Metric/Imperial | American |
|---|---|
| 225 g / 8 oz soya beans | 1 cup soy beans |
| 600 ml / 1 pint water | 2½ cups water |
| 4 tablespoons oil | ¼ cup oil |
| 50 g / 2 oz streaky bacon, derinded and chopped | 3 fatty bacon slices, derinded and chopped |
| 2 onions, peeled and chopped | 2 onions, peeled and chopped |
| 2 celery sticks, sliced | 2 celery stalks, sliced |
| 1 large carrot, peeled and sliced | 1 large carrot, peeled and sliced |
| 100 g / 4 oz mushrooms, sliced | 1 cup sliced mushrooms |
| 4 tomatoes, skinned and chopped | 4 tomatoes, skinned and chopped |
| 1 tablespoon tomato purée | 1 tablespoon tomato paste |
| 1 teaspoon dried marjoram | 1 teaspoon dried marjoram |
| salt | salt |
| freshly ground black pepper | freshly ground black pepper |
| 1 bay leaf | 1 bay leaf |
| 675 g / 1½ lb aubergines, stalks removed and thinly sliced | 1½ lb eggplants, stalks removed and thinly sliced |
| CHEESE SAUCE: | CHEESE SAUCE: |
| 25 g / 1 oz vegetable margarine | 2 tablespoons vegetable margarine |
| 25 g / 1 oz flour | ¼ cup flour |
| 300 ml / ½ pint milk | 1¼ cups milk |
| 100 g / 4 oz Cheddar cheese, grated | 1 cup grated Cheddar cheese |
| 1 egg, beaten | 1 egg, beaten |
| ½ teaspoon prepared mustard | ½ teaspoon prepared mustard |

Put the soya beans in a large bowl, cover with the water, then leave to soak overnight. Alternatively, pour over boiling water and soak for several hours.

Drain the beans, reserving the water. Make up to 1.2 litres / 2 pints / 5 cups with more water.

Place the beans and liquid in a large pan, then bring to the boil. Skim then lower the heat, cover and simmer for about 2 hours until the beans are just tender. Drain and reserve 300 ml / ½ pint / 1¼ cups cooking liquid.

Heat 1 tablespoon oil in a large pan. Add the bacon, onions, celery and carrot and fry gently for 5 minutes. Add the mushrooms and fry for a further 2 minutes. Stir in the reserved cooking liquid together with the tomatoes, tomato purée (paste), marjoram and salt and pepper to taste.

Bring to the boil, stirring constantly. Add the beans and bay leaf, cover and simmer for 1 hour until the beans are tender and most of the liquid has been absorbed to give a moist mixture. Discard the bay leaf.

Meanwhile, put the aubergine (eggplant) slices in a colander, sprinkling the layers with salt. Leave for about 1 hour to allow the water to drain off and remove the bitterness. Rinse under cold running water to remove the salt, then pat dry.

Place the aubergine (eggplant) slices in a single layer on a grill (broiler) pan. Brush lightly with oil and grill (broil) for about 5 minutes until lightly browned, turning once. Repeat with the remaining aubergine (eggplant) slices.

Place one third of the aubergines (eggplants) in the bottom of a 1.75 litre / 3 pint / 7½ cup casserole dish. Cover with half the bean mixture, then another third of the aubergines (eggplants). Spread the remaining bean mixture on top, then finish with a neat layer of aubergines (eggplants).

To make the sauce: melt the margarine in a pan, add the flour and cook for 1 to 2 minutes, stirring constantly. Remove from the heat and stir in the milk gradually, beating vigorously after each addition. Return to the heat and bring to the boil, stirring constantly. Simmer for 2 minutes until thick, then stir in half the cheese and the beaten egg. Add the mustard and salt and pepper to taste.

Pour the cheese sauce over the top of the moussaka, then sprinkle with the remaining cheese. Bake in a preheated moderate oven (180°C / 350°F, Gas Mark 4) for 30 minutes until the topping is browned. Garnish with parsley and serve hot.

**Serves 6**

*Chick pea (garbanzos) salad; Soya bean moussaka Southern baked beans (page 152,*

# Leeks à la Grècque

| Metric/Imperial | American |
|---|---|
| 300 ml / ½ pint water (or 150 ml / ¼ pint dry white wine and 150 ml / ¼ pint water) | 1¼ cups water (or ⅔ cup dry white wine and ⅔ cup water) |
| finely grated rind and juice of 1 lemon | finely grated rind and juice of 1 lemon |
| 2 shallots, peeled and thinly sliced | 2 shallots, peeled and thinly sliced |
| 4 parsley sprigs | 4 parsley sprigs |
| 1 small celery stick, with leaves | 1 small celery stalk, with leaves |
| 1 fennel sprig or few fennel seeds | 1 fennel sprig or few fennel seeds |
| 1 thyme sprig | 1 thyme sprig |
| 6 peppercorns | 6 peppercorns |
| 3 coriander seeds | 3 coriander seeds |
| salt | salt |
| 450 g / 1 lb leeks, trimmed and cleaned | 1 lb leeks, trimmed and cleaned |

Put all the ingredients in a large pan, except the leeks. Bring to the boil, then lower the heat, cover and simmer for 10 minutes.

Add the leeks to the pan, cover and simmer gently for 10 to 15 minutes until tender but not broken up.

Transfer the leeks to a serving dish. Boil the cooking liquid until reduced by half. Strain if preferred, then pour over the leeks and leave to cool. Serve cold.

**Serves 4**

# Courgettes (Zucchini) Provençal

| Metric/Imperial | American |
|---|---|
| 450 g / 1 lb courgettes, sliced | 1 lb zucchini, sliced |
| 4 tomatoes, sliced | 4 tomatoes, sliced |
| 1 small onion, peeled and grated | 1 small onion, peeled and grated |
| 2 tablespoons chopped parsley | 2 tablespoons chopped parsley |
| 1 tablespoon thyme leaves | 1 tablespoon thyme leaves |
| salt | salt |
| freshly ground black pepper | freshly ground black pepper |
| 5 tablespoons stock | ⅓ cup stock |

Arrange the courgettes (zucchini) and tomatoes in layers in a baking dish or casserole, sprinkling each layer with the onion, half of the parsley, the thyme and salt and pepper to taste. Pour in the stock.

Cover and bake in a preheated moderate oven (180°C /

350°F, Gas Mark 4) for 30 to 40 minutes until the courgettes (zucchini) are tender but not soft.

Alternatively, put all the ingredients, except half the parsley, in a large saucepan. Cover and cook gently for 10 minutes until just tender, stirring occasionally.

Taste and adjust the seasoning. Sprinkle with the remaining parsley and serve hot or cold.

**Serves 4**

# Celery with Orange and Nuts

| Metric/Imperial | American |
|---|---|
| 1 celery head, trimmed and cut into 5 cm / 2 inch lengths, leaves reserved | 1 celery head, trimmed and cut into 2 inch lengths, leaves reserved |
| finely grated rind of ½ orange | finely grated rind of ½ orange |
| juice of 1 orange | juice of 1 orange |
| 1 orange, peel and pith removed and divided into segments | 1 orange, peel and pith removed and divided into segments |
| 25 g / 1 oz sultanas | 3 tablespoons seedless white raisins |
| 25 g / 1 oz walnuts | ¼ cup walnuts |
| salt | salt |
| freshly ground black pepper | freshly ground black pepper |

Put the celery and leaves in a baking dish. Add the orange rind, juice and segments, then sprinkle with the sultanas (seedless white raisins), nuts and salt and pepper to taste.

Cover and bake in a preheated moderate oven (180°C / 350°F, Gas Mark 4) for 30 to 40 minutes until the celery is just tender.

Alternatively, put all the ingredients in a large saucepan. Cover and cook gently for 15 to 20 minutes until just tender, stirring occasionally. If necessary, add a little water towards the end of cooking.

Taste and adjust the seasoning. Serve hot.

**Serves 4**

# Spinach Fried with Garlic

*This is a very quick and nutritious way to cook spinach – it is fried quickly with onions and garlic until just tender. To make a quick lunch or supper dish, add 100 g / 4 oz / ½ cup chopped bacon with the onion.*

*The spinach stalks may be cooked separately and served like asparagus spears. Alternatively, they may be chopped and added with the leaves, but they will take a little longer to cook than the leaves.*

| Metric/Imperial | American |
| --- | --- |
| 2 tablespoons oil | 2 tablespoons oil |
| 1 large onion, peeled and chopped | 1 large onion, peeled and chopped |
| 1 large garlic clove, peeled and crushed | 1 large garlic clove, peeled and crushed |
| 450 g / 1 lb spinach leaves | 1 lb spinach leaves |
| 1 tablespoon lemon juice | 1 tablespoon lemon juice |
| salt | salt |
| freshly ground black pepper | freshly ground black pepper |

Heat the oil in a large pan. Add the onion and garlic and fry gently for 5 minutes, stirring frequently.

Wash the spinach thoroughly, then add to the pan with only the water clinging to the leaves. Add the lemon juice and salt and pepper to taste. Fry gently for 3 to 5 minutes until the spinach is just tender but still bright green, stirring constantly. Taste and adjust the seasoning, then serve immediately.

**Serves 4**

# Cabbage Braised with Apple and Yogurt

| Metric/Imperial | American |
| --- | --- |
| 450 g / 1 lb cabbage, shredded | 6 cups shredded cabbage |
| 1 onion, peeled and grated | 1 onion, peeled and grated |
| 1 cooking apple, peeled, cored and grated | 1 baking apple, peeled, cored and grated |
| salt | salt |
| freshly ground white pepper | freshly ground white pepper |
| 150 ml / ¼ pint natural yogurt | ⅔ cup unflavored yogurt |
| pinch of grated nutmeg | pinch of grated nutmeg |

Put half the cabbage in a baking dish. Sprinkle with half the onion and apple and salt and pepper to taste. Spoon over half the yogurt.

Add the remaining cabbage, then top with the remaining apple and onion and sprinkle with salt and pepper to taste. Spoon over the remaining yogurt and sprinkle with the nutmeg.

Bake in a preheated moderately hot oven (190°C / 375°F, Gas Mark 5) for about 20 minutes or until the cabbage is just tender. Serve hot.
**Serves 4**

# Vegetable Strudel

| Metric/Imperial | American |
| --- | --- |
| 2 tablespoons oil | 2 tablespoons oil |
| 1 small onion, peeled and chopped | 1 small onion, peeled and chopped |
| 1 clove garlic, peeled and crushed | 1 clove garlic, peeled and crushed |
| 1 celery stick, sliced | 1 celery stalk, sliced |
| 100 g / 4 oz button mushrooms, sliced | 1 cup sliced button mushrooms |
| 2 tablespoons flour | 2 tablespoons flour |
| 150 ml / ¼ pint light stock | ⅔ cup light stock |
| 1 tablespoon tomato purée | 1 tablespoon tomato paste |
| 225 g / 8 oz tomatoes, skinned and chopped | 2 cups chopped tomatoes |
| 1 small cauliflower, cooked and roughly chopped | 1 small cauliflower, cooked and roughly chopped |
| 1 tablespoon chopped parsley | 1 tablespoon chopped parsley |
| ¼ teaspoon dried basil | ¼ teaspoon dried basil |
| salt | salt |
| freshly ground black pepper | freshly ground black pepper |
| 1 × 375 g / 13 oz packet frozen puff pastry, thawed | 1 × 13 oz package frozen puff paste, thawed |
| 1 egg, beaten | 1 egg, beaten |

Heat the oil in a frying pan (skillet) and sauté the onion, garlic and celery until soft. Add the mushrooms and cook for 1 minute. Add the flour, then gradually stir in the stock and tomato purée (paste). Bring to the boil, stirring.

Remove from the heat, and add the tomatoes, cauliflower and herbs. Season with salt and pepper to taste, then leave to cool.

Roll out the pastry to a 36 cm / 14 inch square. Spread the cooked vegetable filling over the pastry, leaving a 2.5 cm / 1 inch border around the edge. Brush this border with beaten egg. Fold the pastry in half and press the edges together to seal. Brush the pastry with beaten egg and roll up like a Swiss (jelly) roll.

Carefully place on a baking tray. Brush with beaten egg to glaze and make several slits along the top of the strudel. Bake in a moderately hot oven (200°C / 400°F, Gas Mark 6) for 30 minutes. Cut into slices and serve with a crisp green salad.
**Serves 4**

# Leek Pie

*The bacon may be omitted for a vegetarian dish.*

**Metric/Imperial**

PASTRY:

175 g / 6 oz wholemeal flour

pinch each of salt and pepper

75 g / 3 oz vegetable margarine

75 g / 3 oz mature Cheddar cheese, finely grated

2 tablespoons cold water

beaten egg or milk to glaze

FILLING:

1 tablespoon vegetable margarine

100 g / 4 oz streaky bacon, rinds removed and chopped

750 g / 1½ lb leeks, trimmed and sliced into 1 cm / ½ inch rounds

25 g / 1 oz flour

300 ml / ½ pint stock (or milk and water mixed)

finely grated rind and juice of ½ lemon

¼ teaspoon grated nutmeg

50 g / 2 oz shelled hazelnuts

50 g / 2 oz seedless raisins

salt

freshly ground black pepper

**American**

DOUGH:

1½ cups wholewheat flour

pinch each of salt and pepper

⅓ cup vegetable margarine

¾ cup finely grated mature Cheddar cheese

2 tablespoons cold water

beaten egg or milk to glaze

FILLING:

1 tablespoon vegetable margarine

½ cup chopped fatty bacon

1½ lb leeks, trimmed and sliced into ½ inch rounds

¼ cup flour

1¼ cups stock (or milk and water mixed)

finely grated rind and juice of ½ lemon

¼ teaspoon grated nutmeg

⅜ cup shelled filberts

⅓ cup seedless raisins

salt

freshly ground black pepper

To make the pastry dough: put the flour and salt and pepper in a bowl, then add the margarine in pieces. Rub into the flour until the mixture resembles breadcrumbs, then stir in the cheese. Add the water and mix to a firm dough. Chill in the refrigerator until required.

To make the filling: melt the margarine in a pan. Add the bacon and fry gently for 3 minutes, stirring occasionally. Add the leeks and fry gently for a further 5 minutes, stirring constantly until soft but not brown.

Stir in the flour and cook for 1 to 2 minutes, then gradually stir in the stock or milk and water. Bring to the boil, then lower the heat and simmer until the sauce is thick and smooth, stirring constantly. Add the remaining filling ingredients, simmer for 2 minutes, then transfer to a 1 litre / 1¾ pint / 4¼ cup pie dish. Leave to cool.

Meanwhile, roll out the pastry dough on a lightly floured surface until 2.5 cm / 1 inch larger than the circumference of the pie dish. Cut a 1 cm / ½ inch strip from the edge, then press it onto the moistened rim of the dish. Moisten the strip, then cover the dish with the remaining pastry dough, pressing the edges firmly to seal. Trim and flute the edge and decorate the top of the pie with the trimmings.

Brush with beaten egg or milk. Bake in a preheated moderately hot oven (200°C / 400°F, Gas Mark 6) for 30 minutes until the pastry is crisp and golden brown. Serve hot or cold.

**Serves 4**

# Mixed Vegetable Curry

*If you do not have all the individual spices for this curry, substitute 1-2 tablespoons curry powder.*

**Metric/Imperial**

2 tablespoons oil
225 g / 8 oz onions, peeled and sliced
1 garlic clove, peeled and crushed
1 cooking apple, peeled, cored and chopped
2.5 cm / 1 inch piece fresh root ginger, peeled and grated
1 tablespoon mustard seeds
1 teaspoon ground turmeric
1 teaspoon ground coriander
1 teaspoon ground cumin
½ teaspoon ground fenugreek
¼ teaspoon chilli powder
450 ml / ¾ pint stock
finely grated rind and juice of ½ lemon
salt
freshly ground black pepper
225 g / 8 oz potatoes, peeled and diced
225 g / 8 oz carrots, peeled and sliced
225 g / 8 oz tomatoes, skinned and roughly chopped
225 g / 8 oz cauliflower florets
225 g / 8 oz runner beans, sliced
50 g / 2 oz sultanas
50 g / 2 oz shelled Brazil nuts
1 tablespoon grated fresh coconut

**American**

2 tablespoons oil
2 onions, peeled and sliced
1 garlic clove, peeled and crushed
1 baking apple, peeled, cored and chopped
1 inch piece fresh ginger root, peeled and grated
1 tablespoon mustard seeds
1 teaspoon ground turmeric
1 teaspoon ground coriander
1 teaspoon ground cumin
½ teaspoon ground fenugreek
¼ teaspoon chili powder
2 cups stock
finely grated rind and juice of ½ lemon
salt
freshly ground black pepper
1⅓ cups peeled and diced raw potato
1½ cups peeled and sliced carrots
1 cup skinned and roughly chopped tomatoes
2 cups cauliflower florets
1 cup sliced green beans
⅓ cup seedless white raisins
½ cup shelled Brazil nuts
1 tablespoon grated fresh coconut

Heat the oil in a large pan. Add the onions, garlic, apple and ginger and fry gently for 5 minutes, stirring occasionally. Stir in the spices and fry gently for a further 3 minutes, stirring constantly.

Add the stock and bring to the boil, stirring constantly, until the sauce thickens slightly. Add the lemon rind and juice and salt and pepper to taste, then lower the heat and simmer for 2 minutes.

Add the potatoes, carrots and tomatoes. Cover the pan and simmer for 10 minutes.

Add the cauliflower, beans, sultanas (seedless white raisins) and nuts. Cover and simmer for a further 10 minutes or until the vegetables are just tender but still crisp and not broken up.

Taste and adjust the seasoning. Sprinkle with the coconut and serve hot. Alternatively, serve cold as a salad.

**Serves 4**

# Underground Hotpot

*Other root vegetables such as turnips, swedes (rutabaga) or celeriac may be substituted. Whole peanuts are usually obtainable but if not, substitute salted peanuts and decrease the quantity of salt in the recipe.*

| Metric/Imperial | American |
|---|---|
| 450 g / 1 lb potatoes, peeled and thinly sliced | 4 medium potatoes, peeled and thinly sliced |
| 225 g / 8 oz onions, peeled and sliced | 2 onions, peeled and sliced |
| 225 g / 8 oz carrots, peeled and sliced | 1½ cups peeled and sliced carrots |
| 225 g / 8 oz parsnips, peeled and sliced | 1½ cups peeled and sliced parsnips |
| 225 g / 8 oz Jerusalem artichokes, peeled and sliced | 1½ cups peeled and sliced Jerusalem artichokes |
| 2 celery sticks, sliced | 2 celery stalks, sliced |
| 100 g / 4 oz whole peanuts, shelled | ½ cup whole shelled peanuts |
| 100 g / 4 oz mature Cheddar cheese, grated | 1 cup grated mature Cheddar cheese |
| 2 tablespoons rosemary leaves | 2 tablespoons rosemary leaves |
| salt | salt |
| freshly ground black pepper | freshly ground black pepper |
| 300 ml / ½ pint stock | 1¼ cups stock |

Put half the potato slices in the bottom of a 1.75 litre / 3 pint / 7½ cup casserole dish.

Arrange the remaining vegetables in the dish in layers, sprinkling each layer with the nuts, cheese, rosemary and salt and pepper to taste. Reserve a little cheese for the topping.

Finish with a layer of potatoes arranged neatly in circles on top, then pour on the stock and sprinkle with the reserved cheese.

Bake in a preheated moderately hot oven (190°C / 375°F, Gas Mark 5) for 1½ hours until the top is browned and the vegetables are tender when pierced with a skewer. Serve hot.

**Serves 4 to 6**

# Brazil Mushroom Casserole

| Metric/Imperial | American |
|---|---|
| 450 g / 1 lb button mushrooms | 4 cups button mushrooms |
| 4 tomatoes, sliced | 4 tomatoes, sliced |
| 4 spring onions, trimmed and chopped | 4 scallions, trimmed and chopped |
| 1 tablespoon chopped oregano or marjoram | 1 tablespoon chopped oregano or marjoram |
| 1 tablespoon chopped basil | 1 tablespoon chopped basil |
| 1 teaspoon rosemary leaves | 1 teaspoon rosemary leaves |
| salt | salt |
| freshly ground black pepper | freshly ground black pepper |
| 4 tablespoons dry white wine or stock | ¼ cup dry white wine or stock |
| 100 g / 4 oz Brazil nuts, coarsely ground | 1 cup coarsely ground Brazil nuts |
| 50 g / 2 oz fresh wholemeal breadcrumbs | 1 cup fresh wholewheat breadcrumbs |

Wipe the mushrooms and cut the larger ones into halves or quarters, leaving the small ones whole. Arrange the mushrooms, tomatoes and spring onions (scallions) in layers in a casserole dish, sprinkling each layer with the herbs and salt and pepper to taste. Pour on the wine or stock.

Mix the nuts and breadcrumbs together and sprinkle over the top of the casserole. Bake in a preheated moderately hot oven (190°C / 375°F, Gas Mark 5) for 20 to 30 minutes until the mushrooms are tender and the topping is browned. Serve hot.

**Serves 4**

# Stuffed Peppers

| Metric/Imperial | American |
|---|---|
| 175 g / 6 oz brown rice | 1 cup brown rice |
| 300 ml / ½ pint water | 1¼ cups water |
| salt | salt |
| 4 tomatoes, skinned and chopped | 4 tomatoes, skinned and chopped |
| 1 onion, peeled and grated | 1 onion, peeled and grated |
| 50 g / 2 oz pine nuts | ½ cup pine nuts |
| 25 g / 1 oz seedless raisins | 3 tablespoons seedless raisins |
| 100 g / 4 oz Cheddar cheese, grated | 1 cup grated Cheddar cheese |
| 2 tablespoons chopped parsley | 2 tablespoons chopped parsley |
| pinch of ground cinnamon | pinch of ground cinnamon |
| freshly ground black pepper | freshly ground black pepper |
| 4 green peppers, cored and seeded, tops reserved | 4 green peppers, cored and seeded, tops reserved |
| 5 tablespoons stock or water | ⅓ cup stock or water |

Cook the rice in the boiling salted water for 30 minutes or until the rice is tender and all the water has been absorbed. Remove from the heat and gently fold in the tomatoes, onion, pine nuts and raisins.

Fold in most of the cheese, reserving a little for the topping, then fold in the parsley, cinnamon and salt and pepper to taste.

Stand the peppers upright in a baking dish, cutting a small slice off the bottoms if necessary. Divide the filling equally between the peppers, sprinkle with the reserved cheese and replace the lids.

Pour the stock or water into the dish and cover with foil. Bake in a preheated moderately hot oven (190°C / 375°F, Gas Mark 5) for 30 to 40 minutes until the peppers are tender. Serve hot or cold.

**Serves 4**

# Stuffed Marrow (Squash) Rings

*This recipe may also be used to stuff courgettes (zucchini). Cut a wedge from the top of each courgette (zucchini) to make a boat shape for the stuffing, or if they are small scoop out the inside with an apple corer and fill the central hole with stuffing.*

| Metric/Imperial | American |
|---|---|
| 1 × 1 kg / 2 lb marrow, cut crosswise into 5 cm / 2 inch thick rings, seeds removed | 1 × 2 lb squash, cut crosswise into 2 inch thick rings, seeds removed |
| 1 tablespoon oil | 1 tablespoon oil |
| 1 onion, peeled and chopped | 1 onion, peeled and chopped |
| 100 g / 4 oz mushrooms, chopped | 1 cup chopped mushrooms |
| 100 g / 4 oz cooked ham, diced | ½ cup diced cooked ham |
| 25 g / 1 oz fresh wholemeal breadcrumbs | ½ cup fresh wholewheat breadcrumbs |
| 1 tablespoon chopped parsley | 1 tablespoon chopped parsley |
| 1 tablespoon chopped marjoram or oregano | 1 tablespoon chopped marjoram or oregano |
| salt | salt |
| freshly ground black pepper | freshly ground black pepper |

Put the marrow (squash) in a lightly greased baking dish. Set aside.

Heat the oil in a pan. Add the onion and fry gently for 3 minutes, stirring occasionally. Add the mushrooms and fry for a further 3 minutes. Remove from the heat, add the remaining ingredients and mix well.

Spoon the stuffing mixture into the centre of the marrow (squash) rings, then cover the dish with foil. Bake in a preheated moderate oven (180°C / 350°F, Gas Mark 4) for 20 to 30 minutes until the marrow (squash) is just tender. Serve hot.

**Serves 4**

# Wholewheat Pizza

*To save time, substitute 225 g / 8 oz / ½ lb wholemeal scone dough (wholewheat biscuit dough) for the yeast dough specified in this recipe.*

**Metric/Imperial**
DOUGH:
225 g / 8 oz strong wholemeal flour
1 teaspoon salt
7 g / ¼ oz fresh yeast, or 1 teaspoon dried yeast and ¼ teaspoon caster sugar
150 ml / ¼ pint lukewarm water
TOPPING:
1 tablespoon oil
1 large onion, peeled and chopped
1 garlic clove, peeled and crushed (optional)
4 tomatoes, skinned and roughly chopped
1 tablespoon chopped oregano or marjoram
salt
freshly ground black pepper
1 tomato, sliced
100 g / 4 oz Mozzarella or Bel Paese cheese, thinly sliced
1 × 50 g / 2 oz can anchovy fillets, drained
few black olives

**American**
DOUGH:
2 cups wholewheat flour
1 teaspoon salt
¼ cake compressed yeast, or 1 teaspoon active dry yeast and ¼ teaspoon sugar
⅔ cup lukewarm water
TOPPING:
1 tablespoon oil
1 large onion, peeled and chopped
1 garlic clove, peeled and crushed (optional)
4 tomatoes, skinned and roughly chopped
1 tablespoon chopped oregano or marjoram
salt
freshly ground black pepper
1 tomato, sliced
¼ lb Mozzarella or Bel Paese cheese, thinly sliced
1 × 2 oz can anchovy fillets, drained
few ripe olives

To make the dough: put the flour and salt in a bowl. Blend the fresh yeast with the water until dissolved. (For dried yeast, dissolve the sugar in the water, add the yeast, then leave in a warm place for about 15 minutes until frothy.) Pour the yeast liquid into the flour and mix to a firm dough.

Turn the dough out onto a lightly floured surface and knead well for about 10 minutes until no longer sticky. Put the dough in a warm, greased bowl, cover with greased polythene (plastic) and leave to rise in a warm place for about 1 hour or until doubled in size.

Meanwhile, make the topping: heat the oil in a pan. Add the onion and garlic and fry gently for 5 minutes until soft, stirring occasionally. Add the tomatoes and herbs and cook gently for about 10 minutes until reduced to a pulp. Add salt and pepper to taste.

When the dough has risen, turn out onto the floured surface again and knead for 2 minutes. Roll out to a 23 cm / 9 inch circle and place on a lightly greased baking sheet.

Spread the tomato mixture over the dough, then arrange the tomato slices around the edge, and the cheese slices overlapping in the centre. Arrange the anchovies and olives on top. Leave the pizza to rise in a warm place for 15 minutes until puffy.

Bake in a preheated hot oven (220°C / 425°F, Gas Mark 7) for 20 to 25 minutes until risen and light brown around the edge. Serve hot or cold.
**Serves 4**

*Wholewheat pizza; Pasta with ratatouille sauce (page 164); Broccoli pancakes (crêpes)*

# Broccoli Pancakes (Crêpes)

**Metric/Imperial**
PANCAKE BATTER:
100 g / 4 oz wholemeal
  flour
pinch of salt
1 egg, beaten
150 ml / ¼ pint milk
150 ml / ¼ pint water
oil for frying
FILLING:
450 g / 1 lb broccoli spears
salt
25 g / 1 oz vegetable
  margarine
25 g / 1 oz flour
300 ml / ½ pint milk
100 g / 4 oz Gruyère or
  Cheddar cheese, grated
freshly ground black pepper
1 × 50 g / 2 oz can
  anchovy fillets, drained

**American**
CRÊPE BATTER:
1 cup wholewheat flour
pinch of salt
1 egg, beaten
⅔ cup milk
⅔ cup water
oil for frying
FILLING:
1 lb broccoli spears
salt
2 tablespoons vegetable
  margarine
¼ cup flour
1¼ cups milk
1 cup grated Gruyère or
  Cheddar cheese
freshly ground black pepper
1 × 2 oz can anchovy
  fillets, drained

To make the pancakes (crêpes): put the flour and salt in a bowl and make a well in the centre. Add the egg and milk and stir well to give a smooth batter, then beat in the water to give a pouring consistency.

Heat a little oil in a 20 cm / 8 inch frying pan (skillet). When the oil is hot, quickly pour in enough batter to thinly coat the bottom of the pan, tilting the pan to spread the batter evenly. Cook until the top of the batter is set and the underside is golden brown. Turn or toss the pancake (crêpe) over and cook the other side.

Slide onto a warm plate, cover and keep warm by standing the plate over a pan of hot water. Continue making the pancakes (crêpes) in this way until all the batter is used up, making 8 pancakes (crêpes) in all.

To make the filling: cook the broccoli in boiling salted water for 5 to 10 minutes until just tender, then drain thoroughly and keep warm.

Meanwhile, melt the margarine in a pan. Add the flour and cook for 1 to 2 minutes, stirring constantly. Remove from the heat and gradually stir in the milk, beating well after each addition. Return to the heat and simmer until the sauce is thick and smooth, stirring constantly. Stir in the cheese, reserving a little for the topping, then add pepper to taste.

Divide the broccoli and anchovies equally between the pancakes (crêpes), then roll up and place in a baking dish. Pour over the sauce and sprinkle with the reserved cheese.

Bake in a preheated moderately hot oven (200°C / 400°F, Gas Mark 6) for 10 to 15 minutes until heated through. Serve hot.

Alternatively, leave the pancakes (crêpes) until cold before filling, then cover and bake in a preheated moderately hot oven for 15 minutes. Remove the lid and bake for a further 10 to 15 minutes until hot and bubbling. Serve hot.
**Serves 4**

# Cabbage Dolmas

| Metric/Imperial | American |
|---|---|
| 8 large cabbage leaves | 8 large cabbage leaves |
| salt | salt |
| 1 tablespoon oil | 1 tablespoon oil |
| 1 onion, peeled and chopped | 1 onion, peeled and chopped |
| 1 cooking apple, peeled, cored and chopped | 1 baking apple, peeled, cored and chopped |
| 1 garlic clove, peeled and crushed | 1 garlic clove, peeled and crushed |
| 225 g / 8 oz minced pork or veal | 1 cup ground pork or veal |
| 50 g / 2 oz fresh wholemeal breadcrumbs | 1 cup fresh wholewheat breadcrumbs |
| finely grated rind and juice of ½ lemon | finely grated rind and juice of ½ lemon |
| 1 tablespoon chopped sage | 1 tablespoon chopped sage |
| 1 tablespoon chopped parsley | 1 tablespoon chopped parsley |
| freshly ground black pepper | freshly ground black pepper |
| 4 tomatoes, cut into wedges | 4 tomatoes, cut into wedges |

Blanch the cabbage leaves in boiling salted water for 2 minutes or until soft enough to roll up. Drain thoroughly and set aside.

Heat the oil in a pan. Add the onion, apple and garlic and fry gently for 5 minutes, stirring occasionally. Add the pork or veal and fry for a further 5 minutes, stirring constantly to break up the meat. Remove from the heat and stir in the breadcrumbs, lemon rind and juice, herbs and salt and pepper to taste.

Divide the stuffing mixture equally between the cabbage leaves, then roll up, from the stalk end, folding in the edges to enclose the stuffing completely.

Put the stuffed cabbage in a shallow baking dish and surround with the tomato wedges.

Cover and bake in a preheated moderate oven (180°C / 350°F, Gas Mark 4) for 20 to 30 minutes until the cabbage is tender. Serve hot.

**Serves 4**

# Pasta with Ratatouille Sauce

*This Mediterranean vegetable stew is traditionally cooked in oil and served as an accompaniment to meat. In this recipe the vegetables are cooked in their own juices for a healthier, more concentrated flavour. Served with pasta, ratatouille makes a meal in itself. It is also good served cold as a starter, without pasta.*

| Metric/Imperial | American |
|---|---|
| 1 large onion, peeled and chopped | 1 large onion, peeled and chopped |
| 1 garlic clove, peeled and crushed | 1 garlic clove, peeled and crushed |
| 450 g / 1 lb courgettes, sliced | 3 cups sliced zucchini |
| 1 large aubergine, diced | 1 large eggplant, diced |
| 1 green pepper, cored, seeded and diced | 1 green pepper, cored, seeded and diced |
| 450 g / 1 lb tomatoes, skinned and chopped | 2 cups skinned and chopped tomatoes |
| 1 tablespoon chopped oregano or basil | 1 tablespoon chopped oregano or basil |
| salt | salt |
| freshly ground black pepper | freshly ground black pepper |
| 450 g / 1 lb pasta (spaghetti, noodles, etc) | 1 lb pasta (spaghetti, noodles, etc) |
| 1 tablespoon chopped parsley | 1 tablespon chopped parsley |
| grated Parmesan cheese to serve | grated Parmesan cheese to serve |

Put all the ingredients, except the pasta, parsley and cheese, into a large pan. Cover and cook gently for 30 minutes until the vegetables are tender and the juices have thickened slightly, stirring occasionally.

Meanwhile, cook the pasta in a large pan containing plenty of boiling salted water until just tender (about 5 minutes for freshly made pasta and 15 minutes for dried). Drain and pile into a warmed serving dish.

Taste and adjust the seasoning of the sauce, then pour over the pasta. Sprinkle with the parsley and grated Parmesan cheese. Serve hot.

**Serves 4 to 6**

# Cauliflower Cheese Timbale

*In this recipe, cauliflower is cooked in a savoury egg custard, similar to a baked soufflé but much easier to control. It is a very useful way of turning leftover cooked vegetables into a tasty substantial dish.*

| Metric/Imperial | American |
|---|---|
| 450 g / 1 lb cauliflower, chopped, with leaves and stalks finely chopped | 1 lb cauliflower, chopped, with leaves and stalks finely chopped |

1 large onion, peeled and
    chopped
300 ml / ½ pint water
salt
4 eggs, lightly beaten
50 g / 2 oz fresh wholemeal
    breadcrumbs
100 g / 4 oz Cheddar
    cheese, grated
pinch of grated nutmeg
freshly ground white pepper
300 ml / ½ pint milk

1 large onion, peeled and
    chopped
1¼ cups water
salt
4 eggs, lightly beaten
1 cup fresh wholewheat
    breadcrumbs
1 cup grated Cheddar
    cheese
pinch of grated nutmeg
freshly ground white pepper
1¼ cups milk

Put the cauliflower and onion in a large pan with the water and salt. Bring to the boil, then lower the heat, cover and simmer for about 10 minutes until the cauliflower is just tender. Drain thoroughly.

Put the eggs in a bowl with the breadcrumbs, cheese, nutmeg and salt and pepper to taste. Mix well. Heat the milk, but do not allow to boil, then stir into the egg mixture.

Put the cauliflower in a 1.5 litre / 2½ pint / 6¼ cup baking dish or greased ring mould. Pour over the egg custard to cover the cauliflower.

Stand the dish or mould in a roasting pan, half-filled with hot water. Bake in a preheated moderate oven (180°C / 350°F, Gas Mark 4) for 45 minutes or until the custard is set and a skewer comes out clean when inserted in the centre.

Alternatively, cover the dish or mould and steam over boiling water for about 1 hour until set.

Serve straight from the dish, or leave to stand for a few minutes, then turn out of the mould onto a warmed serving platter. Serve hot with a mushroom or tomato sauce.

The timbale can also be served cold, in which case it should be left to cool in the mould before turning out onto a serving platter.

**Serves 4**

# Spinach Roulade

*A simple spinach soufflé mixture is first baked flat, then filled with an onion and mushroom sauce and rolled up like a Swiss (jelly) roll. It makes a delicious light main course.*

| Metric/Imperial | American |
|---|---|
| ROULADE: | ROULADE: |
| 450 g / 1 lb spinach leaves | 1 lb spinach leaves |
| 4 eggs, separated | 4 eggs, separated |
| pinch of grated nutmeg | pinch of grated nutmeg |
| salt | salt |
| freshly ground black pepper | freshly ground black pepper |
| FILLING: | FILLING: |
| 25 g / 1 oz vegetable margarine | 2 tablespoons vegetable margarine |
| 100 g / 4 oz streaky bacon, derinded and chopped | ½ cup chopped fatty bacon |
| | 2 onions, peeled and sliced |

2 onions, peeled and sliced
100 g / 4 oz button
    mushrooms, sliced
25 g / 1 oz flour
300 ml / ½ pint milk
1 teaspoon lemon juice
1 tablespoon grated
    Parmesan cheese

1 cup sliced button
    mushrooms
¼ cup flour
1¼ cups milk
1 teaspoon lemon juice
1 tablespoon grated
    Parmesan cheese

To make the roulade: wash the spinach thoroughly, then put in a large pan with only the water clinging to the leaves. Cook gently for about 5 minutes until tender, then drain thoroughly.

Chop the spinach finely, then put in a bowl with the egg yolks, nutmeg and salt and pepper to taste. Beat well. Whisk the egg whites until stiff, then fold into the spinach mixture.

Line a 32 × 23 cm / 13 × 9 inch roasting pan with oiled greaseproof paper or non-stick parchment so that it comes above the sides of the pan. Spoon in the spinach and smooth the surface.

Bake in a preheated moderately hot oven (200°C / 400°F, Gas Mark 6) for 10 to 15 minutes until the roulade is well risen, firm and just beginning to brown.

Meanwhile, make the filling: melt the margarine in a pan. Add the bacon and onions and fry gently for 5 minutes, stirring occasionally. Add the mushrooms and fry gently for a further 2 minutes.

Add the flour and cook for 1 to 2 minutes, stirring constantly. Remove from the heat and gradually stir in the milk, beating well after each addition. Return to the heat and simmer until the sauce is thick and smooth, stirring constantly. Add the lemon juice and salt and pepper to taste.

Sprinkle the Parmesan cheese over a large sheet of greaseproof (wax) paper. Turn the roulade out onto the paper, then carefully peel off the lining paper on top of the roulade.

Spread the sauce over the roulade, leaving a 2.5 cm / 1 inch margin all round. Roll up the roulade like a Swiss (jelly) roll, gently lifting the paper so that the roulade falls over the filling. Lift carefully onto a warmed serving dish and serve immediately.

**Serves 4**

Heat the oil in a wok or large frying pan (skillet). Add the bacon, onion, garlic, ginger and mushrooms and fry briskly for 3 minutes, stirring constantly.

Add the peas and cabbage and fry for a further 2 minutes, stirring constantly.

Add the remaining ingredients and stir-fry over moderate heat for about 5 minutes until the vegetables are tender but still crisp, and most of the liquid has evaporated. Taste and adjust the seasoning and serve immediately.

**Serves 4**

## Vegetable Kebabs with Pilaf

*Bacon rolls, pieces of chicken breast, cubes of lamb, pork or steak may be substituted for some of the vegetables on the skewers.*

| Metric/Imperial | American |
|---|---|
| PILAF: | PILAF: |
| 2 tablespoons oil | 2 tablespoons oil |
| 1 large onion, peeled and chopped | 1 large onion, peeled and chopped |
| 2 celery sticks, sliced | 2 celery stalks, sliced |
| 225 g / 8 oz brown rice | 1¼ cups brown rice |
| 600 ml / 1 pint stock | 2½ cups stock |
| 50 g / 2 oz seedless raisins | ⅓ cup seedless raisins |
| 50 g / 2 oz dried apricots, roughly chopped | ⅓ cup roughly chopped dried apricots |
| 50 g / 2 oz walnuts, roughly chopped | ½ cup roughly chopped walnuts |
| 1 cinnamon stick | 1 cinnamon stick |
| 1 bay leaf | 1 bay leaf |
| salt | salt |
| freshly ground black pepper | freshly ground black pepper |
| KEBABS: | KEBABS: |
| 225 g / 8 oz courgettes, sliced | 1½ cups sliced zucchini |
| 8 small tomatoes | 8 small tomatoes |
| 1 large onion, cut into wedges with skin | 1 large onion, cut into wedges with skin |
| 8 button mushrooms | 8 button mushrooms |
| 1 green pepper, cored, seeded and cut into 8 pieces | 1 green pepper, cored, seeded and cut into 8 pieces |
| 1 tablespoon oil | 1 tablespoon oil |
| 1 tablespoon lemon juice | 1 tablespoon lemon juice |
| 1 tablespoon thyme leaves | 1 tablespoon thyme leaves |

To make the pilaf: heat the oil in a pan. Add the onion and celery and fry gently for 5 minutes until golden brown. Add the rice and cook for 1 minute, stirring constantly. Pour on the stock, then add the raisins, apricots and walnuts.

Bring to the boil, stirring occasionally, then add the cinnamon, bay leaf and salt and pepper to taste. Lower the heat, cover the pan and simmer for 30 minutes or until the

## Chinese Stir-Fried Vegetables

*Traditionally cooked in a Chinese wok, the vegetables are cooked very quickly to retain their natural flavour and crispness.*
*Whole peanuts are usually obtainable but if not, substitute salted peanuts and decrease the quantity of salt in the recipe.*

| Metric/Imperial | American |
|---|---|
| 1 tablespoon oil | 1 tablespoon oil |
| 50 g / 2 oz streaky bacon, derinded and chopped | ¼ cup chopped fatty bacon |
| 1 large onion, peeled and chopped | 1 large onion, peeled and chopped |
| 1 garlic clove, peeled and crushed | 1 garlic clove, peeled and crushed |
| 1 tablespoon peeled and grated fresh root ginger | 1 tablespoon peeled and grated fresh ginger root |
| 50 g / 2 oz mushrooms, sliced | ½ cup sliced mushrooms |
| 450 g / 1 lb mange-tout peas, topped and tailed | 1 lb snow peas, topped and tailed |
| 450 g / 1 lb Chinese or other cabbage, shredded | 6 cups shredded Chinese or other cabbage |
| 100 g / 4 oz bean sprouts | 2 cups bean sprouts |
| 50 g / 2 oz whole peanuts, shelled | ¼ cup whole shelled peanuts |
| 1 tablespoon soy sauce | 1 tablespoon soy sauce |
| 5 tablespoons stock or water | ⅓ cup stock or water |
| salt | salt |
| freshly ground black pepper | freshly ground black pepper |

rice is tender and all the stock has been absorbed.

To make the kebabs: blanch the courgettes (zucchini) in boiling water for 1 minute, then drain. Thread the vegetables onto 4 large kebab skewers, alternating the different ingredients.

Mix together the oil, lemon juice, thyme and salt and pepper to taste, then brush over the vegetables. Cook on a barbecue or under the grill (broiler) for 5 to 10 minutes until cooked through, turning and basting from time to time.

Spoon the pilaf into a warmed shallow serving dish and arrange the kebabs on top. Serve immediately.

**Serves 4**

# Carrot Soufflé

| Metric/Imperial | American |
|---|---|
| 450 g / 1 lb carrots, peeled and chopped | 3 cups peeled and chopped carrots |
| 1 onion, peeled and chopped | 1 onion, peeled and chopped |
| 450 ml / ¾ pint water | 2 cups water |
| salt | salt |
| freshly ground white pepper | freshly ground white pepper |
| 25 g / 1 oz vegetable margarine | 2 tablespoons vegetable margarine |
| 1 tablespoon flour | 1 tablespoon flour |
| 150 ml / ¼ pint milk | ⅔ cup milk |
| 100 g / 4 oz cooked ham, diced | ½ cup diced cooked ham |
| 4 eggs, separated | 4 eggs, separated |

Put the carrots in a pan with the onion, water and salt. Bring to the boil, then lower the heat, cover and simmer for about 20 minutes or until the carrots are soft. Drain, then mash or work to a purée in an electric blender. Add salt and pepper to taste.

Melt the margarine in a pan. Add the flour and cook for 1 to 2 minutes, stirring constantly. Remove from the heat, and gradually stir in the milk, beating well after each addition. Return to the heat and simmer until the sauce is thick and smooth, stirring constantly.

Stir the sauce into the carrot purée with the ham. Beat in the egg yolks.

Beat the egg whites until stiff, then fold gently into the carrot mixture. Pour into a greased 1.5 litre / 2½ pint / 6¼ cup soufflé dish.

Bake in a preheated moderate oven (180°C / 350°F, Gas Mark 4) for 45 minutes until well risen and set. Serve immediately.

**Serves 4**

*TOP LEFT: Chinese stir-fried vegetables*
*LEFT: Vegetable kebabs with pilaf*
*ABOVE: Carrot soufflé*

# VEGETABLES

Most vegetables are low in calories and it is probably easier to memorize those which are *not* than those which are.

It is vitally important to choose vegetables which are truly fresh, which is why you should go into your greengrocer's shop with an open mind. Although shopping lists are useful to avoid bringing home a basketful of jolly foods which do not go with each other or with your plans, this does not really apply when it comes to buying vegetables. Be flexible and impulsive. Forget that you had planned to cook French beans if the mushrooms look superb.

Many vegetables benefit from being steamed which, by rare and happy chance, is the best method from a calorie viewpoint, too. The flavour, texture and goodness are all so much better that you will feel less tempted to add a nut of butter or a dollop of parsley sauce. If you have no steamer you can improvise, but a fish kettle or steamer is a valuable piece of equipment, especially for the health conscious gourmet.

Do not overcook your vegetables. Serve them while there is still some bite to them. Flavour them well, with plenty of freshly ground black pepper and coarse sea salt.

## Leeks Niçoise

| Metric/Imperial | American |
|---|---|
| 6 leeks, trimmed and cleaned | 6 leeks, trimmed and cleaned |
| 2 tablespoons vegetable oil | 2 tablespoons vegetable oil |
| 1 × 200 g / 7 oz can tomatoes | 7 oz can tomatoes |
| chopped fresh basil | chopped fresh basil |
| 1 garlic clove, crushed | 1 garlic clove, crushed |
| salt and black pepper | salt and black pepper |
| pinch of sugar | pinch of sugar |
| chopped parsley to garnish | chopped parsley to garnish |

Heat the oil in a deep pan. Add the leeks and fry gently until they are soft but not brown. Chop the tomatoes and add them to the pan with their juice, the chopped basil and the garlic. Season to taste with salt and pepper, then stir in the sugar. Bring to the boil, reduce the heat to low and cover the pan. Simmer for about 20 minutes, or until the leeks are tender, stirring occasionally.

Sprinkle over the chopped parsley and serve immediately.

**Serves 4**

## Stuffed Aubergines (Eggplants)

| Metric/Imperial | American |
|---|---|
| 3 large aubergines | 3 large eggplants |
| 1 large onion, chopped | 1 large onion, chopped |
| 100 g / 4 oz tomatoes, peeled, seeded and chopped | ½ cup peeled, seeded and chopped tomatoes |
| 2 tablespoons chopped parsley | 2 tablespoons chopped parsley |
| 50 g / 2 oz mushrooms, chopped | ½ cup chopped mushrooms |
| 1 teaspoon oregano | 1 teaspoon oregano |
| salt | salt |
| freshly ground black pepper | freshly ground black pepper |

Cut the aubergines (eggplants) in half lengthwise. Scoop out some of the flesh and chop it finely.

Boil the onion in very little salted water for 3 to 4 minutes, then drain it well.

Add it to the chopped aubergine (eggplant) flesh, together with the tomatoes, parsley, mushrooms, oregano, salt and pepper. Mix well and fill each aubergine (eggplant) half with this mixture. Brush the top of each with oil and bake in a preheated moderate oven (180°C/350°F, Gas Mark 4) for ³/₄ to 1 hour. Serve hot or cold.

**Serves 4**

*LEFT: Stuffed aubergines (eggplants)*

# Stuffed Tomatoes

**Metric/Imperial**
4 large tomatoes
350 g / 12 oz fresh spinach
salt
freshly ground black pepper
freshly grated nutmeg
1 garlic clove, crushed
2 tablespoons cottage
   cheese

**American**
4 large tomatoes
3/4 lb fresh spinach
salt
freshly ground black pepper
freshly grated nutmeg
1 garlic clove, crushed
2 tablespoons cottage
   cheese

Cut the tops off the tomatoes and carefully scoop out the pulp, taking care not to damage the skins. Use the pulp for soups.

Wash the spinach thoroughly and cook it, without adding any more water, for 7 to 10 minutes in a tightly covered pan. Empty it into a sturdy metal colander and chop it finely, pressing out all the liquid. Season the spinach with salt, pepper and nutmeg. Blend in the garlic and cottage cheese.

Spoon the spinach mixture into the hollowed tomatoes and cook in a preheated moderate oven (180°C/350°F, Gas Mark 4) for 20 to 30 minutes. The tomatoes should be hot but not too soft.

**Serves 4**

# Purée of Swedes (Rutabaga)

**Metric/Imperial**
1 kg / 2 lb swedes
salt
freshly ground black pepper
pinch of ground ginger
4 tablespoons soured cream
chopped parsley to garnish

**American**
2 lb rutabaga
salt
freshly ground black pepper
pinch of ground ginger
4 tablespoons sour cream
chopped parsley to garnish

Peel the swedes (rutabaga) and cut them into even sized pieces. Boil them in salted water until they are soft enough to be rubbed through a sieve (strainer).

Season the swede (rutabaga) purée with more salt, pepper and ginger. Blend in the soured cream and reheat gently, without allowing it to boil.

Serve sprinkled with parsley.

**Serves 4**

# Stuffed Cabbage Leaves

**Metric/Imperial**
4 large cabbage leaves
salt and pepper
1 tablespoon vegetable oil
1 onion, chopped
1 carrot, chopped
225 g / 8 oz tomatoes,
   peeled, seeded and
   chopped
100 g / 4 oz mushrooms,
   chopped
freshly grated nutmeg
2 tablespoons finely
   chopped parsley
2 tablespoons beef stock

**American**
4 large cabbage leaves
salt and pepper
1 tablespoon vegetable oil
1 onion, chopped
1 carrot, chopped
1 cup peeled, seeded and
   chopped tomatoes
1 cup chopped mushrooms
freshly grated nutmeg
2 tablespoons finely
   chopped parsley
2 tablespoons beef stock

Cook the cabbage leaves in a large pan of boiling salted water for 3 to 5 minutes. Drain and cool them. Spread each one out carefully and remove the hard stem from the base.

Heat half of the oil in a frying pan (skillet) and fry the onion and carrot for 5 minutes, stirring all the time. Add the tomatoes, mushrooms, salt, pepper, nutmeg and parsley. Allow to cook until the juice from the tomatoes has evaporated.

Let this mixture cool slightly, then divide it between the cabbage leaves. Fold the sides over, to trap the filling, and roll up the leaves carefully and neatly.

Brush a casserole with the remaining oil, and arrange the stuffed cabbage leaves in it, in a single layer.

Bake in a preheated moderate oven (180°C/350°F, Gas Mark 4) for 45 to 50 minutes, basting with a little stock from time to time. Serve hot.

**Serves 4**

*RIGHT: Stuffed cabbage leaves*

# Ratatouille

| Metric/Imperial | American |
|---|---|
| 1 medium aubergine, diced | 1½ cups diced eggplant |
| 225 g / 8 oz courgettes, sliced | 1½ cups sliced zucchini |
| salt | salt |
| 1 tablespoon olive oil | 1 tablespoon olive oil |
| 4 medium onions, sliced | 4 medium onions, sliced |
| 450 g / 1 lb tomatoes, skinned, seeded and chopped | 2 cups skinned, seeded and chopped tomatoes |
| 2 garlic cloves, chopped | 2 garlic cloves, chopped |
| 1 green pepper, cored, seeded and sliced | 1 green pepper, cored, seeded and sliced |
| 1 red pepper, cored, seeded and sliced | 1 red pepper, cored, seeded and sliced |
| freshly ground black pepper | freshly ground black pepper |
| chopped parsley to garnish | chopped parsley to garnish |

Place the aubergine (eggplant) and courgettes (zucchini) in a colander. Sprinkle them with salt and allow to stand for 30 minutes.

Heat the oil in a large pan. Add the onions, tomatoes and garlic and cook gently until the juice starts to flow from the tomatoes.

Add the green and red peppers, aubergines (eggplant) and courgettes (zucchini), salt and pepper. Stir well and cover with a tightly fitting lid. Simmer gently until the vegetables are cooked but still quite firm.

Serve hot or cold, sprinkled with parsley.

**Serves 4**

# Mushrooms and Tomatoes

| Metric/Imperial | American |
|---|---|
| 1 tablespoon vegetable oil | 1 tablespoon vegetable oil |
| 15 g / ½ oz margarine | 1 tablespoon margarine |
| 1 large onion, sliced | 1 large onion, sliced |
| 350 g / 12 oz mushrooms, sliced | 3 cups sliced mushrooms |
| 225 g / 8 oz tomatoes, peeled, seeded and chopped | 1 cup skinned, seeded and chopped tomatoes |
| salt and pepper | salt and pepper |
| 2 tablespoons finely chopped parsley | 2 tablespoons finely chopped parsley |

Heat together the oil and margarine in a heavy pan. When hot add the onion and fry it for 5 minutes until soft and golden. Add the mushrooms and cook for 5 minutes.

Add the tomatoes, salt, pepper and parsley. Stir, cover the pan and simmer for 8 to 10 minutes.

**Serves 4**

# Pumpkin (Squash) Provençal

| Metric/Imperial | American |
|---|---|
| 4 tablespoons olive oil | 4 tablespoons olive oil |
| 2 large onions, peeled and finely chopped | 2 large onions, peeled and finely chopped |
| 1 garlic clove, crushed | 1 garlic clove, crushed |
| 1 medium pumpkin, peeled, seeded and cut into cubes | 1 medium winter squash, peeled, seeded and cut into cubes |
| 6 large tomatoes, blanched, peeled and chopped | 6 large tomatoes, blanched, peeled and chopped |
| 2 tablespoons tomato purée | 2 tablespoons tomato paste |
| chopped mixed fresh herbs to garnish | chopped mixed fresh herbs to garnish |
| salt and pepper | salt and pepper |

Heat the oil in a large pan. Add the onions and garlic and fry gently until they are soft but not brown, about 5 minutes. Stir in the pumpkin (squash) cubes and fry for a further 5 minutes. Add all the remaining ingredients, season to taste and cover the pan. Simmer for 45 minutes, stirring occasionally, until the vegetables are tender.

Adjust the seasoning and garnish with the chopped herbs before serving.

**Serves 4-6**

# Fenouil à la Grècque

| Metric/Imperial | American |
|---|---|
| 2 tablespoons olive oil | 2 tablespoons olive oil |
| 2 tablespoons water | 2 tablespoons water |
| 2 tomatoes, peeled and chopped | ⅓ cup peeled and chopped tomatoes |
| 6 coriander seeds | 6 coriander seeds |
| 1 bay leaf | 1 bay leaf |
| sprig of thyme | sprig of thyme |
| salt | salt |
| freshly ground black pepper | freshly ground black pepper |
| 3-4 fennel bulbs | 3 or 4 fennel bulbs |
| juice of ½ lemon | juice of ½ lemon |
| chopped parsley to garnish | chopped parsley to garnish |

In a saucepan put the oil, water, tomatoes, coriander seeds, bay leaf, thyme, salt and pepper.

Bring to the boil and simmer for 3 to 4 minutes.

Cut each fennel bulb into 4 pieces. Toss them in lemon juice. Add the fennel and lemon juice to the pan and cook gently until the fennel is tender but not too soft.

Using a slotted spoon transfer the fennel to a serving dish.

Cook the sauce quickly over a high heat until it starts to thicken. Pour this over the fennel and allow to cool.

**Serves 4**

*RIGHT: Fenouil à la Grècque*

# Leeks with Tomato Sauce

| Metric/Imperial | American |
|---|---|
| 1 kg / 2 lb leeks, washed and trimmed | 2 lb leeks, washed and trimmed |
| SAUCE: | SAUCE: |
| 225 g / 8 oz tomatoes, peeled, seeded and chopped | 1 cup peeled, seeded and chopped tomatoes |
| 1 tablespoon fresh orange juice | 1 tablespoon fresh orange juice |
| salt | salt |
| freshly ground black pepper | freshly ground black pepper |
| finely chopped basil or oregano | finely chopped basil or oregano |

Steam the leeks in a double boiler or fish kettle until they are tender but not too soft.

Put the tomatoes, orange juice, salt, pepper and basil or oregano in a heavy pan. Bring to the boil and allow to cook quite quickly until of the required consistency.

Pour this sauce over the leeks and serve hot.

**Serves 4**

# Danish Red Cabbage

| Metric/Imperial | American |
|---|---|
| 1 tablespoon vegetable oil | 1 tablespoon vegetable oil |
| 1 medium red cabbage, finely shredded | 6 cups finely shredded red cabbage |
| 1 large onion, finely sliced | 1 large onion, finely sliced |
| 1 large cooking apple, finely sliced | 1 large baking apple, finely sliced |
| 1 tablespoon caraway seeds | 1 tablespoon caraway seeds |
| 2 tablespoons wine vinegar | 2 tablespoons wine vinegar |
| pinch of soft brown sugar | pinch of light brown sugar |
| salt | salt |
| freshly ground black pepper | freshly ground black pepper |
| 2 tablespoons beef stock | 2 tablespoons beef stock |
| parsley to garnish | parsley to garnish |

Heat the oil in a large pan. Add the cabbage, onion, apple, caraway seeds, vinegar, sugar, salt, pepper and stock. Stir well and cover with a close fitting lid.

Allow to cook gently for 40 to 45 minutes, stirring or shaking from time to time. Garnish with parsley.

**Serves 4**

# French Beans with Garlic and Herbs

| Metric/Imperial | American |
|---|---|
| 450 g / 1 lb French beans | 1 lb French beans |
| salt | salt |
| 1 tablespoon vegetable oil | 1 tablespoon vegetable oil |
| 1 garlic clove, crushed | 1 garlic clove, crushed |
| 2 tablespoons finely chopped parsley | 2 tablespoons finely chopped parsley |
| 2 tablespoons finely chopped chives | 2 tablespoons finely chopped chives |
| pinch of ground cinnamon | pinch of ground cinnamon |
| freshly ground black pepper | freshly ground black pepper |

Steam the beans, or boil them gently in salted water until almost cooked but still slightly crisp.

Heat the oil in a heavy pan. Add the garlic and cook it, over the heat, for 1 minute, then add the parsley, chives and cinnamon. Stir over the heat for a further minute, then add the drained beans.

Reheat gently, stirring to mix the beans, garlic and herbs thoroughly. Sprinkle with pepper before serving.

**Serves 4**

# Courgettes (Zucchini) Milanaise

| Metric/Imperial | American |
|---|---|
| 2 tablespoons olive oil | 2 tablespoons olive oil |
| 450 g / 1 lb courgettes, sliced | 3 cups sliced zucchini |
| 1 garlic clove, crushed | 1 garlic clove, crushed |
| pinch of chopped basil | pinch of chopped basil |
| pinch of paprika | pinch of paprika |
| 4 tomatoes, peeled, seeded and chopped | 4 tomatoes, blanched, peeled, seeded and chopped |
| 1 tablespoon tomato purée | 1 tablespoon tomato paste |
| 1 bay leaf | 1 bay leaf |
| salt and black pepper | salt and black pepper |
| 2 tablespoons dry white wine | 2 tablespoons dry white wine |

Heat the oil in a large pan. Add the courgette (zucchini) slices and garlic and fry for about 5 minutes or until they are lightly browned. Stir in the remaining ingredients and season to taste. Cover and simmer the mixture over low heat for 30 minutes, or until the courgettes (zucchini) are tender.

**Serves 4**

*RIGHT: Danish red cabbage*

# Carrots Vichy

| Metric/Imperial | American |
|---|---|
| 1 kg / 2 lb carrots, chopped | 2 lb carrots, chopped |
| 75 g / 3 oz vegetable margarine | 6 tablespoons vegetable margarine |
| chopped parsley | chopped parsley |
| salt and black pepper | salt and black pepper |

Cook the carrots in boiling salted water for 10 to 15 minutes or until they are just tender. Drain them, then add the margarine and parsley to taste. Cover the pan until the margarine has melted.

Season to taste with salt and pepper before serving.

**Serves 6-8**

# Cabbage with Sweet and Sour Sauce

| Metric/Imperial | American |
|---|---|
| 1 Chinese cabbage, or 1 hard white cabbage, chopped or shredded | 1 head Chinese cabbage, or 1 head hard white cabbage, chopped or shredded |
| SAUCE: | SAUCE: |
| 1 tablespoon vegetable oil | 1 tablespoon vegetable oil |
| 1 large carrot, cut into thin strips | 1 large carrot, cut into thin strips |
| 3 tomatoes, peeled, seeded and chopped | 1/2 cup peeled, seeded and chopped tomatoes |
| 150 ml / 1/4 pint beef stock | 2/3 cup beef stock |
| 2 tablespoons soy sauce | 2 tablespoons soy sauce |
| 1 teaspoon salt | 1 teaspoon salt |
| 1 tablespoon demerara sugar | 1 tablespoon brown sugar |
| 2 tablespoons wine vinegar | 2 tablespoons wine vinegar |
| 1 × 300 g / 11 oz can crushed pineapple | 1 × 11 oz can crushed pineapple |

Heat the oil in a heavy pan. Add the carrots and tomatoes and fry for 2 to 3 minutes, stirring all the time.

Add the stock, soy sauce, salt, sugar, vinegar and pineapple. Bring to the boil and allow to simmer gently for 5 minutes.

Boil the cabbage in salted water for only 3 to 4 minutes. Drain it well, transfer it to a hot vegetable dish and top it with the sauce.

**Serves 4**

# Braised Celery

| Metric/Imperial | American |
|---|---|
| 2 heads celery | 2 heads celery |
| 15 g / 1/2 oz margarine | 1 tablespoon margarine |
| 150 ml / 1/4 pint beef stock | 2/3 cup beef stock |
| 1/2 teaspoon Worcestershire sauce | 1/2 teaspoon Worcestershire sauce |
| salt and pepper | salt and black pepper |
| finely chopped parsley to garnish | finely chopped parsley to garnish |

Trim the celery and cut each head into quarters lengthwise. Any leaves or trimmings should be used to flavour soups or casseroles. Wash the celery well and dry it with paper towels.

Heat the butter in a large frying pan (skillet). Add the celery and toss it in the butter over a gentle heat until lightly browned all over. Add the stock, Worcestershire sauce, salt and pepper. Cover with a lid or plate and cook for 10 to 15 minutes, or until the celery is tender but still crisp.

Serve sprinkled with parsley.

**Serves 4**

# Cauliflower with Tomato Sauce

| Metric/Imperial | American |
|---|---|
| 1 cauliflower, divided into florets | 1 cauliflower, divided into florets |
| chopped parsley to garnish | chopped parsley to garnish |
| SAUCE: | SAUCE: |
| 225 g / 8 oz tomatoes, skinned, seeded and chopped | 1 cup peeled, seeded and chopped tomatoes |
| salt | salt |
| juice of 1/2 orange | juice of 1/2 orange |
| 1/2 teaspoon yeast extract | 1/2 teaspoon Brewer's yeast |
| freshly ground black pepper | freshly ground black pepper |

Put the tomatoes and salt in a pan and cook gently until the juice begins to flow. Add the orange juice, yeast extract (Brewer's yeast) and pepper and continue to cook until the tomatoes are soft enough to be sieved (strained). Sieve (strain) them, check the seasoning and keep this sauce warm.

Either steam the cauliflower, or boil it gently in salted water until tender but not too soft. Drain it well.

Pour the hot sauce over the cauliflower and serve sprinkled with parsley.

**Serves 4**

*LEFT: Cabbage with sweet and sour sauce*

# FRUIT & NUTS

Like vegetables, the main contribution that fruits give to the diet are vitamins (especially vitamin C), minerals and fibre. They also provide a wide variety of colour, texture and flavour and a refreshing juiciness. This juiciness is due to the high water content – up to 95 per cent depending on the type of fruit.

Fruits especially high in vitamin C are black and red currants, strawberries, citrus fruits, gooseberries, raspberries and blackberries. Those high in vitamin A are apricots, peaches, blackcurrants, oranges and bananas. As vitamin C is easily destroyed by heat, it is best to eat fruit raw, although obviously some fruits like gooseberries, rhubarb and cooking apples, are inedible raw and therefore must be cooked. As far as possible avoid peeling fruit – especially apples, pears, plums, peaches and grapes – as their skins provide fibre and look attractive.

Served as a dessert, fruit is all too frequently combined with generous amounts of sugar and rich foods, such as butter and cream, which dilute the flavour of the fruit and render the dish less satisfactory from a health point of view. Fruit desserts can be delicious without being sweet or rich. For example, a lemon mousse has a more refreshing flavour when the cream is eliminated; all that is required is lemons, eggs, a little sugar and gelatine. In many recipes, cream can be replaced by yogurt and, or, whisked egg whites which give added volume and texture without the richness. Instead of using whipped cream for decoration, try draining natural (unflavored) yogurt through a sieve lined with muslin (cheesecloth) until it is the consistency of whipped cream and can be piped. The yogurt gives a refreshing flavour which goes well with many fruits.

A little sugar has to be added to many fruits to make them appetizing; if possible use unrefined sugars or honey, which impart a better flavour.

## Dried fruit

Fruit is primarily dried as a means of preservation. In the drying process, nutritional content, flavour, texture and colour are changed, giving us an even wider variety of fruits to include in our diet. Most common of the dried fruits are grapes in the form of raisins, sultanas (white raisins) and currants, but dried peaches, figs, dates, plums, pears, apples and bananas are also available.

They can all be eaten or added to dishes in their dried form, but if reconstituted and cooked with water they are extremely useful in sauces, mousses and soufflés, as they cook to a thick purée which needs no extra thickening and only a little sugar. The nutrients are of course more diluted then, but if you cook the fruit in its soaking water you will retain much of their goodness.

Dried fruit can easily be prepared at home, which is particularly useful if you have an abundance of apples or pears in the garden during autumn. To prepare dried apples: peel, core and slice into rings, about 5 mm/¼ inch thick, and immediately immerse in a salt solution (1 tablespoon salt to 1.2 litres/2 pints/5 cups) water. Leave for 1 minute, then drain and dry thoroughly. Spread the apple rings on a slatted drying tray and leave in a warm place for several hours until they are soft and springy to touch. Cool, then pack in polythene (plastic) bags.

Dried fruits are normally used in sweet dishes, but they can also be added to savoury foods to give extra flavour, colour and texture.

## Nuts

Nuts are increasingly being recognized as a valuable food, lending themselves to both sweet and savoury dishes. Almonds, walnuts, hazelnuts and similar filberts, brazils, chestnuts, pistachios, cashews, peanuts and coconut are the most popular varieties. Pecans, pine kernels, sesame and sunflower seeds can also be included in the diet.

The different varieties vary in their nutritional content but, in general, nuts are a rich source of nutrients. They are widely used by vegetarians to make savoury dishes because of their high protein content.

Mixed with breadcrumbs and flavourings, nuts make substantial dishes; they can also be added to meat dishes, soups or stuffings. Ground or chopped, they make a good base for mousses, soufflés, flans or cakes; very finely ground nuts can replace flour completely in a whisked sponge cake. Used simply on their own, they make attractive and nutritious decorations for sweet dishes.

# Walnut and Cheese Burgers

| Metric/Imperial | American |
|---|---|
| 175 g / 6 oz shelled walnuts | 1½ cups shelled walnuts |
| 50 g / 2 oz wholemeal bread, cubed | 2 large slices wholewheat bread, cubed |
| 100 g / 4 oz Cheddar cheese, grated | 1 cup grated Cheddar cheese |
| 1 onion, peeled and grated | 1 onion, peeled and grated |
| salt | salt |
| freshly ground black pepper | freshly ground black pepper |
| 1 egg | 1 egg |
| 1 tablespoon tomato purée | 1 tablespoon tomato paste |
| oil for shallow frying | oil for shallow frying |
| TO GARNISH: | TO GARNISH: |
| tomatoes | tomatoes |
| watercress | watercress |

Put the nuts in an electric blender, reserving 50 g / 2 oz / ½ cup for the coating. Add the bread and grind coarsely. Transfer to a bowl, add the cheese, onion and salt and pepper to taste and stir well. Beat the egg with the tomato purée (paste). Add to the nut mixture and stir until well combined.

Divide the mixture into 4 on a lightly floured surface. Shape into burgers, about 8 cm / 3½ inches in diameter and 1 cm / ½ inch thick. Chop the reserved walnuts and press into both sides of the burgers.

Heat a little oil in a frying pan (skillet), add the burgers and fry for about 5 minutes until browned on both sides, turning once. Alternatively, place the burgers on a lightly greased baking sheet and bake in a preheated moderately hot oven (200°C / 400°F, Gas Mark 6) for 20 minutes until browned.

Serve hot or cold, garnished with tomatoes and watercress.
**Serves 4**

*RIGHT: Preparing Walnut and cheese burgers*
*ABOVE RIGHT: Preparing Herb and nut roast; Brazil nut loaf*

# Herb and Nut Roast

| Metric/Imperial | American |
|---|---|
| 100 g / 4 oz hazelnuts | ¾ cup filberts |
| 100 g / 4 oz wholemeal bread, cubed | 2 large slices wholewheat bread, cubed |
| 100 g / 4 oz vegetable margarine | ½ cup vegetable margarine |
| 450 g / 1 lb onions, peeled and chopped | 1 lb onions, peeled and chopped |
| 1 tablespoon yeast extract | 1 tablespoon yeast extract |
| 100 g / 4 oz unsalted cashews or peanuts | 1 cup unsalted cashews or peanuts |
| 2 tablespoons chopped parsley | 2 tablespoons chopped parsley |
| 2 tablespoons chopped mixed herbs | 2 tablespoons chopped mixed herbs |
| salt | salt |
| freshly ground black pepper | freshly ground black pepper |

Put the hazelnuts (filberts) in an electric blender, reserving about 12 whole ones. Add the bread and grind coarsely.

Melt the margarine in a large pan, add the onions and fry gently for 10 minutes until soft. Stir in the yeast extract.

Remove from the heat, then stir in the ground nuts and bread, cashews or peanuts, herbs, salt and pepper to taste.

Press the mixture into a 900 ml / 1½ pint / 3¾ cup pie dish or casserole. Press the reserved nuts into the top. Bake in a preheated moderate oven (180°C / 350°F, Gas Mark 4) for 40 minutes until lightly browned on top. Serve hot.

**Serves 4 to 6**

# Brazil Nut Loaf

| Metric/Imperial | American |
|---|---|
| 225 g / 8 oz shelled Brazil nuts | ½ lb shelled Brazil nuts |
| 100 g / 4 oz wholemeal bread, cubed with crusts | 2 large slices wholewheat bread, cubed with crusts |
| 1 tablespoon oil | 1 tablespoon oil |
| 100 g / 4 oz bacon, derinded and chopped | 4 bacon slices, derinded and chopped |
| 2 onions, peeled and chopped | 2 onions, peeled and chopped |
| 1 garlic clove, peeled and crushed | 1 garlic clove, peeled and crushed |
| 1 tablespoon chopped parsley | 1 tablespoon chopped parsley |
| 1 tablespoon chopped thyme | 1 tablespoon chopped thyme |
| salt | salt |
| freshly ground black pepper | freshly ground black pepper |
| 1 egg | 1 egg |
| 1 teaspoon Worcestershire sauce | 1 teaspoon Worcestershire sauce |

Put the nuts and bread in an electric blender and grind coarsely.

Heat the oil in a pan, add the bacon, onions and garlic and fry gently for 4 to 5 minutes until soft. Remove the pan from the heat, then add the ground nuts and bread, herbs and salt and pepper to taste. Mix well. Beat the egg with the Worcestershire sauce, add to the nut mixture and bind thoroughly.

Press the mixture into a lightly greased 450 g / 1 lb / 4½ × 2½ × 1½ inch loaf tin and level the surface. Bake in a preheated moderately hot oven (190°C / 375°F, Gas Mark 5) for 40 minutes until the top is crisp and lightly browned.

Turn the loaf out onto a serving dish and serve hot. Alternatively leave to cool in the tin, then turn out and serve cold with sliced tomatoes.

**Serves 4 to 6**

# Chestnut Soup

*This soup will have a better flavour if the chestnuts are first roasted to remove their skins, rather than boiled.*

| Metric/Imperial | American |
|---|---|
| 450 g / 1 lb chestnuts | 1 lb chestnuts |
| 1 large onion, peeled and chopped | 1 large onion, peeled and chopped |
| 2 celery sticks, chopped | 2 celery stalks, chopped |
| 1.2 litres / 2 pints turkey or chicken stock | 5 cups turkey or chicken stock |
| 1 bay leaf | 1 bay leaf |
| salt | salt |
| freshly ground black pepper | freshly ground black pepper |

Make a small cut through the skins of the chestnuts, then place on a baking sheet and bake on the top shelf of a moderately hot oven (200°C / 400°F, Gas Mark 6) until the skins crack. Alternatively, put the chestnuts in a pan, cover with water and bring to the boil. Peel off both layers of skin while the nuts are still hot.

Put the peeled chestnuts in a pan, add the remaining ingredients and bring to the boil. Lower the heat, cover and simmer for 45 minutes until the chestnuts and celery are tender. Discard the bay leaf.

Transfer the soup to an electric blender, reserving a few whole chestnuts for the garnish. Blend to a smooth purée, then return to the rinsed-out pan. Reheat gently, then taste and adjust the seasoning. Stir in a little milk if the soup is too thick.

Serve hot, garnished with the reserved chestnuts.

**Serves 6**

# Spinach and Peanut Galette

| Metric/Imperial | American |
|---|---|
| PANCAKES: | PANCAKES: |
| 100 g / 4 oz wholemeal flour | 1 cup wholewheat flour |
| 1 egg, beaten | 1 egg, beaten |
| 300 ml / ½ pint milk | 1¼ cups milk |
| oil for shallow frying | oil for shallow frying |
| FILLING: | FILLING: |
| 1 tablespoon oil | 1 tablespoon oil |
| 1 small onion, peeled and sliced | 1 small onion, peeled and sliced |
| 225 g / 8 oz button mushrooms, sliced | 1 cup sliced button mushrooms |
| 450 g / 1 lb frozen spinach, cooked and drained | 1 lb frozen spinach, cooked and drained |
| salt | salt |
| freshly ground black pepper | freshly ground black pepper |
| SAUCE: | SAUCE: |
| 25 g / 1 oz butter | 2 tablespoons butter |
| 50 g / 2 oz shelled peanuts | ½ cup shelled peanuts |
| 2 tablespoons flour | 2 tablespoons flour |
| 300 ml / ½ pint chicken stock | 1¼ cups chicken stock |

To make the pancakes: put the flour in a bowl and make a well in the centre. Pour in the egg and milk and beat well to give a smooth batter.

Heat a little oil in a 20 cm / 8 inch frying pan (skillet). Pour in enough batter to coat the bottom of the pan thinly. Cook until set and golden brown underneath, then turn the pancake and cook the other side. Repeat with the remaining batter to make 8 pancakes.

To prepare the filling: heat the oil in a pan and sauté the onion and mushrooms until soft. Stir in the spinach and season with salt and pepper to taste.

Spread each pancake with a little of the spinach filling and pile the pancakes on top of one another in a straight-sided ovenproof serving dish.

To make the sauce: heat the butter in a pan and fry the peanuts until golden brown. Stir in the flour and cook for 1 minute. Add the stock gradually, stirring constantly. Cook, stirring, until thickened.

Pour the sauce over the galette and cook in a preheated moderately hot oven (200°C / 400°F, Gas Mark 6) for 30 minutes. Serve hot.

**Serves 4 to 6**

# Greek Rice Ring

| Metric/Imperial | American |
|---|---|
| 3 tablespoons oil | 3 tablespoons oil |
| 1 onion, peeled and sliced | 1 onion, peeled and sliced |
| 1 clove garlic, peeled and crushed | 1 clove garlic, peeled and crushed |
| 225 g / 8 oz brown rice | 1⅓ cups brown rice |
| 750 ml / 1¼ pints water | 3 cups water |
| salt | salt |
| 1 green pepper, cored, seeded and chopped | 1 green pepper, cored, seeded and chopped |
| 50 g / 2 oz dried apricots, soaked and sliced | ⅓ cup dried apricots, soaked and sliced |
| 50 g / 2 oz dried prunes, soaked, stoned and sliced | ⅓ cup dried prunes, soaked pitted and sliced |
| 75 g / 3 oz walnuts, roughly chopped | ¾ cup roughly chopped walnuts |
| 50 g / 2 oz black olives, halved and stoned | ⅓ cup ripe olives, halved and pitted |
| freshly ground black pepper | freshly ground black pepper |

Heat the oil in a large pan and sauté the onion and garlic until soft. Stir in the rice and cook, stirring, for 1 minute. Add the water and salt. Bring to the boil, cover and simmer for 20 minutes.

Stir in the green pepper, apricots and prunes. Continue to simmer, covered, for about 20 minutes or until the rice is cooked and the liquid absorbed. Stir in the walnuts, olives and salt and pepper to taste.

Turn the mixture into a greased 900 ml / 1½ pint / 3¾ cup ring mould and cook in a preheated moderate oven (180°C / 350°F, Gas Mark 4) for 30 minutes. Turn out and serve hot or cold. Fill the centre with courgettes (zucchini) provençal (page 156) or a crisp green salad if preferred.

**Serves 4**

# Broccoli and Almonds

| Metric/Imperial | American |
|---|---|
| 450 g / 1 lb broccoli spears | 4 cups broccoli spears |
| salt | salt |
| 2 tablespoons olive oil | 2 tablespoons olive oil |
| 1 onion, peeled and sliced | 1 onion, peeled and sliced |
| 1 clove garlic, peeled and crushed | 1 clove garlic, peeled and crushed |
| 50 g / 2 oz blanched almonds | ½ cup blanched almonds |
| 5 tomatoes, skinned and chopped | 5 tomatoes, skinned and chopped |
| freshly ground black pepper | freshly ground black pepper |
| 1 tablespoon chopped parsley | 1 tablespoon chopped parsley |

Cook the broccoli spears in boiling salted water for about 15 minutes until just tender.

Heat the oil in a pan and sauté the onion, garlic and almonds until the onion is soft and the almonds are beginning to brown. Stir in the tomatoes and heat through. Season with salt and pepper to taste.

Drain the broccoli and place in a heated serving dish. Spoon the sauce over the broccoli and sprinkle with chopped parsley. Serve hot.

**Serves 4**

# Apricot Tart

| Metric/Imperial | American |
|---|---|
| PASTRY: | DOUGH: |
| 100 g / 4 oz wholemeal flour | 1 cup wholewheat flour |
| 75 g / 3 oz vegetable margarine | 1/3 cup vegetable margarine |
| 75 g / 3 oz ground almonds | 3/4 cup ground almonds |
| 50 g / 2 oz sugar | 1/4 cup sugar |
| 1 egg yolk, mixed with 2 teaspoons cold water | 1 egg yolk, mixed with 2 teaspoons cold water |
| 4 drops almond essence | 4 drops almond extract |
| FILLING: | FILLING: |
| 300 ml / 1/2 pint milk | 1 1/4 cups milk |
| 2 eggs | 2 eggs |
| 2 tablespoons cornflour | 2 tablespoons cornstarch |
| 2 tablespoons caster sugar | 2 tablespoons sugar |
| 150 ml / 1/4 pint natural yogurt | 2/3 cup unflavored yogurt |
| 1 tablespoon sherry | 1 tablespoon sherry |
| 450 g / 1 lb apricots | 1 lb apricots |
| 4 tablespoons apricot jam | 1/4 cup apricot jam |
| 2 tablespoons orange juice | 2 tablespoons orange juice |
| 25 g / 1 oz shelled almonds | 1/4 cup shelled almonds |

To make the pastry dough: put the flour in a bowl. Add the margarine and rub into the flour until the mixture resembles breadcrumbs. Stir in the almonds and sugar, then the egg yolk mixture and almond essence (extract). Mix to a firm dough.

Turn onto a lightly floured surface, roll out and use to line a 20 cm / 8 inch flan dish or flan ring placed on a baking sheet. Line the dough with foil, then fill with baking beans or rice.

Bake in a preheated moderately hot oven (200°C / 400°F, Gas Mark 6) for 15 minutes, then remove the beans or rice and foil and bake for a further 5 to 10 minutes until the bottom of the pastry is crisp. Remove from the oven and leave to cool.

To make the filling: heat the milk to just below boiling point. Put the eggs in a bowl with the cornflour (cornstarch) and sugar. Beat lightly, then gradually stir in the hot milk. Return to the pan and bring to the boil, stirring constantly. Simmer for 2 minutes until the custard is thick and smooth.

Leave to cool, stirring occasionally to prevent a skin forming. Whisk in the yogurt and sherry, then spoon the custard into the flan case and level the surface.

Cut the apricots in half and remove the stones (seeds). Put the jam and orange juice in a pan and heat gently until the jam has melted. Add the apricots to the pan, cut side down, and simmer for 5 to 10 minutes until tender. Arrange the apricots and almonds on top. Pour over the syrup from the pan, then leave to cool and set. Serve cold.

**Serves 4 to 6**

# Hazelnut (Filbert) and Raspberry Torte

*Use hazelnuts (filberts) with their skins on to give colour and flavour to this torte. Ground hazelnuts (filberts) are used instead of flour for the cake mixture, and the filling is a purée of apples and raspberries.*

| Metric/Imperial | American |
|---|---|
| TORTE: | TORTE: |
| 4 eggs, separated | 4 eggs, separated |
| 100 g / 4 oz soft brown sugar | 2/3 cup brown sugar |
| 100 g / 4 oz shelled hazelnuts, coarsely ground | 3/4 cup shelled filberts, coarsely ground |
| FILLING: | FILLING: |
| 450 g / 1 lb cooking apples, peeled, cored and sliced | 1 lb baking apples, peeled, cored and sliced |
| finely grated rind and juice of 1/2 lemon | finely grated rind and juice of 1/2 lemon |
| 225 g / 8 oz raspberries | 1 3/4 cups raspberries |
| 50 g / 2 oz light soft brown sugar | 1/3 cup light brown sugar |
| TO DECORATE: | TO DECORATE: |
| 150 ml / 1/4 pint natural yogurt | 2/3 cup unflavored yogurt |
| few whole hazelnuts | few whole filberts |

To make the torte: beat the egg yolks and sugar together until thick and creamy. Beat the egg whites until just stiff. Fold the ground hazelnuts (filberts) and egg whites carefully into the creamed mixture.

*Apricot tart; Spiced fruit compote; Hazelnut (filbert) and raspberry torte*

Line the bottoms of two greased 23 cm / 9 inch sandwich tins (layer cake pans) with greased greaseproof paper or non-stick parchment. Divide the mixture equally between the tins and level the surface.

Bake in a preheated moderate oven (180°C / 350°F, Gas Mark 4) for 30 minutes until risen and firm to touch. Leave in the tins until cold; do not turn out onto a wire rack or the cakes will stick.

To make the filling: put the apples in a pan with the lemon rind and juice, raspberries and sugar. Cook for 10 to 15 minutes until pulpy, stirring occasionally. Remove from the heat and beat until smooth, or rub through a sieve (strainer) for a smoother texture. Leave to cool.

Meanwhile, place a sieve (strainer) over a bowl and line with a piece of muslin (cheesecloth). Pour in the yogurt and leave to drain for about 3 hours until most of the liquid has drained through, leaving the yogurt with a smooth, creamy consistency in the sieve (strainer).

To assemble the torte: lift the cakes carefully out of the tins and peel off the paper. Place one cake on a serving plate and spread with the filling mixture. Cover with the other cake, then pipe the creamy yogurt in rosettes on the top. Decorate with whole hazelnuts (filberts).

**Serves 6 to 8**

# Spiced Fruit Compote

| Metric/Imperial | American |
|---|---|
| 450 g / 1 lb mixed dried fruit (apples, apricots, figs, peaches, pears, prunes, sultanas, etc) | 3 cups mixed dried fruit (apples, apricots, figs, peaches, pears, prunes, seedless white raisins, etc) |
| 300 ml / ½ pint orange juice | 1¼ cups orange juice |
| 300 ml / ½ pint water | 1¼ cups water |
| 1 cinnamon stick | 1 cinnamon stick |
| 2 cloves | 2 cloves |
| 50 g / 2 oz blanched slivered almonds | ½ cup blanched slivered almonds |

Put the dried fruit in a bowl and pour over the orange juice and water. Add the spices and leave to soak overnight. Alternatively, pour over boiling juice and water and soak for a few hours.

Transfer to a pan and bring to the boil. Lower the heat, cover and simmer for about 20 minutes or until the fruit is tender, adding more water if the syrup becomes absorbed.

Sprinkle with the almonds and serve warm or cold.

**Serves 4 to 6**

# Pears in Cassis

*Pears cooked in white wine and blackcurrants turn a beautiful rich crimson colour – perfect for a dinner party as they can be cooked in advance.*

| Metric/Imperial | American |
|---|---|
| 300 ml / ½ pint medium or sweet white wine | 1¼ cups medium or sweet white wine |
| 100 g / 4 oz blackcurrants, stalks removed | 1 cup blackcurrants, stalks removed |
| 4 tablespoons honey | ¼ cup honey |
| 1 cinnamon stick | 1 cinnamon stick |
| 2 strips lemon rind | 2 strips lemon rind |
| 4-6 pears | 4-6 pears |
| 1 teaspoon arrowroot | 1 teaspoon arrowroot |

Pour the wine into a pan, then add the blackcurrants, honey, cinnamon and lemon rind. Heat gently until the honey has dissolved, then bring to the boil. Boil for 1 minute.

Peel the pears, leaving the stalks attached. Put the pears in the pan, submerging them as much as possible in the wine mixture. Cover and cook gently for about 20 minutes until the pears are tender, turning occasionally.

Lift the pears carefully out of the pan and transfer to a serving bowl. Discard the cinnamon stick and lemon rind.

Blend the arrowroot with a little cold water, then pour into the wine mixture. Bring to the boil, then lower the heat and simmer for 1 minute until the sauce thickens, stirring constantly. Pour over the pears. Serve hot or cold.

**Serves 4 to 6**

# Almond and Strawberry Malakoff

| Metric/Imperial | American |
|---|---|
| 18 sponge fingers | 18 ladyfingers |
| finely grated rind and juice of 2 oranges | finely grated rind and juice of 2 oranges |
| 2 tablespoons sherry | 2 tablespoons sherry |
| FILLING: | FILLING: |
| 100 g / 4 oz vegetable margarine | ½ cup vegetable margarine |
| 100 g / 4 oz light soft brown sugar | ⅔ cup light brown sugar |
| 225 g / 8 oz curd cheese | 1 cup cottage cheese |
| 175 g / 6 oz ground almonds | 1½ cups ground almonds |
| 350 g / 12 oz strawberries | ¾ lb strawberries |

Line the bottom of a 15 × 7 cm / 6 × 3 inch round cake tin with greased greaseproof paper or non-stick parchment. Trim one end off the sponge fingers (ladyfingers) so that they fit the depth of the tin; reserve the trimmings.

Mix the orange juice with the sherry. Dip in the sponge fingers (ladyfingers), one at a time, for a few seconds to soften slightly, then arrange them, rounded end down, around the edge of the tin. Reserve any remaining juice for the filling.

To make the filling: beat together the margarine and sugar until light and creamy. Add the cheese, ground almonds, orange rind and reserved juice and beat well. Set aside about one third of the strawberries; slice the remainder.

Spread one third of the almond mixture in the bottom of the tin. Cover with half the sliced strawberries and sponge trimmings. Spread another third of the almond mixture on top, then the remaining sliced strawberries and sponge trimmings. Finish with the remaining almond mixture and level the surface.

Cover with a small plate or saucer, place a weight on top, then chill in the refrigerator for at least 4 hours until firm.

To serve: invert the malakoff onto a serving plate and decorate the top with the reserved strawberries.

**Serves 6**

# Peach and Raspberry Cheesecake

*If you do not have a loose-bottomed cake tin, make this cheesecake in an ordinary cake tin and turn it out onto a serving plate so that the crust is on top rather than underneath.*

| Metric/Imperial | American |
|---|---|
| BISCUIT CRUST: | CRACKER CRUST: |
| 75 g / 3 oz vegetable margarine | 1/3 cup vegetable margarine |
| 175 g / 6 oz digestive biscuits, crushed | 1 1/2 cups Graham crackers, crushed |
| 1 tablespoon demerara sugar | 1 tablespoon raw sugar |
| FILLING: | FILLING: |
| 350 g / 12 oz cottage cheese, sieved | 1 1/2 cups cottage cheese, sieved |
| 150 ml / 1/4 pint natural yogurt | 2/3 cup unflavored yogurt |
| 50 g / 2 oz caster sugar | 1/4 cup sugar |
| finely grated rind and juice of 1 lemon | finely grated rind and juice of 1 lemon |
| 15 g / 1/2 oz gelatine | 1 envelope unflavored gelatin |
| 2 tablespoons water | 2 tablespoons water |
| 2 egg whites | 2 egg whites |
| TOPPING: | TOPPING: |
| 2 large peaches | 2 large peaches |
| 225 g / 8 oz raspberries | 2 cups raspberries |

To make the crust: melt the margarine in a pan, then stir in the biscuits (crackers) and sugar. Spoon the mixture into a lightly greased 18-20 cm / 7-8 inch loose-bottomed cake tin, spread evenly and press down with the back of a spoon. Chill in the refrigerator.

Meanwhile, make the filling: put the cottage cheese in a bowl with the yogurt, sugar, lemon rind and juice, reserving 1 tablespoon of lemon juice for the topping. Beat well.

Sprinkle the gelatine over the water in a small cup. Stand the cup in a pan of hot water and stir until the gelatine has dissolved. Fold into the cheese mixture.

Beat the egg whites until stiff, then fold into the cheese mixture. Pour on top of the crust in the tin and level the surface. Chill in the refrigerator until set.

To serve: run a knife around the edge of the cheesecake, then remove from the tin. Cut the peaches in half, remove the stones (seeds), then slice the flesh. Brush the cut surfaces with the reserved lemon juice. Arrange the peach slices on top of the cheesecake with the raspberries. Serve chilled.

**Serves 6 to 8**

# Apricot Syllabub

| Metric/Imperial | American |
|---|---|
| 225 g / 8 oz dried apricots | 1½ cups dried apricots |
| 600 ml / 1 pint water | 2½ cups water |
| finely grated rind and juice of 1 lemon | finely grated rind and juice of 1 lemon |
| 150 ml / ¼ pint natural yogurt | 1¼ cups unflavored yogurt |
| 2 tablespoons Grand Marnier or other liqueur | 2 tablespoons Grand Marnier or other liqueur |
| 50 g / 2 oz soft brown sugar | ⅓ cup brown sugar |
| 2 egg whites | 2 egg whites |
| lemon twists or chopped nuts, to decorate | lemon twists or chopped nuts, to decorate |

Put the apricots in a bowl, pour over the water, then add the lemon rind and juice. Leave to soak overnight. Alternatively, pour over boiling water and soak for a few hours.

Transfer to a pan and bring to the boil. Lower the heat, cover and simmer for 20 to 30 minutes until the apricots are soft, adding more water if necessary.

Work the mixture to a smooth purée in an electric blender, then transfer to a bowl and leave to cool.

Stir the yogurt, liqueur and sugar into the purée until well blended. Beat the egg whites until just stiff, then fold into the mixture.

Spoon into a serving bowl or 6 individual dishes or glasses, then chill in the refrigerator for at least 1 hour before serving. Decorate with lemon twists or nuts.

**Serves 6**

ABOVE: Raspberry chantilly; Strawberry and orange soufflé; Peach and raspberry cheesecake (page 187)
BELOW LEFT: Apricot syllabub

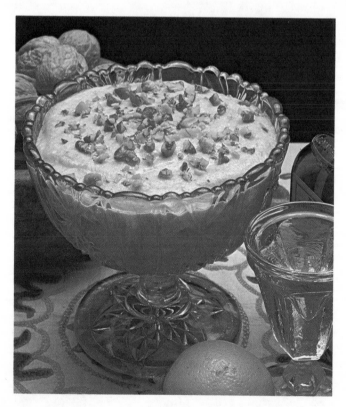

# Raspberry Chantilly

| Metric/Imperial | American |
|---|---|
| 450 g / 1 lb raspberries | 3 cups raspberries |
| 2 tablespoons Grand Marnier or other liqueur | 2 tablespoons Grand Marnier or other liqueur |
| 2 egg whites | 2 egg whites |
| grated rind of ½ lemon | grated rind of ½ lemon |
| 1 tablespoon caster sugar | 1 tablespoon sugar |
| 25 g / 1 oz flaked almonds, toasted | ¼ cup toasted sliced almonds |

Put the raspberries in 4 glasses and spoon over the liqueur.

Just before serving, beat the egg whites until stiff. Fold in the yogurt carefully with the lemon rind and sugar. Spoon over the raspberries and sprinkle with the almonds.

**Serves 4**

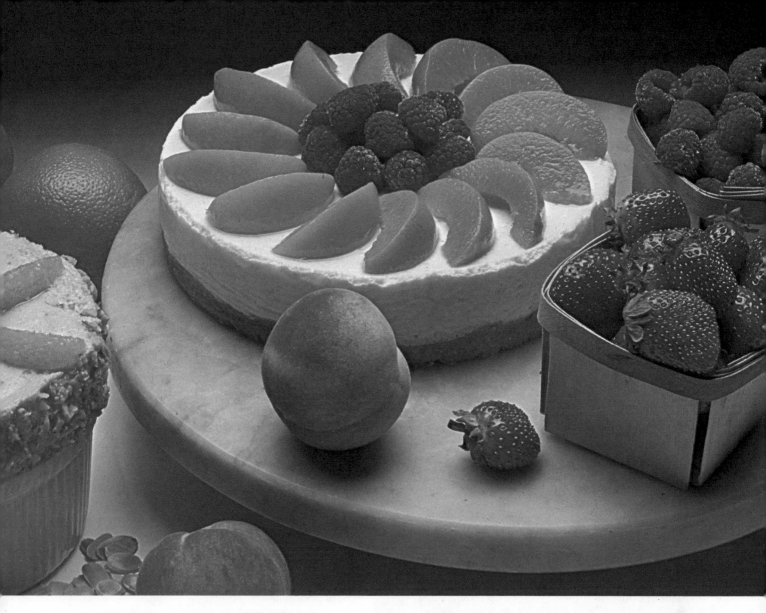

# Strawberry and Orange Soufflé

*The flavour of orange combines well with strawberries. This soufflé has a strong natural flavour as no cream is used to mask the flavour of the fruit and the yogurt gives it a tangy, refreshing taste.*

| Metric/Imperial | American |
|---|---|
| 450 g / 1 lb strawberries, hulled | 3 cups hulled strawberries |
| 4 eggs, separated | 4 eggs, separated |
| 100 g / 4 oz caster sugar | ½ cup sugar |
| finely grated rind and juice of 1 large orange | finely grated rind and juice of 1 large orange |
| 15 g / ½ oz gelatine | 1 envelope gelatin |
| 150 ml / ¼ pint natural yogurt | ⅔ cup unflavored yogurt |
| 25 g / 1 oz flaked almonds, toasted and chopped | ¼ cup toasted sliced almonds, chopped |
| 1 orange, peeled and segmented, to decorate | 1 orange, peeled and segmented, to decorate |

Mash the strawberries or work to a purée in an electric blender, reserving a few whole ones for decoration.

Put the egg yolks in a bowl with the sugar, orange rind and half the juice. Stand the bowl over a pan of gently simmering water and whisk until the mixture is thick and pale. Remove from the heat and continue whisking until cool.

Pour the remaining orange juice into a small cup and sprinkle the gelatine on top. Stand the cup in a pan of hot water and stir until the gelatine has dissolved.

Stir the strawberry purée into the egg mixture with the yogurt and mix well. Stir in the dissolved gelatine. Leave in a cool place until thick and just beginning to set. Beat the egg whites until just stiff and fold into the mixture.

Tie a collar of greaseproof (wax) paper around a 900 ml / 1½ pint / 3¾ cup soufflé dish so that it stands 5 cm / 2 inches above the rim of the dish. Pour in the soufflé mixture. Chill in the refrigerator for at least 2 hours before serving.

Remove the collar carefully before serving. Press the chopped nuts around the side. Decorate the top with the reserved strawberries and the orange segments.

**Serves 4 to 6**

# Rhubarb, Orange and Ginger Fool

| Metric/Imperial | American |
|---|---|
| 450 g / 1 lb rhubarb, trimmed and chopped | 1 lb rhubarb, trimmed and chopped |
| finely grated rind and juice of 1 orange | finely grated rind and juice of 1 orange |
| 4 tablespoons light soft brown sugar | ¼ cup light brown sugar |
| 150 ml / ¼ pint milk | ⅔ cup milk |
| 1 egg, lightly beaten | 1 egg, lightly beaten |
| 1 tablespoon cornflour | 1 tablespoon cornstarch |
| 1 tablespoon sugar | 1 tablespoon sugar |
| ¼ teaspoon vanilla essence | ¼ teaspoon vanilla extract |
| 150 ml / ¼ pint natural yogurt | ⅔ cup unflavored yogurt |
| 1 tablespoon finely chopped preserved ginger | 1 tablespoon finely chopped preserved ginger |
| few orange slices to decorate | few orange slices to decorate |

Put the rhubarb in a pan with the orange rind and juice and the brown sugar. Cover and simmer gently for 10 to 15 minutes until tender. Mash the rhubarb to a pulp by beating vigorously with a wooden spoon, or work to a purée in an electric blender. Leave to cool.

Heat the milk to just below boiling point. Put the egg in a bowl with the cornflour (cornstarch)), sugar and vanilla essence (extract). Beat lightly, then gradually stir in the hot milk. Pour the mixture back into the pan and bring to the boil slowly, stirring constantly. Cook, stirring, until the custard thickens.

Leave to cool, stirring occasionally to prevent a skin from forming, then whisk in the yogurt. Stir the custard into the rhubarb purée with the ginger.

Spoon into a large serving bowl or individual dishes or glasses. Chill in the refrigerator, then decorate with orange slices before serving. Serve chilled.

**Serves 4**

# Bramble Mousse

| Metric/Imperial | American |
|---|---|
| 450 g / 1 lb blackberries | 4 cups blackberries |
| 225 g / 8 oz cooking apples, peeled, cored and sliced | 1½ cups peeled, cored and sliced baking apples |
| finely grated rind and juice of 1 orange or lemon | finely grated rind and juice of 1 orange or lemon |
| 4 tablespoons soft brown sugar | ¼ cup brown sugar |
| 15 g / ½ oz gelatine | 1 envelope gelatin |
| 2 tablespoons water | 2 tablespoons water |
| 150 ml / ¼ pint natural yogurt | ⅔ cup unflavored yogurt |
| 2 egg whites | 2 egg whites |

Put the blackberries in a pan, reserving a few for decoration. Add the apples, orange or lemon rind and juice and the sugar. Cover and heat gently for 10 to 15 minutes until the fruit is soft, stirring occasionally. Rub through a sieve (strainer) into a bowl.

Sprinkle the gelatine over the water in a small cup. Stand the cup in a pan of hot water and stir until the gelatine has dissolved.

Stir the gelatine into the fruit purée with the yogurt and mix well. Leave in a cool place until thick and just beginning to set.

Beat the egg whites until just stiff, then fold into the mousse. Transfer to a large serving bowl or individual dishes or glasses. Chill in the refrigerator until set, then decorate with the reserved blackberries. Serve chilled.

**Serves 4 to 6**

# Gingered Pear and Yogurt Mousse

| Metric/Imperial | American |
|---|---|
| 1 kg / 2 lb pears, peeled, cored and chopped | 2 lb pears, peeled, cored and chopped |
| finely grated rind and juice of 1 lemon | finely grated rind and juice of 1 lemon |
| ¼ teaspoon ground ginger | ¼ teaspoon ground ginger |
| 3-4 pieces stem ginger in syrup | 3-4 pieces preserved ginger in syrup |
| 2 eggs, separated | 2 eggs, separated |
| 300 ml / ½ pint natural yogurt | 1¼ cups unflavored yogurt |
| 15 g / ½ oz gelatine | 2 envelopes gelatin |
| 2 tablespoons water | 2 tablespoons water |

Put the pears in a pan with the lemon rind and juice, ginger and 2 tablespoons syrup from the preserved ginger. Cover and cook gently for 10 to 15 minutes until the pears are tender, stirring occasionally. Take out the preserved ginger; chop one of the pieces, slice the remainder and set aside.

Put the pears and juice, egg yolks and yogurt in an electric blender and blend to a smooth purée. Alternatively, rub the pears and juice through a sieve (strainer), then beat in the egg yolks and yogurt.

Sprinkle the gelatine over the water in a small cup. Stand the cup in a pan of hot water and stir until the gelatine has dissolved. Stir into the pear purée, with the chopped ginger. Leave in a cool place until thick and just beginning to set.

Beat the egg whites until stiff, then fold into the mixture. Spoon into 6 individual glasses or dishes and chill in the refrigerator until set. Decorate with slices of preserved ginger. Serve chilled.

**Serves 6**

# Prune and Orange Ring

| Metric/Imperial | American |
|---|---|
| 225 g / 8 oz prunes | 1⅓ cups prunes |
| finely grated rind of 1 orange | finely grated rind of 1 orange |
| juice of 2 large oranges | juice of 2 large oranges |
| 15 g / ½ oz gelatine | 1 envelope gelatin |
| juice of 1 lemon | juice of 1 lemon |
| 2 egg whites | 2 egg whites |
| 2 oranges, peel and pith removed and sliced, to serve | 2 oranges, peel and pith removed and sliced, to serve |

Put the prunes and orange rind in a bowl. Make the orange juice up to 300 ml / ½ pint / 1¼ cups with water, then pour over the prunes. Leave to soak overnight. Alternatively, pour over boiling juice and water and soak for a few hours.

Transfer to a pan and bring to the boil. Lower the heat, cover and simmer for 20 minutes until the prunes are tender, then drain, reserving the juice.

Measure the juice and make up to 300 ml / ½ pint / 1¼ cups with water. Remove the stones (seeds) from the prunes. Put the prune flesh and juice in an electric blender and work to a smooth purée.

Sprinkle the gelatine over the lemon juice in a small cup. Stand the cup in a pan of hot water and stir until the gelatine has dissolved. Stir into the prune purée.

Beat the egg whites until just stiff, then fold into the mixture. Pour into a 900 ml / 1½ pint / 3¾ cup ring mould or serving bowl and chill in the refrigerator until set.

To serve: dip the mould in hot water for a few seconds, then invert onto a serving plate. Fill the centre of the ring with the orange slices.

**Serves 4 to 6**

# Chestnut Whip

*If fresh chestnuts are unobtainable, use one 450 g /
1 lb can unsweetened chestnut purée instead of
making your own.*

| Metric/Imperial | American |
| --- | --- |
| 450 g / 1 lb chestnuts | 1 lb chestnuts |
| 600 ml / 1 pint water | 2½ cups water |
| 200 ml / ⅓ pint milk | 1 cup milk |
| ¼ teaspoon vanilla essence | ¼ teaspoon vanilla extract |
| finely grated rind and juice of 1 small orange | finely grated rind and juice of 1 small orange |
| 2 tablespoons rum | 2 tablespoons rum |
| 100 g / 4 oz soft brown sugar | ⅔ cup brown sugar |
| 2 egg whites | 2 egg whites |
| orange twists, to decorate | orange twists, to decorate |

*Chestnut whip*

Put the chestnuts in a pan and cover with the water. Bring to the boil, then lower the heat and simmer for 10 minutes. Drain and leave until cool enough to handle.

Peel off the skins with a sharp knife, then return the chestnuts to the pan and add the milk and vanilla essence (extract). Cover and cook gently for about 15 minutes until the chestnuts are soft and have absorbed the milk, stirring occasionally.

Rub through a sieve (strainer) to give a thick, dry purée, then stir in the orange rind and juice, rum and sugar. Beat the egg whites until just stiff, then fold into the chestnut mixture.

Spoon into a serving bowl or 6 individual dishes or glasses. Chill in the refrigerator for at least 1 hour before serving, then decorate with orange twists.
**Serves 6**

# Orange and Lemon Mousse

| Metric/Imperial | American |
| --- | --- |
| 4 large eggs, separated | 4 large eggs, separated |
| 100 g / 4 oz light soft brown sugar | ⅔ cup light brown sugar |
| finely grated rind and juice of 2 lemons | finely grated rind and juice of 2 lemons |
| finely grated rind and juice of 2 oranges | finely grated rind and juice of 2 oranges |
| 15 g / ½ oz gelatine | 1 envelope gelatin |
| 150 ml / ¼ pint natural yogurt | ⅔ cup unflavored yogurt |

Put the egg yolks and sugar in a bowl. Add the lemon rind and juice, orange rind and half of the orange juice.

Pour the remaining orange juice into a small cup and sprinkle on the gelatine. Stand the cup in a pan of hot water and stir until the gelatine has dissolved.

Stand the bowl with the egg yolk mixture over a pan of gently simmering water and whisk until the mixture is thick and pale. Remove from the heat and continue whisking until cool.

Stir the yogurt into the mixture with the dissolved gelatine. Leave in a cool place until thick and just beginning to set.

Beat the egg whites until just stiff, then fold into the mousse. Pour into a serving bowl and chill in the refrigerator for at least 2 hours before serving. Serve chilled.

Alternatively, pour into a 900 ml / 1½ pint / 3¾ cup soufflé dish tied with a collar of greaseproof (wax) paper so that the mousse will set above the rim of the dish. Remove the collar carefully before serving.
**Serves 4 to 6**

*LEFT: Orange and lemon mousse*

*ABOVE: Minted apple snow*

# Minted Apple Snow

**Metric/Imperial**

1 kg / 2 lb cooking apples, peeled, cored and sliced
finely grated rind and juice of 1 orange
3 tablespoons honey
4 large mint sprigs
2 large egg whites

**American**

6 cups peeled, cored and sliced baking apples
finely grated rind and juice of 1 orange
3 tablespoons honey
4 large mint sprigs
2 large egg whites

Put the apples in a pan, then add the orange rind and juice and the honey. Add the mint, reserving the top leaves for decoration. Cover and cook gently for about 15 minutes until the apples are cooked to a pulp, stirring occasionally.

Discard the mint, then beat the pulp vigorously with a wooden spoon until smooth. Alternatively, rub through a sieve (strainer) or work to a purée in an electric blender. Leave to cool.

Beat the egg whites until stiff, then fold into the apple purée. Spoon into a serving bowl or individual dishes or glasses. Decorate with the reserved mint leaves. Serve chilled.

**Serves 4**

# Sunshine Fruit Salad

| **Metric/Imperial** | **American** |
|---|---|
| juice of 2 large oranges | juice of 2 large oranges |
| juice of 1 lemon | juice of 1 lemon |
| 2 tablespoons Cointreau, Grand Marnier or other liqueur (optional) | 2 tablespoons Cointreau, Grand Marnier or other liqueur (optional) |
| 225 g / 8 oz strawberries, hulled and halved | 2 cups strawberries, hulled and halved |
| 2 large peaches | 2 large peaches |
| 2 large bananas | 2 large bananas |
| 2 passion fruit or pomegranates | 2 passion fruit or pomegranates |

Put the orange and lemon juices in a serving bowl, then stir in the liqueur, if using. Add the strawberries.

Cut the peaches in half, remove the stones (seeds), then slice the flesh. Peel and slice the bananas. Cut the passion fruit or pomegranates in half, then scoop out the flesh with the seeds. Add the prepared fruit to the strawberries and fold gently to coat with the juice. Serve chilled.

**Serves 4**

# Frosted Almond Creams

| **Metric/Imperial** | **American** |
|---|---|
| 2 eggs, separated | 2 eggs, separated |
| 50 g / 2 oz soft brown sugar | 1/3 cup brown sugar |
| 50 g / 2 oz chopped almonds, toasted | 1/2 cup toasted chopped almonds |
| 300 ml / 1/2 pint natural yogurt | 1 1/4 cups unflavored yogurt |
| 2 tablespoons Grand Marnier or other liqueur | 2 tablespoons Grand Marnier or other liqueur |
| 25 g / 1 oz toasted slivered almonds, to decorate | 1/4 cup toasted slivered almonds, to decorate |

Beat the egg yolks and sugar together until thick and creamy. Stir in the chopped almonds, yogurt and liqueur. Beat the egg whites until just stiff, then fold into the almond mixture. Pour into 6 individual ramekin dishes and freeze until firm.

To serve: remove from the freezer and leave to soften slightly at room temperature for 15 minutes, or in the refrigerator for 30 minutes. Sprinkle with slivered almonds before serving.

**Serves 6**

# Blackcurrant and Orange Ice Cream

*Something between an ice cream and a sorbet (sherbet), this rich-flavoured dessert uses yogurt and egg yolks as well as the usual egg whites.*

| Metric/Imperial | American |
|---|---|
| 225 g / 8 oz blackcurrants, stalks removed | 2 cups blackcurrants, stalks removed |
| finely grated rind and juice of 1 orange | finely grated rind and juice of 1 orange |
| 6-8 mint leaves | 6-8 mint leaves |
| 4 tablespoons soft brown sugar | ¼ cup brown sugar |
| 300 ml / ½ pint natural yogurt | 1¼ cups unflavored yogurt |
| 2 eggs, separated | 2 eggs, separated |
| 4-6 small mint sprigs to decorate | 4-6 small mint sprigs to decorate |

Put the blackcurrants in an electric blender, reserving a few for decoration. Add the orange rind and juice, the mint leaves, sugar, yogurt and egg yolks. Blend until smooth.

Transfer the purée to a bowl, then place in the freezer, or freezing compartment of the refrigerator; freeze until half frozen and beginning to thicken.

Beat the egg whites until stiff, then fold into the ice cream. Freeze until half frozen, then beat again to prevent large ice crystals forming, then freeze until firm.

To serve: allow the ice cream to soften slightly at room temperature for about 10 minutes, or in the refrigerator for 20 minutes. Spoon into individual dishes or glasses, then decorate with the reserved blackcurrants and the mint sprigs.

**Serves 4 to 6**

# Pineapple Sorbet (Sherbet)

*Traditionally, sorbets (sherbets) are made with a sweet sugar syrup, but this recipe simply uses puréed pineapple flavoured with orange and folded in with the beaten egg whites.*

| Metric/Imperial | American |
|---|---|
| 1 × 1.5 kg / 3 lb pineapple | 1 × 3 lb pineapple |
| finely grated rind and juice of 1 large orange | finely grated rind and juice of 1 large orange |
| sugar to taste | sugar to taste |
| 2 egg whites | 2 egg whites |

Cut the pineapple in half lengthwise, leaving the green leaves attached. Scoop out the pineapple flesh and discard the central core. Reserve the pineapple shells for serving. Alternatively, slice the top off the pineapple and scoop out the flesh.

Work the pineapple flesh to a purée with the orange rind and juice in an electric blender. Add sugar to taste. Transfer the purée to a bowl, then place in the freezer, or freezing compartment of the refrigerator; freeze until half frozen and beginning to thicken.

Beat the egg whites until stiff. Beat the sorbet (sherbet) well to break down the ice crystals, then fold in the beaten egg whites. Spoon the mixture into the pineapple shells and return to the freezer or freezing compartment. If there is too much sorbet (sherbet) to fill the shells, freeze in a separate container.

To serve: allow the sorbet (sherbet) to soften slightly at room temperature for 10 to 15 minutes, or in the refrigerator for 20 minutes.

**Serves 6 to 8**

# Walnut Pie

**Metric/Imperial**

PASTRY:
175 g / 6 oz wholemeal
  flour
100 g / 4 oz vegetable
  margarine
50 g / 2 oz soft brown sugar
1 tablespoon ground mixed
  spice
2 tablespoons beaten egg
FILLING:
2 eggs, separated
100 g / 4 oz soft brown
  sugar
100 g / 4 oz walnut halves,
  chopped
finely grated rind and juice
  of 1 lemon
few walnut halves, to
  decorate

**American**

DOUGH:
1½ cups wholewheat flour
½ cup vegetable margarine
⅓ cup brown sugar
2 teaspoons ground allspice
1 teaspoon ground
  cinnamon
2 tablespoons beaten egg
FILLING:
2 eggs, separated
⅔ cup brown sugar
1 cup chopped walnuts
finely grated rind and juice
  of 1 lemon
few walnut halves, to
  decorate

To make the pastry dough: put the flour in a bowl, then rub in the margarine until the mixture resembles breadcrumbs. Stir in the sugar and spice, then the egg. Mix to a firm dough.

Turn the dough out onto a lightly floured surface, then roll out and use to line a 20 cm / 8 inch flan dish or flan ring placed on a baking sheet. Line the dough with foil, then fill with baking beans or rice. Bake in a preheated moderately hot oven (200°C / 400°F, Gas Mark 6) for 15 minutes, then remove the foil and beans or rice.

Meanwhile, make the filling: beat the egg yolks and sugar together until light and creamy. Stir in the walnuts and lemon rind and juice. Beat the egg whites until just stiff, then fold into the walnut mixture.

Pour the filling into the flan case. Bake in a preheated moderate oven (180°C / 350°F, Gas Mark 4) for 30 minutes until lightly browned and risen. Decorate with walnut halves and serve hot or cold.

**Serves 6**

# Spiced Cranberry and Apple Pie

**Metric/Imperial**

PASTRY:
175 g / 6 oz wholemeal
  flour
50 g / 2 oz soft brown sugar
1 tablespoon ground mixed
  spice
100 g / 4 oz vegetable
  margarine
50 g / 2 oz chopped nuts
1 egg, beaten
FILLING:
450 g / 1 lb cooking apples,
  peeled, cored and sliced
finely grated rind and juice
  of 1 orange
225 g / 8 oz cranberries
75 g / 3 oz sugar

**American**

DOUGH:
1½ cups wholewheat flour
⅓ cup brown sugar
2 teaspoons ground allspice
1 teaspoon ground
  cinnamon
½ cup vegetable margarine
½ cup chopped nuts
1 egg, beaten
FILLING:
4 cups peeled, cored and
  sliced baking apples
finely grated rind and juice
  of 1 orange
2 cups cranberries
⅓ cup sugar

To make the pastry dough: put the flour, sugar and spice in a bowl and mix well. Add the margarine in pieces and rub into the flour until the mixture resembles breadcrumbs.

Stir in the nuts, then 2 tablespoons of beaten egg and mix to a firm dough. Turn out onto a lightly floured surface and knead lightly, then cover and chill until required.

To make the filling: put all the ingredients in a bowl and mix well. Spoon into a 900 ml / 1½ pint / 3¾ cup pie dish.

Roll out the dough on the lightly floured surface to a shape 2.5 cm / 1 inch larger than the circumference of the pie dish. Cut a 1 cm / ½ inch strip of dough from around the edge and press it onto the moistened rim of the pie dish. Moisten the strip, then place the large piece of dough on top. Press firmly to seal, then trim and flute the edge.

Decorate the top of the pie with the trimmings and make a slit in the centre. Brush with the remaining beaten egg.

Bake in a preheated moderately hot oven (200°C / 400°F, Gas Mark 6) for 30 to 40 minutes until the pastry is crisp and brown. Serve hot.

**Serves 4 to 6**

*Spiced cranberry and apple pie; Walnut pie; French orange flans (page 198)*

# Plum and Orange Cobbler

**Metric/Imperial**
FILLING:
450 g / 1 lb Victoria plums
juice of 2 oranges
1 orange, peel and pith
    removed and divided into
    segments
3 tablespoons honey
SCONES:
225 g / 8 oz wholemeal
    flour
1 teaspoon ground mixed
    spice
2 teaspoons baking powder
½ teaspoon salt
25 g / 1 oz vegetable
    margarine
25 g / 1 oz soft brown sugar
finely grated rind of 1
    orange
150 ml / ¼ pint natural
    yogurt or milk
milk or beaten egg to glaze

**American**
FILLING:
1 lb purple plums
juice of 2 oranges
1 orange, peel and pith
    removed and divided into
    segments
3 tablespoons honey
BISCUITS:
2 cups wholewheat flour
½ teaspoon ground allspice
½ teaspoon ground
    cinnamon
2 teaspoons baking powder
½ teaspoon salt
2 tablespoons vegetable
    margarine
3 tablespoons brown sugar
finely grated rind of 1
    orange
⅔ cup unflavored yogurt
milk or beaten egg to glaze

To make the filling: place the plums in a baking dish. Add the orange juice and segments and spoon over the honey.

To make the scones (biscuits): put the flour, spice, baking powder and salt in a bowl and stir well. Rub in the margarine, then stir in the sugar and orange rind. Add the yogurt and mix to a soft dough.

Turn the dough out onto a lightly floured surface and roll out to about 1 cm / ½ inch thickness. Cut out 8 to 10 rounds with a 4 cm / 1½ inch biscuit cutter, then arrange overlapping around the edge of the dish. Brush with a little milk or beaten egg.

Bake in a preheated hot oven (220°C / 425°F, Gas Mark 7) for about 15 minutes until the scones (biscuits) are risen and brown and the plums are just tender when pierced with a skewer. Serve hot.

**Serves 4**

# French Orange Flans

**Metric/Imperial**
PASTRY:
175 g / 6 oz wholemeal
    flour
50 g / 2 oz soft brown sugar
1 tablespoon ground mixed
    spice
100 g / 4 oz vegetable
    margarine
2 tablespoons beaten egg
TOPPING:
2 small thin-skinned
    oranges, thinly sliced
2 tablespoons clear honey
FILLING:
1 egg, beaten
50 g / 2 oz ground almonds
1 tablespoon sugar

**American**
DOUGH:
1½ cups wholewheat flour
⅓ cup brown sugar
2 teaspoons ground allspice
1 teaspoon ground
    cinnamon
½ cup vegetable margarine
2 tablespoons beaten egg
TOPPING:
2 small thin-skinned
    oranges, thinly sliced
2 tablespoons clear honey
FILLING:
1 egg, beaten
½ cup ground almonds
1 tablespoon sugar

To make the pastry dough: put the flour, sugar and spice in a bowl and mix well. Add the margarine in pieces and rub into the flour until the mixture resembles breadcrumbs.

Add the beaten egg and mix to a firm dough. Turn out onto a lightly floured surface and knead lightly. Cover and chill in the refrigerator until required.

To make the topping: put the orange slices in a pan and simmer for about 30 minutes until the peel is tender. Drain.

Divide the dough into 4 pieces. Roll out on a lightly floured surface and use to line individual flan rings, about 10 cm / 4 inches in diameter. Alternatively, roll out four 10 cm / 4 inch circles and place on a baking sheet.

Line the dough with foil, then fill with baking beans or rice. Bake in a preheated moderately hot oven (200°C / 400°F, Gas Mark 6) for 15 minutes, then remove the beans or rice and foil.

To make the filling: put the egg, almonds and sugar in a bowl and beat well to mix. Spread in the bottom of the flan cases then arrange the orange slices on top, overlapping each other. Spoon over the honey.

Bake in a moderate oven (180°C / 350°F, Gas Mark 4) for 20 minutes. Serve hot or cold.

**Serves 4**

# Black Pear Pudding

| Metric/Imperial | American |
|---|---|
| 4 pears, peeled, cored and sliced | 4 pears, peeled, cored and sliced |
| 100 g / 4 oz blackberries | 1 cup blackberries |
| finely grated rind and juice of 1 lemon | finely grated rind and juice of 1 lemon |
| 75 g / 3 oz soft brown sugar | ½ cup brown sugar |
| 50 g / 2 oz vegetable margarine | ¼ cup vegetable margarine |
| 1 large egg, beaten | 1 large egg, beaten |
| 100 g / 4 oz wholemeal flour | 1 cup wholewheat flour |
| 1 teaspoon ground cinnamon | 1 teaspoon ground cinnamon |
| 2 teaspoons baking powder | 2 teaspoons baking powder |
| 1 tablespoon milk | 1 tablespoon milk |

Put the pears and blackberries in a 900 ml / 1½ pint / 3¾ cup pie dish. Sprinkle over the lemon rind and juice and 2 tablespoons sugar.

Cream the margarine and remaining sugar together until pale and fluffy. Beat in the egg with a little of the flour and the cinnamon.

Fold in the remaining flour and baking powder to give a soft dropping consistency, then spread the mixture over the fruit and level the surface.

Bake in a preheated moderate oven (180°C / 350°F, Gas Mark 4) for 45 minutes until the topping is risen and brown. Serve hot.

**Serves 4**

# Cherry Custard Pudding

*This pudding separates out on cooking to give a layer of custard and cherries with a light sponge topping.*

| Metric/Imperial | American |
|---|---|
| 350 g / 12 oz cherries, stoned | 3 cups pitted cherries |
| 50 g / 2 oz vegetable margarine | ¼ cup vegetable margarine |
| 50 g / 2 oz caster sugar | ¼ cup sugar |
| finely grated rind and juice of 1 large lemon | finely grated rind and juice of 1 large lemon |
| 2 eggs, separated | 2 eggs, separated |
| 300 ml / ½ pint milk | 1¼ cups milk |
| 50 g / 2 oz self-raising flour | ½ cup self-rising flour |
| ½ teaspoon ground cinnamon | ½ teaspoon ground cinnamon |

Put the cherries in a baking dish.

Cream together the margarine, sugar and lemon rind until pale and fluffy. Beat in the egg yolks a little at a time, then stir in the milk, lemon juice, flour and cinnamon to give a loose, curd-like mixture.

Beat the egg whites until just stiff, then fold into the mixture and spoon on top of the cherries.

Place the dish in a roasting pan, then pour in enough hot water to come half way up the sides of the pan. Bake in a preheated moderate oven (180°C / 350°F, Gas Mark 4) for 40 to 45 minutes until the top is set, firm and golden. Serve hot.

**Serves 4**

# Gooseberry and Almond Crumble

| Metric/Imperial | American |
|---|---|
| 450 g / 1 lb gooseberries, topped and tailed | 2¾ cups gooseberries, topped and tailed |
| 2 tablespoons sugar | 2 tablespoons sugar |
| finely grated rind and juice of 1 orange | finely grated rind and juice of 1 orange |
| CRUMBLE: | CRUMBLE: |
| 100 g / 4 oz wholemeal flour or rolled oats | 1 cup wholewheat flour or rolled oats |
| 50 g / 2 oz vegetable margarine | ¼ cup vegetable margarine |
| 50 g / 2 oz soft brown sugar | ⅓ cup brown sugar |
| 50 g / 2 oz blanched almonds, flaked or chopped | ½ cup flaked or chopped blanched almonds |

Put the gooseberries in a 900 ml / 1½ pint / 3¾ cup pie dish. Sprinkle over the sugar, then pour over the orange juice, reserving the rind for the crumble.

To make the crumble: put the flour in a bowl, then rub in the margarine. Stir in the brown sugar, almonds and reserved orange rind, then spoon on top of the gooseberries to cover them completely.

Bake in a preheated moderately hot oven (200°C / 400°F, Gas Mark 6) for 30 minutes until the crumble is crisp and brown. Serve hot.

**Serves 4**

# Blackberry and Orange Stuffed Apples

**Metric/Imperial**
4 large cooking apples
225 g / 8 oz blackberries
finely grated rind and juice
   of 1 large orange
4 tablespoons soft brown
   sugar
1 tablespoon chopped mint

**American**
4 large baking apples
2 cups blackberries
finely grated rind and juice
   of 1 large orange
1/4 cup brown sugar
1 tablespoon chopped mint

Remove the cores from the apples, making a large hole for the stuffing. Make a shallow cut through the skin around the centre of each apple to prevent the skins bursting.

To make the stuffing: mix the blackberries with the orange rind, sugar and mint. Place the apples in a baking dish and divide the stuffing equally between the apples, pressing it well down into the centres. Spoon any remaining stuffing around the apples, then spoon over the orange juice.

Bake in a preheated moderate oven (180°C / 350°F, Gas Mark 4) for 45 minutes or until the apples are tender. Serve hot.

**Serves 4**

# Baked Grapefruit Soufflé

| Metric/Imperial | American |
|---|---|
| finely grated rind of 2 large grapefruit | finely grated rind of 2 large grapefruit |
| 25 g / 1 oz vegetable margarine | 2 tablespoons vegetable margarine |
| 25 g / 1 oz flour | ¼ cup flour |
| juice of 1 large grapefruit | juice of 1 large grapefruit |
| 1 grapefruit, peel and pith removed and divided into segments | 1 grapefruit, peel and pith removed and divided into segments |
| 50 g / 2 oz sugar | ¼ cup sugar |
| 4 egg yolks | 4 egg yolks |
| 5 egg whites | 5 egg whites |

Put the grapefruit rind and margarine in a pan and heat gently until the margarine has melted. Stir in the flour, then the grapefruit juice. Bring to the boil, stirring constantly to give a thick smooth sauce.

Add the grapefruit segments and simmer for 1 minute. Stir in the sugar, then remove from the heat and leave to cool slightly.

Beat the egg yolks into the grapefruit sauce. Beat the egg whites until stiff, then fold gently into the grapefruit mixture.

Pour into a 1.5 litre / 2½ pint / 6¼ cup soufflé dish. Bake in a preheated moderate oven (180°C / 350°F, Gas Mark 4) for 45 minutes until the soufflé is well risen, set and golden brown on top. Serve immediately.

**Serves 4**

*LEFT: Blackberry and orange stuffed apples; Spiced stuffed peaches*
*BELOW: Grapefruit soufflé*

# Spiced Stuffed Peaches

| Metric/Imperial | American |
|---|---|
| 4 large peaches | 4 large peaches |
| juice of 2 oranges | juice of 2 oranges |
| 2 tablespoons redcurrant jelly | 2 tablespoons redcurrant jelly |
| 1 cinnamon stick | 1 cinnamon stick |
| 2 cloves | 2 cloves |
| ½ teaspoon whole allspice | ½ teaspoon whole allspice |
| 2-3 tablespoons brandy (optional) | 2-3 tablespoons brandy (optional) |
| FILLING: | FILLING: |
| 1 egg, lightly beaten | 1 egg, lightly beaten |
| 50 g / 2 oz ground almonds | ½ cup ground almonds |
| 1 tablespoon finely chopped preserved ginger | 1 tablespoon finely chopped preserved ginger |
| 1 tablespoon soft brown sugar | 1 tablespoon brown sugar |

Cut the peaches in half. Remove the stones (seeds). Scoop out and reserve some of the flesh from the centre of each peach half to allow room for the filling.

To make the filling: put the egg in a bowl with the almonds, ginger, sugar and reserved peach flesh. Mix well, then spoon into the peach halves. Place the peaches in a baking dish.

Put the orange juice, redcurrant jelly and spices in a small pan. Heat gently until the jelly has dissolved, then bring to the boil. Pour over the peaches.

Bake in a preheated moderate oven (180°C / 350°F, Gas Mark 4) for about 20 minutes until the peaches are tender when pierced with a skewer. If liked, warm the brandy, pour over the peaches and set alight. Serve hot or cold.

**Serves 4**

# Hot Berry Snow

**Metric/Imperial**
450 g / 1 lb mixed red
  berries (strawberries,
  raspberries, redcurrants),
  hulled and stalks
  removed
1 tablespoon honey
150 ml / ¼ pint natural
  yogurt
2 eggs, separated
1 tablespoon flour
25 g / 1 oz ground almonds
2 tablespoons soft brown
  sugar

**American**
3-4 cups mixed red berries
  (strawberries, raspberries,
  redcurrants), hulled and
  stalks removed
1 tablespoon honey
⅔ cup unflavored yogurt
2 eggs, separated
1 tablespoon flour
¼ cup ground almonds
2 tablespoons brown sugar

Wash the fruit and place in a baking dish. Spoon over the honey.

Put the yogurt in a bowl, then beat in the egg yolks, flour and almonds.

Beat the egg whites until stiff, then fold into the yogurt mixture. Spoon over the fruit and sprinkle with the sugar.

Bake in a preheated moderately hot oven (200°C / 400°F, Gas Mark 6) for 15 to 20 minutes until the topping is risen and golden brown. Serve immediately.

**Serves 4**

# Hot Harlequin Soufflé

**Metric/Imperial**
175 g / 6 oz mixed dried
  fruit
450 ml / ¾ pint water
finely grated rind and juice
  of 1 lemon
25 g / 1 oz soft brown sugar
4 egg whites

**American**
1 cup mixed dried fruit
2 cups water
finely grated rind and juice
  of 1 lemon
3 tablespoons brown sugar
4 egg whites

Put the dried fruit in a bowl, pour over the water and lemon rind and juice and leave to soak overnight. Alternatively, pour over boiling water and soak for a few hours.

Transfer to a pan and bring to the boil. Lower the heat, cover and simmer for 30 minutes or until the fruit is tender. Drain and reserve the liquid.

Remove any stones (seeds) from the fruit. Make up the liquid to 150 ml / ¼ pint / ⅔ cup with water if necessary, then work the fruit and liquid to a smooth purée in an electric blender. Transfer to a large bowl, stir in the sugar and leave to cool.

Beat the egg whites until just stiff, then fold into the purée. Pour into a 1.5 litre / 2½ pint / 6¼ cup soufflé dish.

Bake in a preheated moderately hot oven (200°C / 400°F, Gas Mark 6) for 20 minutes until the soufflé has risen and the top is lightly browned. Serve immediately.

**Serves 4**

# Hot Fruit Compote

| **Metric/Imperial** | **American** |
|---|---|
| 175 g / 6 oz dried apricots | 1 cup dried apricots |
| 450 ml / ¾ pint dry cider | 2 cups hard cider |
| 3 tablespoons clear honey | 3 tablespoons clear honey |
| 150 ml / ¼ pint water | ⅔ cup water |
| 1 cinnamon stick | 1 cinnamon stick |
| 2 cloves | 2 cloves |
| 50 g / 2 oz seedless raisins | ⅓ cup seedless raisins |
| 1 large grapefruit, peel and pith removed and divided into segments | 1 large grapefruit, peel and pith removed and divided into segments |
| 2 bananas, peeled and cut into chunks | 2 bananas, peeled and cut into chunks |

Soak the apricots in the cider for 2 to 3 hours.

Place the apricots, cider, honey, water, cinnamon and cloves in a large pan. Bring to the boil, then lower the heat, cover and simmer gently for 15 to 25 minutes, until the apricots are just soft. Add the raisins and simmer for 5 minutes.

Discard the cinnamon stick and cloves. Add the grapefruit segments and banana chunks to the pan and heat through gently. Serve warm, with yogurt if liked.

**Serves 4**

# Strawberries

Strawberries are surprisingly – and gratifyingly – low in calories. It is only when you feel the need to sprinkle them with sugar and shroud them in cream that the trouble starts.

Learn some new strawberry habits. In Scotland, where they eat their porridge with salt, they eat strawberries with just a dusting of white pepper. Sceptics can prove for themselves that this really does release the flavour.

Or, try them sprinkled with fresh lemon or orange juice.

Or, make a sauce by puréeing some of the softer, over-ripe strawberries together with some raspberries or redcurrants and a little grated orange rind. Serve the more beautiful, whole strawberries on a layer of this and you will not miss the cream.

If you really must have cream with your strawberries, remember that soured cream is less fattening than single (light) cream, and only half as fattening as double (heavy) cream. Eke it out with some stiffly beaten egg white and the damage will be still less.

But best of all, for your waistline's sake, enjoy strawberries just as nature intended.

# Oven Baked Damsons

| Metric/Imperial | American |
| --- | --- |
| 450 g/ 1 lb damsons | 4 cups damsons |
| 1/2 teaspoon ground cinnamon | 1/2 teaspoon ground cinnamon |
| juice of 1 orange | juice of 1 orange |
| grated rind of 1 orange | grated rind of 1 orange |
| 2 tablespoons clear honey | 2 tablespoons clear honey |
| 1 tablespoon dry vermouth | 1 tablespoon dry vermouth |
| 2 tablespoons water | 2 tablespoons water |

Wipe but do not stone (pit) the damsons. Place them in a casserole.

In a saucepan, bring to the boil the cinnamon, orange juice, orange rind, honey, vermouth and water.

Pour this over the damsons. Cover with foil and bake in a preheated moderate oven (180°C/350°F, Gas Mark 4) for 30 minutes.

Serve either hot or cold.

This recipe is suitable for any member of the plum family.

**Serves 4**

# Cottage Pears

| Metric/Imperial | American |
| --- | --- |
| 4 ripe dessert pears | 4 ripe dessert pears |
| 1 tablespoon lemon juice | 1 tablespoon lemon juice |
| 100 g/ 4 oz cottage cheese, sieved | 1/2 cup cottage cheese, strained |
| 1/4 teaspoon freshly grated nutmeg | 1/4 teaspoon freshly grated nutmeg |
| 8 strawberries to decorate | 8 strawberries to decorate |

Chill the pears. Peel them if necessary, then halve them lengthwise, discarding pips and cores. Sprinkle the pears with lemon juice.

Blend together the cottage cheese and nutmeg.

Fill each hollowed pear half with the cheese mixture. Top each one with a strawberry.

**Serves 4**

# Tangy Fresh Orange Jelly

| Metric/Imperial | American |
| --- | --- |
| 3 large oranges | 3 large oranges |
| 1 lemon | 1 lemon |
| 300 ml/ 1/2 pint water | 1 1/4 cups water |
| 15 g/ 1/2 oz gelatine | 1 envelope gelatin |
| clear honey | clear honey |

Using a potato peeler, peel the oranges and lemon very thinly, taking care to leave the pith behind. Put the orange and lemon peel in a saucepan with the water, bring to the boil and allow to simmer for 10 minutes.

Put 4 tablespoons cold water in a basin. Sprinkle in the gelatine and allow to soak for 5 minutes. Add this to the pan containing the peel and water, away from the heat, and stir well until completely dissolved. Strain this into a measuring jug, add the strained juice of the oranges and lemon and make up to 600 ml/ 1 pint (2 1/2 cups), adding cold water if necessary.

Sweeten to taste with honey but keep it tangy. Pour into a moistened jelly mould and chill until set.

**Serves 4**

*ABOVE: A selection of berry fruits with a container of raspberry purée*

## Fresh Peaches with Raspberry Sauce

| Metric/Imperial | American |
|---|---|
| 6 ripe peaches | 6 ripe peaches |
| 225 g / 8 oz raspberries | 1½ cups raspberries |
| 1 tablespoon clear honey | 1 tablespoon clear honey |
| pinch of ground cinnamon | pinch of ground cinnamon |
| 1 tablespoon fresh orange juice | 1 tablespoon fresh orange juice |

Peel the peaches. If the skins are reluctant to come off, pour boiling water over the peaches, allow to stand for 30 seconds only, then plunge them immediately into cold water. Slice the peeled peaches into a serving bowl and chill.

Rub the raspberries through a nylon sieve (strainer), using a wooden spoon. Blend the honey, cinnamon and orange juice into the raspberry purée. Chill well before pouring over the peaches.

**Serves 4**

## Greek Fruit Salad

| Metric/Imperial | American |
|---|---|
| 2 bananas | 2 bananas |
| 1 apple | 1 apple |
| 2 oranges | 2 oranges |
| 1 tablespoon dry sherry | 1 tablespoon dry sherry |
| 250 ml / 8 fl oz natural yogurt | 1 cup unflavored yogurt |
| 2 tablespoons clear honey | 2 tablespoons clear honey |

Peel the bananas, apple and oranges. Cut all the fruit into very small pieces. Stir in the sherry and allow to stand in a cool place for at least 1 hour.

Whisk together the yogurt and honey. Stir this lightly into the fruit. Chill for a further 1 hour before serving.

**Serves 4**

# Banana Yogurt

| Metric/Imperial | American |
| --- | --- |
| 4 very ripe bananas | 4 very ripe bananas |
| 250 ml / 8 fl oz natural yogurt | 1 cup unflavored yogurt |
| 4 teaspoons clear honey | 4 teaspoons clear honey |

Peel and chop the bananas. Work the bananas and yogurt to a purée in an electric blender.

Serve chilled, in individual glasses, topping each one with a swirl of honey.

**Serves 4**

*BELOW: Melon balls with lemon sauce*

# Melon and Grapes

| Metric/Imperial | American |
| --- | --- |
| 1 small melon (Honeydew, Cantaloup or Rock) | 1 small melon (Honeydew, Cantaloup or Rock) |
| juice of 1 lemon | juice of 1 lemon |
| 1 small bunch seedless grapes, peeled | 1 cup seedless grapes, peeled |

Remove the skin and seeds carefully from the melon and cut the flesh into neat cubes. Pour the lemon juice over them and toss well.

Mix together the grapes and melon cubes. Chill well before serving.

**Serves 4**

# Melon Balls with Lemon Sauce

| Metric/Imperial | American |
| --- | --- |
| 1 ripe melon (Honeydew, Charentais, Cantaloup or Ogen) | 1 ripe melon (Honeydew, Charentais, Cantaloup or Ogen) |
| 2 lemons | 2 lemons |
| 1 tablespoon sugar | 1 tablespoon sugar |
| TO GARNISH: | TO GARNISH: |
| sprigs of mint | sprigs of mint |
| lemon slices | lemon slices |

Halve the melon and remove the seeds. Using a vegetable scoop make as many melon balls as possible. Chill them thoroughly while making the sauce.

Grate the rind of the lemons into a small pan. Squeeze the juice from the 2 lemons and measure it, adding enough water to make up to 150 ml / ¼ pint (⅔ cup). Add this to the rind, together with the sugar and any untidy scraps of melon which remain after the 'balling' process. Bring to the boil and allow to simmer for 5 minutes. Work this mixture to a purée in an electric blender, chill and put it in the bottom of a glass dish. Top it with the melon balls, mint and lemon slices.

**Serves 4**

*RIGHT: Melon and grapes*

# Pineapple Baskets

This is not so much a recipe as a method of serving fresh pineapple, making it attractive and easy to eat.

Halve the pineapple lengthwise, or, if it is very large, quarter it lengthwise, including the leaves.

Using a very sharp grapefruit knife, penetrate the flesh of the pineapple just underneath the hard centre core. Cut all the way along, then down and along the bottom edge, just inside the prickly skin.

Turn the half pineapple round and do the same at the other side.

When this is done it should be possible to remove all the tender flesh in one piece. But do not do this. Instead, cut it into neat, bite size pieces, but leave it looking like an intact demi-pineapple.

When the pineapple has been eaten you are left with a basket shape which is made up of all the inedible parts of the fruit – the centre core, prickly skin and leaves.

For a special party effect, you could remove just one or two of the cubes of pineapple and replace them with perfect whole strawberries or huge black grapes.

# Oranges and Grapes

| Metric/Imperial | American |
|---|---|
| 6 oranges, peel and pith removed | 6 oranges, peel and pith removed |
| juice of 1 lemon | juice of 1 lemon |
| rind of 1/2 lemon | rind of 1/2 lemon |
| 1 tablespoon demerara sugar | 1 tablespoon brown sugar |
| few drops vanilla essence | few drops vanilla extract |
| 225 g / 8 oz black grapes, seeded | 2 cups seeded pitted purple grapes |

Slice the oranges across thinly, taking care to catch all the juice. Put this juice in a small pan, together with the lemon juice. Using a potato peeler or sharp knife, remove the rind from 1/2 lemon. Add it to the pan, together with the sugar and vanilla essence (extract). Bring to the boil, and allow to cook quickly until well reduced.

Allow to cool, then pour this over the oranges, discarding the lemon rind. Add the grapes and chill before serving.

**Serves 4**

# Stuffed Pineapple

| Metric/Imperial | American |
|---|---|
| 2 small pineapples | 2 small pineapples |
| 2 oranges, peel and pith removed | 2 oranges, peel and pith removed |
| 1 tablespoon finely chopped stem ginger | 1 tablespoon finely chopped preserved ginger |

Halve the pineapples lengthwise, leaving any leaves, and scoop out the flesh. A grapefruit knife is useful for this process.

Dice the pineapple flesh. Divide the oranges into segments, carefully discarding any pips or membrane.

Mix together the pineapple, orange and ginger and fill each hollowed pineapple with this fruit mixture. Serve chilled.

**Serves 4**

# Compôte

| Metric/Imperial | American |
|---|---|
| 50 g / 2 oz sugar | 1/4 cup sugar |
| 150 ml / 1/4 pint water | 2/3 cup water |
| 1 lemon | 1 lemon |
| juice of 1 orange | juice of 1 orange |
| 1 large cooking apple, peeled, cored and sliced | 2 cups peeled, cored and sliced baking apple |
| 100 g / 4 oz blackberries | 1 cup blackberries |
| 100 g / 4 oz damsons, stoned | 1 cup damsons, pitted |
| 100 g / 4 oz black plums, stoned | 4 oz black plums, pitted |
| 100 g / 4 oz golden plums, stoned | 4 oz golden plums, pitted |

Put the sugar and water in a large, heavy pan. Add 2 or 3 large pieces of lemon rind and the strained juice of the lemon and the orange.

Bring to the boil, stirring, until the sugar has dissolved. Add the apple, blackberries, damsons and plums.

Simmer gently until the fruit is cooked. Remove the lemon rind and serve either hot or cold.

**Serves 4**

*RIGHT: Oranges and grapes*

# Rhubarb Meringue

| Metric/Imperial | American |
|---|---|
| 450 g / 1 lb rhubarb | 1 lb rhubarb |
| pinch of freshly grated nutmeg | pinch of freshly grated nutmeg |
| 2 tablespoons sugar | 2 tablespoons sugar |
| 3 egg whites | 3 egg whites |
| 2 tablespoons sifted icing sugar | 2 tablespoons sifted confectioner's sugar |

Wipe the rhubarb and cut it into 2.5 cm / 1 inch pieces. Put them in a deep casserole and sprinkle them with the nutmeg and sugar.

Whisk the egg whites until they are so stiff that the bowl may be safely turned upside down without them falling out. Carefully fold in the icing (confectioner's) sugar.

Pile this meringue on top of the rhubarb and bake in a preheated moderate oven (180°C / 350°F, Gas Mark 4) for 30 minutes.

This same 'meringue' treatment may be applied to any other fruit. Try it with plums, a mixture of apple and blackberries, apricots or gooseberries.

**Serves 4**

# Coeur à la Crême

| Metric/Imperial | American |
|---|---|
| 350 g / 12 oz cottage cheese | 1½ cups cottage cheese |
| 150 ml / ¼ pint natural yogurt | ⅔ cup unflavored yogurt |
| juice of ½ lemon | juice of ½ lemon |
| rind of ½ lemon | rind of ½ lemon |
| 2 teaspoons gelatine | 2 teaspoons gelatin |
| 2 tablespoons warm water | 2 tablespoons warm water |
| 4 teaspoons demerara sugar | 4 teaspoons brown sugar |
| ground cinnamon | ground cinnamon |

Using a wooden spoon, press the cottage cheese through a sieve (strainer), into a mixing bowl.

Blend in the yogurt, lemon juice and lemon rind.

Dissolve the gelatine in the warm water. Stir this into the cheese mixture, making sure that it is evenly distributed.

Line individual pierced moulds (heart-shaped, if possible) with cheesecloth. Fill each one with the cheese mixture and chill overnight.

Turn them out on to individual plates and sprinkle each one with a spoonful of brown sugar and a dusting of cinnamon.

To show them at their best, serve these pretty heart-shaped desserts on brightly coloured plates. Alternatively, line plain white plates with freshly washed blackcurrant leaves or fig leaves.

**Serves 4**

# Rhubarb and Yogurt Fool

| Metric/Imperial | American |
|---|---|
| 450 g / 1 lb rhubarb | 1 lb rhubarb |
| 2 tablespoons demerara sugar | 2 tablespoons brown sugar |
| 1 tablespoon grated orange rind | 1 tablespoon grated orange rind |
| 1 tablespoon fresh orange juice | 1 tablespoon fresh orange juice |
| pinch of ground ginger | pinch of ground ginger |
| 600 ml / 1 pint natural yogurt | 2½ cups unflavored yogurt |

Cut the rhubarb into 2.5 cm / 1 inch lengths. Gently stew the rhubarb with the sugar, orange rind, orange juice and ginger until very soft. Allow it to cool.

Stir in the yogurt, check for sweetness and chill for at least 1 hour before serving.

**Serves 4**

# Raspberry Sorbet (Sherbet)

*This dessert can also be made with blackcurrants.*

| Metric/Imperial | American |
|---|---|
| 450 g / 1 lb frozen raspberries in sugar | 3 cups frozen raspberries in sugar |
| 100 g / 4 oz sugar | ½ cup sugar |
| 300 ml / ½ pint water | 1¼ cups water |
| 2 egg whites | 2 egg whites |

Allow the raspberries to defrost at room temperature for 3 to 4 hours, then beat them to a rough purée.

Put the sugar and water into a pan. Heat gently, stirring, until the sugar dissolves. Bring to the boil, then boil, without stirring, for 8 minutes. Remove from the heat and set aside to cool.

Blend the cooled syrup and raspberry purée together, then pour into an ice cube tray or freezerproof container and place in the freezer or freezing compartment of the refrigerator. Freeze for 1 hour until half frozen and beginning to solidify. Scrape the purée into a bowl and beat briskly for a few minutes to prevent large crystals forming.

Beat the egg whites until stiff, then fold into the purée. Return the mixture to the freezerproof container and replace it in the freezer or freezing compartment and continue to freeze until set.

To serve: allow the sorbet (sherbet) to soften slightly at room temperature for about 10 minutes, or in the refrigerator for 20 minutes. Spoon into individual serving bowls and serve.

**Serves 6**

*RIGHT: Rhubarb and yogurt fool*

# Poached Apples

| Metric/Imperial | American |
|---|---|
| 4 eating apples | 4 dessert apples |
| juice of ½ lemon | juice of ½ lemon |
| 150 ml / ¼ pint fresh orange juice | ⅔ cup fresh orange juice |
| 2 tablespoons water | 2 tablespoons water |
| pinch of ground cinnamon | pinch of ground cinnamon |

Peel the apples carefully, without removing the stalks. Roll each apple in lemon juice to prevent browning. Poach them gently in the orange juice and water, flavoured with cinnamon, until cooked but not too soft. A frying pan (skillet) is useful for this process as it allows space for turning the apples without damaging them.

Serve hot or cold.

For a special occasion, flambé the poached apples. Gin is the least calorific of the spirits and you need only 1 tablespoon for quite a spectacular effect. Warm the gin in a soup ladle and ignite it just as you pour it over the hot poached apples.

**Serves 4**

# Apple Slices with Honey

| Metric/Imperial | American |
|---|---|
| 8 eating apples, peeled, cored and sliced | 6 cups peeled, cored and sliced dessert apples |
| 2 cloves | 2 cloves |
| juice of 1 orange | juice of 1 orange |
| rind of 1 orange | rind of 1 orange |
| 2 tablespoons clear honey | 2 tablespoons clear honey |
| 2 tablespoons water | 2 tablespoons water |

Place the apples and cloves in a baking dish.

Mix together the orange juice, orange rind, honey and water. Pour this over the apples. Cover with foil and bake in a preheated moderate oven (180°C / 350°F, Gas Mark 4) for 20 to 25 minutes.

Serve either hot or cold.

**Serves 4**

*BELOW: Poached apples*

# Baked Apricots

**Metric/Imperial**
450 g / 1 lb apricots, halved and stoned
1 tablespoon fresh orange juice
25 g / 1 oz vanilla sugar*

**American**
1 lb apricots, halved and pitted
1 tablespoon fresh orange juice
2 tablespoons vanilla sugar*

Arrange the apricots in an ovenproof dish. Sprinkle them with the orange juice, then the vanilla sugar.

Bake in a preheated cool oven (140°C / 275°F, Gas Mark 1) for 1 hour.

Serve hot or cold.

**Serves 4**

*Vanilla sugar can be bought in rather expensive small packets, or it can be made at home by storing a vanilla pod (bean) in an airtight container of caster (superfine) sugar. The vanilla pod (bean) flavours the sugar and will not need replacing for months. Just fill up with more sugar as it is needed.

# Snowy Apple

**Metric/Imperial**
50 g / 2 oz sugar
150 ml / ¼ pint water
700 g / 1½ lb cooking apples, peeled, cored and sliced
1 egg yolk, beaten
2 egg whites, stiffly beaten
ground cinnamon

**American**
4 tablespoons sugar
⅔ cup water
6 cups peeled, cored and sliced baking apples
1 egg yolk, beaten
2 egg whites, stiffly beaten
ground cinnamon

Put the sugar and water in a heavy pan and heat gently, stirring, until the sugar has dissolved. Add the apples and allow to simmer gently until they are very soft.

Work the apples to a purée in an electric blender, or rub them through a sieve (strainer). Allow to cool slightly, then blend in the egg yolk. Mix well and allow to cool completely. Fold in the egg whites.

Transfer the snowy apple to a glass serving dish and top with a sprinkling of cinnamon.

**Serves 4**

# Baked Apple with Orange

**Metric/Imperial**
4 medium cooking apples
2 tablespoons marmalade
2 tablespoons fresh orange juice
1 teaspoon grated orange rind
thin strips of orange peel to garnish

**American**
4 medium baking apples
2 tablespoons marmalade
2 tablespoons fresh orange juice
1 teaspoon grated orange rind
thin strips of orange peel to garnish

Carefully core but do not peel the apples. Make small slits in the top of each apple to prevent the skin from bursting during cooking.

Blend together the marmalade, orange juice and orange rind.

Fill the centre of each apple with this mixture. Bake them in the centre of a preheated moderate oven (180°C / 350°F, Gas Mark 4) for 1 hour.

Garnish each baked apple with thin strips of orange peel.

**Serves 4**

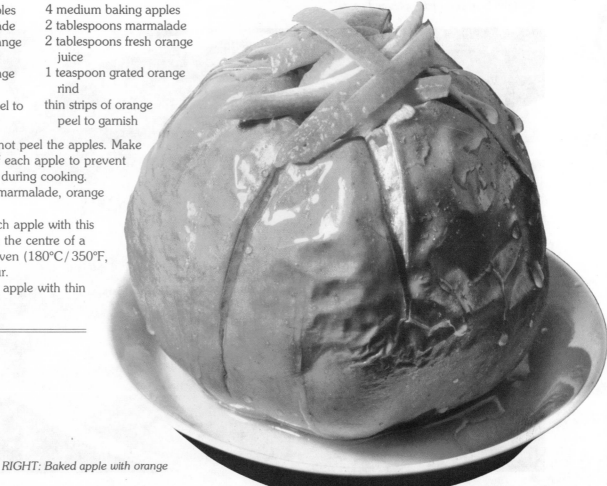

*RIGHT: Baked apple with orange*

# Pink Poached Apples and Pears

| Metric/Imperial | American |
|---|---|
| 450 g/ 1 lb red fruit, such as stoned plums, redcurrants, raspberries, loganberries or rhubarb, either a mixture or a single variety | 3 cups red fruit, such as pitted plums, redcurrants, raspberries, loganberries or rhubarb, either a mixture or a single variety |
| sugar, if needed | sugar, if needed |
| 2 eating apples | 2 dessert apples |
| 2 dessert pears | 2 dessert pears |

Poach the red fruit gently in very little water, with sugar if a sour fruit is chosen. Cook until quite soft then work to a purée in an electric blender. Check for sweetness.

Peel the apples and pears carefully, without removing the stalks. Gently poach them in the red purée until cooked but not too soft.

Serve either hot or cold.

**Serves 4**

# West Country Pears

| Metric/Imperial | American |
|---|---|
| 300 ml/ ½ pint dry cider | 1¼ cups hard cider |
| 2 strips lemon rind | 2 strips lemon rind |
| 1 stick of cinnamon, or ¼ teaspoon ground cinnamon | 1 stick of cinnamon, or ¼ teaspoon ground cinnamon |
| few drops cochineal (optional) | few drops cochineal (optional) |
| 4 dessert pears | 4 dessert pears |

Place the cider, lemon rind, cinnamon and cochineal, if used, in a pan. Bring to the boil, cover and boil for 1 minute.

Peel the pears carefully, without removing the stalks. Stand them upright in a casserole dish, cutting a thin slice from the base of any pear which threatens to fall over.

Pour over the hot cider, cover and cook in a preheated moderate oven (180°C/350°F, Gas Mark 4) for 30 to 40 minutes, basting from time to time.

Carefully transfer the cooked pears to a serving dish, and strain the liquid over them.

Serve hot or cold.

**Serves 4**

BELOW: Pink poached apples and pears

RIGHT: West country pears

# WHOLEGRAIN BAKING

Home-baked cakes, scones and biscuits (cookies) might seem inevitably to contain too many 'unhealthy ingredients' and too many calories to have any place in a healthy diet, but this need not follow, if ingredients are chosen carefully. The recipes in this chapter are based upon wholewheat flour and natural sugars rather than the refined ingredients normally used for baking.

A wheat grain has three components: the starchy inner endosperm, the outer bran, and the wheatgerm. The refining of flour removes the bran and the wheatgerm, leaving only the starchy endosperm. The extraction rate describes the percentage of the original grain that remains in the flour.

Wholewheat (or wholemeal) flour has a 100 per cent extraction rate because it contains all the original grain and it has a coarse texture. Wheatmeal or brown flour, with an 80 or 90 per cent extraction rate, contains a proportion of bran and germ and the texture is finer than that of wholewheat flour. Wheaten flour is brown flour with extra pieces of whole grain added. Granary flour has malted wheat and rye grains added to a brown flour base.

Although the vitamin and mineral contents are lowered as the extraction rate drops, millers are required by law to restore them to that of an 80 or 90 per cent extraction rate. White flour should therefore be as nutritious as brown flour, but all the fibre supplied by the bran is lost.

Most people prefer white bread, yet wholewheat bread is certainly better for us because of the higher proportion of roughage it provides and it is delicious – especially when home-made. A number of other cereals can be used in baking. Oatmeal and muesli make good and nourishing cakes and biscuits (cookies) with a distinctive 'nutty' flavour.

Fats are required for most cakes and biscuits (cookies). To moderate the intake of animal fats use vegetable margarine rather than butter; it gives an excellently light texture to cakes and is easier to blend.

Sweetening is essential in cake-baking, but refined sugars can easily be avoided. Natural brown sugars, to which nothing is added or taken away, impart excellent flavour and colour to cakes and biscuits (cookies). Demerara (raw) sugar has a crunchy texture and is good for biscuits (cookies) and cake toppings. Unrefined Muscovado or Barbados sugar is soft and sticky, finely grained, and comes in dark and light varieties so that it can be used in all types of cakes. Molasses or Black Barbados sugar is very dark and strongly flavoured – perfect for gingerbread and fruit cakes.

Honey is a natural sweetener which has traces of minerals and vitamins. The simple sugars contained in honey – glucose and fructose – are quickly absorbed by the body and utilized for energy. A little honey added to bread dough, cakes and biscuits (cookies) will greatly improve the flavour. In cake recipes, a proportion of one-quarter honey to three-quarters sugar will give an excellent flavour and the cake will keep longer. Honey whipped into a little cream or vegetable margarine makes a good filling for cakes or a topping for wholewheat biscuits (cookies).

There is no special trick in wholewheat baking, except to remember that flours have different absorption rates. Liquid should be added gradually and mixed in carefully until completely absorbed. If wholewheat flour is substituted for white flour in a recipe, it may be necessary to add a little more liquid to get a satisfactory consistency.

Wholewheat recipes are generally a little more 'chewy' and flavoursome than those made with white flour, and are delicious served at any time of the day.

*Farmhouse bread (page 218); Fruit malt loaf (page 219);*
*Bran bread (page 218); Wholewheat baps (page 218)*

# Farmhouse Bread

| Metric/Imperial | American |
|---|---|
| 1.5 kg / 3 lb wholemeal bread flour | 12 cups wholewheat flour |
| 25 g / 1 oz sea salt | 1 tablespoon coarse salt |
| 25 g / 1 oz Muscovado sugar | 1½ tablespoons Barbados sugar |
| 25 g / 1 oz fresh yeast | 1 cake compressed yeast |
| 900 ml / 1½ pints lukewarm water | 3¾ cups lukewarm water |
| 1 tablespoon vegetable oil | 1 tablespoon vegetable oil |
| beaten egg to glaze | beaten egg to glaze |

Put the flour, salt and sugar in a warm bowl and mix well. Blend the yeast with a little of the water, then stir into the remaining water and add to the dry ingredients with the oil. Mix to a soft dough.

Turn out onto a lightly floured surface and knead for 5 minutes until smooth. Place the dough in a warm, greased bowl. Cover with a damp cloth and leave in a warm place for about 1 hour until doubled in size.

Turn out onto the floured surface and knead again for 5 minutes, then divide the dough into 4 pieces. Fold each piece into 3, then place in greased, warmed 450 g / 1 lb / 8 × 4½ × 2½ inch loaf tins. Cover with a damp cloth and leave in a warm place for about 30 minutes until the dough rises to the tops of the tins.

Brush the dough with beaten egg, then bake in a preheated hot oven (230°C / 450°F, Gas Mark 8) for 40 minutes. Turn out onto a wire rack and leave to cool.

**Makes four 450 g / 1 lb loaves**

# Bran Bread

| Metric/Imperial | American |
|---|---|
| 550 g / 1¼ lb wholemeal bread flour | 5 cups wholewheat flour |
| 100 g / 4 oz bran | 2 cups bran |
| 15 g / ½ oz sea salt | 1½ teaspoons coarse salt |
| 25 g / 1 oz Muscovado sugar | 1½ tablespoons Barbados sugar |
| 25 g / 1 oz fresh yeast | 1 cake compressed yeast |
| 450 ml / ¾ pint lukewarm water | 2 cups lukewarm water |
| 1 tablespoon corn oil | 1 tablespoon corn oil |
| TO FINISH: | TO FINISH: |
| 2 tablespoons cold water | 2 tablespoons cold water |
| pinch of salt | pinch of salt |
| 2 tablespoons rolled oats | 2 tablespoons rolled oats |

Put the flour, bran, salt and sugar in a warm bowl and mix well. Blend the yeast with a little of the water, then stir into the remaining water and add to the dry ingredients with the oil. Mix to a firm dough.

Turn out onto a lightly floured surface and knead for 5 minutes until smooth. Shape the dough into a ball and place in a greased polythene (plastic) bag. Tie loosely and leave in a warm place for about 1 hour until doubled in size.

Remove the dough and knead again on the floured surface for 5 minutes, then divide in half. Shape each piece of dough and place in greased, warmed 450 g / 1 lb / 8 × 4½ × 2½ inch loaf tins, tucking in the corners lightly but firmly. Cover with greased polythene (plastic) and leave in a warm place for about 30 minutes until the dough rises to the tops of the tins.

Mix the cold water and salt together, then brush over the tops of the loaves and sprinkle with the oats. Bake in a preheated hot oven (230°C / 450°F, Gas Mark 8) for 35 minutes until well-risen and crisp. Turn out onto a wire rack and leave to cool.

**Makes two 450 g / 1 lb loaves**

# Wholewheat Baps (Buns)

| Metric/Imperial | American |
|---|---|
| 675 g / 1½ lb wholemeal bread flour | 6 cups wholewheat flour |
| 1 teaspoon sea salt | 1 teaspoon coarse salt |
| 25 g / 1 oz Muscovado sugar | 1½ tablespoons Barbados sugar |
| 25 g / 1 oz fresh yeast | 1 cake compressed yeast |
| 450 ml / ¾ pint lukewarm water | 2 cups lukewarm water |
| 1 tablespoon oil | 1 tablespoon oil |

Put the flour, salt and sugar in a warm bowl and mix well. Blend the yeast with a little of the water, then stir into the remaining water and add to the dry ingredients with the oil. Mix to a soft dough.

Turn out onto a lightly floured surface and knead for 5 minutes until smooth. Place the dough in a warm, greased bowl. Cover and leave in a warm place for about 15 minutes until doubled in size.

Turn out onto the floured surface and knead again for 2 minutes, then divide the dough into 12 pieces and shape into round flat baps (buns). Place the baps (buns) on greased, warmed baking sheets and sprinkle with a little wholemeal (wholewheat) flour. Cover with a piece of oiled polythene (plastic) and leave to rise in a warm place until doubled in size.

Bake in a preheated hot oven (220°C / 425°F, Gas Mark 7) for 15 minutes. Remove the baps (buns) from the baking sheets, then wrap them in a clean cloth; this will keep them soft by trapping the steam as they cool.

**Makes 12 baps (buns)**

# Cheese Loaf

| Metric/Imperial | American |
| --- | --- |
| 225 g / 8 oz wholemeal bread flour | 2 cups wholewheat flour |
| 1 teaspoon sea salt | 1 teaspoon coarse salt |
| 1 teaspoon mustard powder | 1 teaspoon mustard powder |
| 100 g / 4 oz Cheddar cheese, grated | 1 cup grated Cheddar cheese |
| 15 g / ½ oz fresh yeast | ½ cake compressed yeast |
| 150 ml / ¼ pint lukewarm water | ⅔ cup lukewarm water |

Put the flour, salt, mustard and cheese in a warm bowl and mix well. Blend the yeast with a little of the water, then stir into the remaining water and add to the dry ingredients. Mix to a soft dough.

Turn out onto a lightly floured surface and knead for 5 minutes until smooth. Place the dough in a warm, greased bowl. Cover and leave in a warm place for about 1 hour until doubled in size.

Turn out onto the floured surface and knead again for 2 minutes, then fold into 3 and place in a greased, warmed 450 g / 1 lb / 8 × 4½ × 2½ inch loaf tin. Cover with a clean cloth and leave in a warm place for about 20 minutes until the dough rises to the top of the tin.

Bake in a preheated hot oven (220°C / 425°F, Gas Mark 7) for 10 minutes, then reduce the heat to moderately hot (190°C / 375°F, Gas Mark 5) and bake for a further 35 minutes. Turn out onto a wire rack and leave to cool.

**Makes one 450 g / 1 lb loaf**

# Fruit Malt Loaf

| Metric/Imperial | American |
| --- | --- |
| 225 g / 8 oz wholemeal flour | 2 cups wholewheat flour |
| ¼ teaspoon sea salt | ¼ teaspoon coarse salt |
| 100 g / 4 oz sultanas | ¾ cup seedless white raisins |
| 25 g / 1 oz vegetable margarine | 2 tablespoons vegetable margarine |
| 50 g / 2 oz malt extract | 3 tablespoons malt extract |
| 25 g / 1 oz black treacle | 1½ tablespoons molasses |
| 25 g / 1 oz fresh yeast | 1 cake compressed yeast |
| 75 ml / 2½ fl oz lukewarm water | ⅓ cup lukewarm water |
| 1 tablespoon clear honey to glaze | 1 tablespoon clear honey to glaze |

Put the flour, salt and sultanas (seedless white raisins) in a warm bowl and mix well. Put the margarine, malt extract and black treacle (molasses) in a pan and heat gently until the margarine has melted. Leave to cool for 5 minutes.

Blend the yeast with the water, then add to the dry ingredients with the melted mixture. Mix to a soft dough.

Turn out onto a lightly floured surface and knead for 5 minutes until smooth. Place the dough in a warmed, greased bowl. Cover and leave in a warm place for about 1 hour until doubled in size.

Turn out onto the floured surface and knead again for 5 minutes. Fold the dough into 3, then place in a greased, warmed 450 g / 1 lb / 8 × 4½ × 2½ inch loaf tin. Cover with a clean damp cloth and leave in a warm place for about 20 minutes until the dough rises to the top of the tin.

Bake in a preheated moderately hot oven (200°C / 400°F, Gas Mark 6) for 45 minutes. Turn out onto a wire rack, brush with honey, then leave to cool.

**Makes one 450 g / 1 lb loaf**

# Farmhouse Scones

| Metric/Imperial | American |
|---|---|
| 225 g / 8 oz wholemeal flour | 2 cups wholewheat flour |
| pinch of sea salt | pinch of coarse salt |
| 1 teaspoon baking powder | 1 teaspoon baking powder |
| 50 g / 2 oz vegetable margarine | 1/4 cup vegetable margarine |
| 25 g / 1 oz Muscovado sugar | 1 1/2 tablespoons Barbados sugar |
| 25 g / 1 oz sultanas | 3 tablespoons seedless white raisins |
| 1 egg | 1 egg |
| 5 tablespoons milk | 1/3 cup milk |
| milk to glaze | milk to glaze |

Put the flour, salt and baking powder in a bowl and mix well. Rub in the margarine until the mixture resembles coarse breadcrumbs, then stir in the sugar and sultanas (seedless white raisins). Beat the egg with the milk, then gradually add to the dry mixture and mix to a soft dough.

# Cottage Cheese Griddlecakes

| Metric/Imperial | American |
|---|---|
| 25 g / 1 oz vegetable margarine, melted | 2 tablespoons vegetable margarine, melted |
| 100 g / 4 oz cottage cheese | 1/2 cup cottage cheese |
| 2 eggs, beaten | 2 eggs, beaten |
| 50 g / 2 oz wholemeal self-raising flour | 1/2 cup wholewheat self-rising flour |
| 1 tablespoon milk | 1 tablespoon milk |

Put the margarine and cottage cheese in a bowl and mix well. Beat in the eggs, then stir in the flour and milk and beat to a smooth thick batter.

Grease a griddle or heavy-based frying pan (skillet) very lightly with fat, then heat until very hot.

Drop tablespoonfuls of the batter onto the hot surface. Cook for 1 minute until just set, then turn over and cook for a further 1 minute. Turn over again and continue cooking until the griddlecakes are set and golden in colour.

Transfer to a wire rack and cover with a clean cloth to keep hot while cooking the remaining batter. Serve hot with honey or a savoury spread.

**Makes 10 to 12 griddlecakes**

*ABOVE: Cottage cheese griddlecakes*
*RIGHT: Yogurt wholewheat scones; Farmhouse scones*

Turn out onto a lightly floured surface and roll out to 1 cm / ½ inch thickness. Cut out 12 rounds with a 5 cm / 2 inch biscuit cutter and place on a greased baking sheet.

Brush the tops with a little milk to glaze, then bake in a preheated moderately hot oven (200°C / 400°F, Gas Mark 6) for 15 minutes. Transfer to a wire rack and leave to cool.

**Makes 12 scones**

# Yogurt Wholewheat Scones

| **Metric/Imperial** | **American** |
|---|---|
| 225 g / 8 oz wholemeal flour | 2 cups wholewheat flour |
| ½ teaspoon salt | ½ teaspoon salt |
| 1½ teaspoons baking powder | 1½ teaspoons baking powder |
| 25 g / 1 oz vegetable margarine | 2 tablespoons vegetable margarine |
| 150 ml / ¼ pint natural yogurt | ⅔ cup unflavored yogurt |

Put the flour, salt and baking powder in a bowl and stir well to mix. Rub in the margarine, then stir in the yogurt and mix to a soft dough.

Turn out onto a lightly floured surface and knead lightly for 30 seconds. Roll out to 2 cm / ¾ inch thickness, cut out 10 rounds with a 5 cm / 2 inch biscuit cutter and place on a greased baking sheet.

Bake in a preheated moderately hot oven (200°C / 400°F, Gas Mark 6) for 12 minutes. Transfer to a wire rack and leave to cool. Serve with honey or a cheese spread.

**Makes 10 scones**

# Honey Fruit Loaf

| Metric/Imperial | American |
|---|---|
| 75 g / 3 oz vegetable margarine | 1/3 cup vegetable margarine |
| 75 g / 3 oz Muscovado sugar | 1/2 cup Barbados sugar |
| 1 egg, beaten | 1 egg, beaten |
| 2 tablespoons honey | 2 tablespoons honey |
| 225 g / 8 oz wholemeal self-raising flour | 2 cups wholewheat self-rising flour |
| 1/4 teaspoon salt | 1/4 teaspoon salt |
| 1 teaspoon ground mixed spice | 1/2 teaspoon ground allspice |
| 175 g / 6 oz mixed dried fruit | 1/2 teaspoon ground cinnamon |
| 4 tablespoons milk | 1 cup mixed dried fruit |
| | 1/4 cup milk |

Cream the margarine and sugar until light and fluffy, then beat in the egg and honey. Stir in the flour, salt and spice, then beat in the fruit and milk until thoroughly mixed.

Spoon the mixture into a greased 750 g / 1 1/2 lb / 10 × 4 × 4 inch loaf pan, then bake in a preheated moderately hot oven (190°C / 375°F, Gas Mark 5) for 45 minutes. Turn out onto a wire rack and leave to cool.

**Makes one 750 g / 1 1/2 lb fruit loaf**

# Walnut Squares

| Metric/Imperial | American |
|---|---|
| 1 egg, beaten | 1 egg, beaten |
| 225 g / 8 oz Muscovado sugar | 1 1/3 cups Barbados sugar |
| 75 g / 3 oz wholemeal flour | 3/4 cup wholewheat flour |
| 1 teaspoon bicarbonate of soda | 1 teaspoon baking soda |
| 1/4 teaspoon salt | 1/4 teaspoon salt |
| 100 g / 4 oz walnuts, finely chopped | 1 cup finely chopped walnuts |

Put the egg and sugar in a bowl and mix well. Mix the flour, soda and salt together, then stir into the egg mixture. Stir in the nuts.

Spread the mixture in a greased 20 cm / 8 inch square tin (pan). Bake in a preheated moderate oven (180°C / 350°F, Gas Mark 4) for 20 minutes. Leave to cool in the tin, then cut into squares before serving.

**Makes 16 squares**

# Honey Cake

| Metric/Imperial | American |
|---|---|
| 100 g / 4 oz vegetable margarine | 1/2 cup vegetable margarine |
| 50 g / 2 oz Muscovado sugar | 1/3 cup Barbados sugar |
| 3 tablespoons honey | 3 tablespoons honey |
| 2 eggs, lightly beaten | 2 eggs, lightly beaten |
| 225 g / 8 oz wholemeal flour | 2 cups wholewheat flour |
| 1 tablespoon baking powder | 1 tablespoon baking powder |
| 1 teaspoon ground cinnamon | 1 teaspoon ground cinnamon |
| 120 ml / 4 fl oz milk (approximately) | 1/2 cup milk (approximately) |
| 25 g / 1 oz flaked almonds | 1/4 cup sliced almonds |

Cream the margarine and sugar until light and fluffy, then beat in the honey. Add the eggs a little at a time, adding a little of the flour after each addition.

Mix the remaining flour with the baking powder and cinnamon, then beat into the creamed mixture with enough milk to make a soft dropping consistency.

Sprinkle the almonds over the base of a greased 18 cm / 7 inch square cake tin. Spoon in the mixture.

Bake in a preheated moderate oven (180°C / 350°F, Gas Mark 4) for 1 hour. Turn out onto a wire rack and leave to cool.

**Makes one 18 cm / 7 inch square cake**

# Parkin

| Metric/Imperial | American |
|---|---|
| 100 g / 4 oz wholemeal flour | 1 cup wholewheat flour |
| 350 g / 12 oz medium oatmeal | 2 cups medium oatmeal |
| 1 teaspoon ground ginger | 1 teaspoon ground ginger |
| 100 g / 4 oz vegetable margarine | ½ cup vegetable margarine |
| 100 g / 4 oz honey | ⅓ cup honey |
| 100 g / 4 oz black treacle | ⅓ cup molasses |
| 4 tablespoons milk | ¼ cup milk |
| ½ teaspoon bicarbonate of soda | ½ teaspoon baking soda |

Put the flour, oatmeal and ginger in a bowl and mix well. Put the margarine, honey and black treacle (molasses) in a pan and heat gently until the margarine has melted. Add to the dry ingredients and mix well.

Heat the milk until lukewarm, stir in the soda, then add to the flour mixture and beat well. Pour the mixture into a greased 28 × 18 cm / 11 × 7 inch cake tin.

Bake in a preheated moderate oven (160°C / 325°F, Gas Mark 3) for 1½ hours. Leave to cool in the tin for 10 minutes, then turn out onto a wire rack and leave to cool completely.

Store in an airtight tin for 3 to 4 days before cutting.

**Makes one 28 × 18 cm / 11 × 7 inch cake**

# Ginger Honey Cake

| Metric/Imperial | American |
|---|---|
| 75 g / 3 oz vegetable margarine | ⅓ cup vegetable margarine |
| 50 g / 2 oz Muscovado sugar | ⅓ cup Barbados sugar |
| 2 tablespoons honey | 2 tablespoons honey |
| 1 egg, beaten with 1 egg yolk | 1 egg, beaten with 1 egg yolk |
| 175 g / 6 oz wholemeal self-raising flour | 1½ cups wholewheat self-rising flour |
| pinch of salt | pinch of salt |
| 1 teaspoon ground ginger | 1 teaspoon ground ginger |
| 1 teaspoon ground cinnamon | 1 teaspoon ground cinnamon |
| 6 tablespoons milk (approximately) | 6 tablespoons milk (approximately) |

Cream the margarine and sugar until light and fluffy, then beat in the honey. Add the egg mixture a little at a time, adding a little of the flour after each addition.

Mix the remaining flour with the salt, ginger and cinnamon, then beat into the creamed mixture with enough milk to make a soft dropping consistency.

Spoon the mixture into a greased 18 cm / 7 inch round cake tin lined with greased greaseproof paper or non-stick parchment.

Bake in a preheated moderate oven (170°C / 325°F, Gas Mark 4) for 50 minutes. Turn out onto a wire rack, carefully remove the paper and leave to cool.

**Makes one 18 cm / 7 inch round cake**

*Oatmeal crunchies (page 226); Wholewheat cheese*

# Nutty Fruit Chews

*For these, use a mixture of raisins, sultanas (seedless white raisins), figs, dates, prunes and apricots.*

| Metric/Imperial | American |
|---|---|
| 450 g / 1 lb mixed dried fruit | 3 cups mixed dried fruit |
| 100 g / 4 oz chopped mixed nuts | 1 cup chopped mixed nuts |
| 100 g / 4 oz clear honey | ⅓ cup clear honey |

Put the large fruit in a bowl and pour on enough boiling water to cover. Leave to stand for 5 minutes, then drain off the water. Put all the fruit through the fine blade of a mincer (grinder), then stir in the nuts and honey until well mixed.

Spread the mixture in a 20 cm / 8 inch square tin lined with foil. Cover with more foil, then place weights on top so that the surface is evenly pressed down. Leave in a cool place for 12 hours. Cut into squares before serving.

**Makes 16 squares**

# Fruit Slices

| Metric/Imperial | American |
|---|---|
| wholewheat pastry made with 225 g / 8 oz flour (see page 227) | wholewheat dough made with 2 cups flour (see page 227) |
| 100 g / 4 oz currants | 2/3 cup currants |
| 100 g / 4 oz sultanas | 2/3 cup seedless white raisins |
| 1 large cooking apple, peeled, cored and grated | 1 large baking apple, peeled, cored and grated |
| finely grated rind of 1 orange | finely grated rind of 1 orange |
| juice of 1/2 lemon | juice of 1/2 lemon |
| 50 g / 2 oz demerara sugar | 1/3 cup raw sugar |
| TOPPING: | TOPPING: |
| 1 egg white, lightly beaten | 1 egg white, lightly beaten |
| little demerara sugar | little raw sugar |

Divide the pastry dough in half. Roll out one piece and use to line the base of a shallow 28 × 20 cm / 11 × 8 inch tin.

Mix the fruit, orange rind, lemon juice and sugar together, then spread this mixture over the dough. Roll out the remaining dough and use to cover the fruit mixture.

Brush with egg white and sprinkle with sugar. Bake in a preheated hot oven (220°C / 425°F, Gas Mark 7) for 25 minutes. Leave to cool in the tin. Cut into slices before serving.

**Makes 16 slices**

# Digestive Biscuits (Graham Crackers)

| Metric/Imperial | American |
|---|---|
| 350 g / 12 oz wholemeal flour | 3 cups wholewheat flour |
| 2 teaspoons sea salt | 2 teaspoons coarse salt |
| 150 g / 5 oz vegetable margarine | 5/8 cup vegetable margarine |
| 50 g / 2 oz Muscovado sugar | 1/3 cup Barbados sugar |
| 1 egg, beaten with 4 tablespoons cold water | 1 egg, beaten with 1/4 cup cold water |

Put the flour and salt in a bowl, then rub in the margarine until the mixture resembles fine breadcrumbs. Stir in the sugar, then add the egg and water mixture and mix to a soft dough.

Turn out onto a lightly floured surface and knead lightly. Roll out to 5 mm / 1/4 inch thickness, then cut out 40 rounds with a 6 cm / 2 1/2 inch biscuit cutter.

Place the rounds on greased baking sheets and prick each one 4 times with a fork. Bake in a preheated moderate oven (180°C / 350°F, Gas Mark 4) for 25 minutes. Transfer to a wire rack and leave to cool.

**Makes 40 biscuits (crackers)**

# Wholewheat Cheese Biscuits (Crackers)

| Metric/Imperial | American |
|---|---|
| 100 g / 4 oz wholemeal flour | 1 cup wholewheat flour |
| 1/2 teaspoon sea salt | 1/2 teaspoon coarse salt |
| 1 teaspoon mustard powder | 1 teaspoon mustard powder |
| 25 g / 1 oz vegetable margarine | 2 tablespoons vegetable margarine |
| 225 g / 8 oz Cheddar cheese, finely grated | 2 cups finely grated Cheddar cheese |
| 2 tablespoons cold water | 2 tablespoons cold water |

Put the flour, salt and mustard in a bowl and mix well. Rub in the margarine, then stir in the cheese. Add the water and mix to a firm dough.

Turn out onto a lightly floured surface and knead lightly. Roll out to 5 mm / 1/4 inch thickness, then cut out 30 rounds with a 5 cm / 2 inch biscuit cutter.

Place the rounds on greased baking sheets and prick each one 3 times with a fork. Bake in a preheated hot oven (230°C / 450°F, Gas Mark 8) for 6 minutes. Transfer to a wire rack and leave to cool.

**Makes 30 biscuits (crackers)**

# Honey Cookies

| Metric/Imperial | American |
|---|---|
| 100 g / 4 oz vegetable margarine | 1/2 cup vegetable margarine |
| 100 g / 4 oz demerara sugar | 2/3 cup raw sugar |
| 1 egg, beaten | 1 egg, beaten |
| 1 tablespoon honey | 1 tablespoon honey |
| 225 g / 8 oz self-raising flour | 2 cups self-rising flour |
| pinch of salt | pinch of salt |
| 50 g / 2 oz chopped mixed nuts | 1/2 cup chopped mixed nuts |

Cream the margarine and sugar until light and fluffy, then beat in the egg and honey. Sift the flour and salt together, then beat gradually into the creamed mixture. Add the nuts and mix well.

Divide the dough into 36 pieces, about the size of walnuts, and roll each one into a ball. Place on greased baking sheets, flattening each ball with a fork dipped in cold water. Bake in a preheated moderate oven (180°C / 350°F, Gas Mark 4) for 12 minutes. Transfer carefully to a wire rack and leave to cool.

**Makes 36 cookies**

# Oatmeal Crunchies

| Metric/Imperial | American |
|---|---|
| 225 g / 8 oz wholemeal flour | 2 cups wholewheat flour |
| 75 g / 3 oz medium oatmeal | 1/2 cup oatmeal |
| 75 g / 3 oz bran | 1 1/2 cups bran |
| 150 g / 5 oz Muscovado sugar | 3/4 cup Barbados sugar |
| 1/2 teaspoon ground ginger | 1/2 teaspoon ground ginger |
| 1/2 teaspoon ground mixed spice | 1/4 teaspoon ground allspice |
| 100 g / 4 oz vegetable margarine | 1/4 teaspoon ground cinnamon |
| 150 ml / 1/4 pint cold water (approximately) | 1/2 cup vegetable margarine |
| | 2/3 cup cold water (approximately) |

Put the dry ingredients in a bowl and mix well. Rub in the margarine until the mixture resembles coarse breadcrumbs, then add enough water to make a stiff dough.

Turn out onto a lightly floured surface, then roll out to 1 cm / 1/2 inch thickness. Cut out 48 rounds with a 6 cm / 2 1/2 inch biscuit cutter.

Place on greased baking sheets, then bake in a preheated moderate oven (180°C / 350°F, Gas Mark 4) for 25 minutes. Transfer to a wire rack and leave to cool.

**Makes 48 crunchies**

# Muesli Flapjacks

| Metric/Imperial | American |
|---|---|
| 150 g / 5 oz vegetable margarine | 2/3 cup vegetable margarine |
| 75 g / 3 oz Muscovado sugar | 1/2 cup Barbados sugar |
| 1 tablespoon honey | 1 tablespoon honey |
| 225 g / 8 oz muesli | 1 1/2 cups muesli |
| 50 g / 2 oz hazelnuts, chopped | 1/2 cup chopped filberts |

Heat the margarine gently in a pan until melted. Remove from the heat and stir in the sugar and honey. Add the muesli and nuts and mix thoroughly.

Press the mixture firmly into a greased 18 cm / 7 inch square cake tin. Bake in a preheated moderately hot oven (190°C / 375°F, Gas Mark 5) for 25 minutes. Mark into 9 squares while still hot, then leave in the tin until almost cold. Transfer carefully to a wire rack and leave to cool completely.

**Makes 9 flapjacks**

# Wholewheat Pastry

*The best flour to use for this pastry is 85 per cent wholemeal (wholewheat). For sweet pies and flans, 25 g / 1 oz / 1 1/2 tablespoons Muscovado (Barbados) sugar may be added to the pastry, before mixing in the liquid.*

| Metric/Imperial | American |
|---|---|
| 225 g / 8 oz wholemeal flour | 2 cups wholewheat flour |
| pinch of salt | pinch of salt |
| 100 g / 4 oz vegetable margarine | 1/2 cup vegetable margarine |
| 2 egg yolks | 2 egg yolks |
| 1 tablespoon cold water | 1 tablespoon cold water |

Put the flour and salt in a bowl, then rub in the margarine until the mixture resembles fine breadcrumbs. Beat the egg yolks with the water, then add to the dry mixture and mix to a dough.

As this pastry is a little difficult to handle, it is best to roll it out on a piece of foil so that it can be easily lifted.

# Date and Hazelnut (Filbert) Fingers

| Metric/Imperial | American |
|---|---|
| 2 eggs | 2 eggs |
| 175 g / 6 oz Muscovado sugar | 1 cup Barbados sugar |
| 75 g / 3 oz wholemeal self-raising flour | 3/4 cup wholewheat self-rising flour |
| pinch of salt | pinch of salt |
| 50 g / 2 oz bran cereal | 1 cup bran cereal |
| 50 g / 2 oz hazelnuts, chopped | 1/2 cup chopped filberts |
| 100 g / 4 oz stoned dates, chopped | 2/3 cup chopped, pitted dates |

Put the eggs and sugar in a bowl and whisk until light and creamy. Stir in the remaining ingredients and mix thoroughly.

Spread the mixture evenly in a 28 × 18 cm / 11 × 7 inch tin lined with greased greaseproof paper or non-stick parchment.

Bake in a preheated moderate oven (180°C / 350°F, Gas Mark 4) for 30 minutes. Leave to cool in the tin. Cut into slices before serving.

**Makes 12 fingers**

# DRINKS

A healthy body requires a considerable amount of liquid to function properly. Drinks can vary from a refreshing thirst-quenching drink, containing very few nutrients, to a complete healthy meal in a glass; they can be a slimming fruit juice or a herbal tea, or a body building milky drink.

Juices made from vegetables and fruits will provide all the nutrients of the particular food, though considerably less if diluted with water. Milk shakes, made by blending fresh fruit with milk, provide a very healthy drink; they are also very refreshing made with yogurt instead of milk.

Hot milk drinks, sometimes enriched with eggs and flavoured with liqueurs and spices, make a satisfying bedtime or winter drink. Herbal tea has long been thought to cure minor ailments. Such claims may not be true, but it is certainly a refreshing drink – especially mixed with lemon juice.

Some people find it difficult or time-consuming to eat a proper breakfast – a nourishing drink based on fruits, milk, yogurt and eggs is the perfect solution.

If you drink a lot of fruit and vegetable juice it might be worth investing in a special juice extractor, but the following juices can all be made using an electric blender.

## Citrus Sparkler

| Metric/Imperial | American |
|---|---|
| 1 small grapefruit | 1 small grapefruit |
| 2 small oranges | 2 small oranges |
| 1 lemon | 1 lemon |
| 50 g / 2 oz soft brown sugar | 1/3 cup brown sugar |
| 600 ml / 1 pint water | 2 1/2 cups water |
| 1 small orange or lemon, sliced, to serve | 1 small orange or lemon, sliced, to serve |

Wash the fruit, then chop coarsely, including the peel, pith and pips (seeds). Place in an electric blender with the sugar and water. Blend for about 5 seconds until the fruit is chopped into small pieces. (Do not blend any longer or the pith will make the juice bitter.)

Strain into a bowl, then chill in the refrigerator until required. Pour into individual glasses, add ice cubes and float orange or lemon slices on the top before serving.

**Makes about 750 ml / 1 1/4 pints / 3 cups juice**

## Peach Yogurt Shake

*This refreshing, creamy drink can be served at any time of day.*

| Metric/Imperial | American |
|---|---|
| 2 large ripe peaches, skinned, halved and stoned | 2 large ripe peaches, skinned, halved and pitted |
| juice of 2 oranges | juice of 2 oranges |
| 600 ml / 1 pint natural yogurt | 2 1/2 cups unflavored yogurt |

Put all the ingredients in an electric blender and work to a smooth purée. Transfer to a bowl, then chill in the refrigerator until required.

**Makes about 900 ml / 1 1/2 pints / 3 3/4 cups juice**

# Rose Hip Syrup

*Rose hips are rich in vitamin C. This syrup makes a refreshing drink when diluted with water, or added to milk shakes.*

| Metric/Imperial | American |
|---|---|
| 1 kg / 2 lb ripe rose hips | 2 lb ripe rose hips |
| 2 lemons, coarsely chopped | 2 lemons, coarsely chopped |
| 2 litres / 3½ pint water | 4½ pints (9 cups) water |
| 450 g / 1 lb sugar | 2 cups sugar |

Mince (grind) the rose hips and lemons coarsely together, then place in a large pan. Pour over the water, bring to the boil, then simmer for 5 minutes. Strain through a jelly bag and leave to drip overnight, or for at least 2 hours.

Transfer the juice to a pan and bring to the boil. Add the sugar and heat gently until the sugar has dissolved, stirring constantly. Bring to the boil, then boil for 5 minutes.

Pour the hot syrup into warmed bottles. Seal with screw tops or corks, then store in the refrigerator for up to 2 weeks.

If longer storage is required, preserve the syrup by heat process: fill sterilized screw-topped bottles with hot syrup to within 2.5 cm / 1 inch of the top. Loosely fit the screw tops, then place the bottles in a deep pan as for bottling.

Fill the pan with cold water up to the level of the syrup in the bottles, bring to simmering point, then simmer for 20 minutes. Remove the bottles from the water and screw the tops tightly. Rose hip syrup preserved by this method will keep for up to 6 months.

**Makes about 1.2 litres / 2 pints / 5 cups juice**

# Mulled Apple Juice

| Metric/Imperial | American |
|---|---|
| 450 g / 1 lb cooking apples, peeled, cored and sliced | 1 lb baking apples, peeled, cored and sliced |
| 600 ml / 1 pint water | 2½ cups water |
| finely grated rind and juice of 2 oranges | finely grated rind and juice of 2 oranges |
| 6 tablespoons honey | 6 tablespoons honey |
| 6 cloves, or large pinch of ground cloves | 6 cloves, or large pinch of ground cloves |
| 1 cinnamon stick, or pinch of ground cinnamon | 1 cinnamon stick, or pinch of ground cinnamon |
| pinch of ground ginger | pinch of ground ginger |
| 2 tablespoons rum or brandy | 2 tablespoons rum or brandy |

Put all the ingredients in a pan, except the rum or brandy. Bring to the boil, then lower the heat, cover and simmer for 10 minutes until the apples are reduced to a pulp.

Transfer to an electric blender and blend until the apples are smooth, but the whole spices, if used, are still in pieces.

Strain, stir in the rum or brandy and serve hot.

**Makes 900 ml / 1½ pints / 3¾ cups juice**

# Old-Fashioned Raspberry Vinegar

*This old-fashioned recipe is said to be good for sore throats. It can be drunk neat as a liqueur, or diluted with water or soda and served as a refreshing drink with ice cubes.*

| Metric/Imperial | American |
|---|---|
| 450 g / 1 lb raspberries, washed and hulled | 3 cups raspberries, washed and hulled |
| 600 ml / 1 pint wine vinegar | 2½ cups wine vinegar |
| 450 g / 1 lb sugar | 2 cups sugar |

Put the raspberries in a bowl, then crush with a wooden spoon. Pour over the vinegar, cover and leave to stand for about 4 days, stirring occasionally.

Strain the vinegar into a pan without pressing the pulp through the sieve (strainer). Add the sugar and heat gently until dissolved, stirring constantly. Bring to the boil, then boil for 5 minutes until syrupy.

Leave to cool, then pour into clean, dry bottles. Seal with a cork or screw top and store in the refrigerator for up to 6 months.

**Makes about 750 ml / 1½ pints / 3 cups juice**

# Tomato and Orange Juice

| Metric/Imperial | American |
|---|---|
| 450 g / 1 lb tomatoes, roughly chopped | 2 cups roughly chopped tomatoes |
| 1 small onion, peeled and chopped | 1 small onion, peeled and chopped |
| finely grated rind and juice of 2 oranges | finely grated rind and juice of 2 oranges |
| 300 ml / ½ pint water | 1¼ cups water |
| 1 mint sprig | 1 mint sprig |
| 1 tablespoon soft brown sugar | 1 tablespoon brown sugar |
| 1 teaspoon Worcestershire sauce | 1 teaspoon Worcestershire sauce |
| salt | salt |
| freshly ground black pepper | freshly ground black pepper |
| few mint sprigs to garnish | few mint sprigs to garnish |

Put all the ingredients, except the garnish, in a pan. Bring to the boil, then lower the heat, cover and simmer for 10 minutes until the tomatoes are reduced to a pulp.

Transfer the mixture to an electric blender. Work to a smooth purée, then rub through a sieve (strainer) into a bowl.

Chill in the refrigerator until required. Garnish with mint sprigs just before serving.

**Makes about 600 ml / 1 pint / 2½ cups juice**

# Salad Vegetable Juice

*This is similar to a gazpacho soup – a variety of vegetables are blended with yogurt, then sieved to give a thick vegetable juice.*

| Metric/Imperial | American |
|---|---|
| 4 tomatoes, quartered | 4 tomatoes, quartered |
| 1 onion, peeled and chopped | 1 onion, peeled and chopped |
| 1 green pepper, cored, seeded and chopped | 1 green pepper, cored, seeded and chopped |
| 2 carrots, peeled and chopped | 2 carrots, peeled and chopped |
| 10 cm / 4 inch piece cucumber, chopped | 4 inch piece cucumber, chopped |
| finely grated rind and juice of ½ lemon | finely grated rind and juice of ½ lemon |
| 300 ml / ½ pint natural yogurt | 1¼ cups unflavored yogurt |
| 150 ml / ¼ pint water | ⅔ cup water |
| salt | salt |
| freshly ground white pepper | freshly ground white pepper |
| TO GARNISH: | TO GARNISH: |
| few thin lemon slices | few thin lemon slices |
| few thin cucumber slices | few thin cucumber slices |

Put all the ingredients, except the garnish, in an electric blender. Work to a smooth purée, then rub through a sieve (strainer) into a jug.

Chill in the refrigerator until required. Garnish with lemon and cucumber slices just before serving.

**Makes about 900 ml / 1½ pints / 3¾ cups juice**

# Herb and Lemon Tea

*Herbs and lemon make a refreshing hot drink, which is said to be good for all sorts of minor ailments such as headaches, colds, etc.*

| Metric/Imperial | American |
|---|---|
| 1 tablespoon coarsely chopped herbs (mint, rosemary, thyme) | 1 tablespoon coarsely chopped herbs (mint, rosemary, thyme) |
| finely grated rind and juice of ½ small lemon | finely grated rind and juice of ½ small lemon |
| 600 ml / 1 pint boiling water | 2½ cups boiling water |

Put the herbs, lemon rind and juice in a bowl. Pour over the boiling water, cover and leave to infuse for 3 to 5 minutes. Strain into cups and serve hot.

**Makes 600 ml / 1 pint / 2½ cups tea**

# Spiced Orange Tea

*Tea, flavoured with orange and spices, makes a refreshing drink that can be served hot or cold.*

| Metric/Imperial | American |
|---|---|
| 1 litre / 1¾ pints water | 4¼ cups water |
| finely grated rind and juice of 2 large oranges | finely grated rind and juice of 2 large oranges |
| 1 cinnamon stick | 1 cinnamon stick |
| ½ teaspoon cloves | ½ teaspoon cloves |
| 2 tablespoons tea leaves | 2 tablespoons tea leaves |
| 1 small orange, sliced, to serve | 1 small orange, sliced, to serve |

Put the water, orange rind, juice and spices in a pan. Bring to the boil, then pour over the tea leaves in a warmed tea pot or bowl. Cover and leave to infuse for 5 to 10 minutes. Strain and serve hot or cold with the orange slices floating on top.

**Makes about 1.2 litres / 2 pints / 5 cups tea**

# Egg Nog

*This foamy hot milk drink is best at bedtime.*

| Metric/Imperial | American |
|---|---|
| 300 ml / ½ pint milk | 1½ cups milk |
| 1 egg, separated | 1 egg, separated |
| 1 tablespoon soft brown sugar | 1 tablespoon brown sugar |
| 1 tablespoon ground almonds | 1 tablespoon ground almonds |
| 1 tablespoon brandy, rum or sherry | 1 tablespoon brandy, rum or sherry |
| TO SERVE: | TO SERVE: |
| grated nutmeg | grated nutmeg |
| ground cinnamon | ground cinnamon |

Heat the milk in a pan to just below boiling point. Whisk the egg yolk in a bowl with the sugar and almonds, then stir in the brandy, rum or sherry. Pour on the hot milk, whisking constantly.

Beat the egg white until just stiff, then fold into the milk. Pour into mugs and sprinkle generously with nutmeg and cinnamon. Serve hot.

**Serves 2**

# MENUS

## Daily Menus for Vegetarians

Breakfast
Fruit Muesli with Yogurt

Lunch
Mixed Vegetable Curry
Brown Rice
Cucumber and Tomato Raita
Rhubarb, Orange and Ginger Fool

Supper
Broccoli Pancakes (Crêpes)
Spiced Fruit Compote

Breakfast
Morning Starter
Scrambled Eggs, Wholewheat Toast

Lunch
Cheese and Bread Salad
Blackberry and Orange Stuffed Apples

Supper
Minestrone Soup
Wholewheat Baps (Buns)
Fruit Slices

Breakfast
Breakfast in a Glass

Lunch
Herb and Nut Roast
Broccoli
Plum and Orange Cobbler

Supper
Wholewheat Pizza
Green Salad
Sunshine Fruit Salad

Breakfast
Citrus Starter
Poached Eggs and Wholewheat Toast

Lunch
Mediterranean Lentil Stew
Mixed Salad
Wholewheat Bread
Minted Apple Snow

Supper
Cauliflower Cheese Timbale
Walnut Pie

# Dinner Party Menus

### Starter
Guacamole, Wholewheat Toast

### Main Course
Baked Trout
French Beans   Duchesse Potatoes
Green Salad

### Dessert
Peach and Raspberry Cheesecake

### Starter
Marinated Mushrooms with
Prawns (Shrimp)

### Main Course
Roast Veal with Orange Juice
Spinach Fried with Garlic
Creamed Potatoes

### Dessert
Almond and Strawberry Malakoff

### Starter
Prawn (Shrimp) Quiches

### Main Course
Lamb Skewers
Courgette (Zucchini) Provençal
Pilaf

### Dessert
Pears in Cassis

### Starter
Sailors' Mussels
Wholewheat Bread

### Main Course
Spring Beef Casserole
Celery with Orange and Nuts
Baked Potatoes in their skins

### Dessert
Bramble Mousse

### Starter
Avocado, Grapefruit and
Sesame Salad

### Main Course
Italian Liver
Brown Rice   Spinach
Mixed Salad

### Dessert
Spiced Apple and Cranberry Pie

### Starter
Black Eye Fish Hors d'Oeuvres

### Main Course
Chicken and Olive Bake
Broccoli   Noodles

### Dessert
Strawberry and Orange Soufflé

### Vegetarian Menu

Starter
*Slimmers' Watercress Soup*
*Wholewheat Bread*

Main Course
*Soyabean Moussaka*
*Braised Cabbage    Creamed Potatoes*

Dessert
*Raspberry Chantilly*

# Summer Menus

### Monday

Breakfast
*Meusli*

Lunch
*Baked Crab*
*Peach Yogurt Shake*

Dinner
*Cucumber, Lemon and Mint Soup*
*Spring Beef Casserole*
*Hot Berry Snow*

### Tuesday

Breakfast
*Scrambled Eggs*

Lunch
*Swedish Pickled Shrimp*
*Pineapple Sorbet (Sherbet)*

Dinner
*Fish Roe Stuffed Eggs*
*Lamb Skewers*
*Rhubarb, Orange and Ginger Fool*

### Wednesday

Breakfast
*Poached Eggs on Wholewheat Toast*

Lunch
*Tomato and Orange Juice*
*Smoked Haddock Flan*
*Hazelnut (Filbert) and Raspberry Torte*

Dinner
*Chick Pea (Garbanzos) Salad*
*Chicken and Olive Bake*
*Gooseberry and Almond Crumble*

### Thursday

Breakfast
*Baked Tomato Eggs*

Lunch
*Summer Fish Salad*
*Apricot Tart*

Dinner
*Chilled Pea Soup*
*Lamb and Vegetable Casserole*
*Blackcurrant and Orange Ice Cream*

## Friday

### Breakfast
*Banana Flip*

### Lunch
*Salad Vegetable Juice*
*Pasta with Ratatouille Sauce*
*Spiced Stuffed Peaches*

### Dinner
*Tomato Tart*
*Swedish Baked Fish*
*Strawberry and Orange Soufflé*

## Saturday

### Breakfast
*Fruit Muesli with Yogurt*

### Lunch
*Egg Mousse*
*Seafood Curry*
*Cherry Custard Pudding*

### Tea
*Cottage Cheese Griddlecakes*
*Fruit Slices*

## Sunday

### Breakfast
*Country Grill (Broil)*

### Lunch
*Baked Stuffed Tomatoes*
*Roast Veal with Orange Juice*
*Peach and Raspberry Cheesecake*

### Tea
*Farmhouse Scones*
*Muesli Flapjacks*

# Winter Menus

## Monday

### Breakfast
*Prune Fluff*

### Lunch
*Soft Roes on Toast*
*Spiced Fruit Compote*

### Dinner
*Leeks à la Grècque*
*Meat-Stuffed Marrow (Squash)*
*Orange and Lemon Mousse*

## Tuesday

### Breakfast
*Wholewheat Crêpes*

### Lunch
*Cold Lamb in Mint Aspic*
*Baked Grapefruit Soufflé*

### Dinner
*Italian Bean Soup*
*Trout in Yogurt Sauce*
*Black Pear Pudding*

## Wednesday

### Breakfast
*Granola*

### Lunch
*Spiced Fish Casserole*
*French Orange Flans*

### Dinner
*Herb Pâté*
*Vegetable Kebabs with Pilaf*
*Minted Apple Snow*

## Thursday

### Breakfast
*Citrus Starter*

### Lunch
*Fish in a Packet*
*Walnut Pie*

### Dinner
*Jerusalem Cocottes*
*Oxtail and Kidney Casserole*
*Pears in Cassis*

## Friday

### Breakfast
*Spiced Grapefruit Refresher*

### Lunch
*Sailors' Mussels*
*Apricot Syllabub*

### Dinner
*Slimmers' Watercress Soup*
*Stuffed Cabbage Leaves*
*Bramble Mousse*

## Saturday

### Breakfast
*Poached Haddock and Eggs*

### Lunch
*Minestrone*
*Baked Liver in Yogurt Sauce*
*Plum and Orange Cobbler*

### Tea
*Bran Bread with honey*
*Parkin*

### Bedtime Drink
*Egg Nog*

## Sunday

### Breakfast
*Farmhouse Scramble*

### Lunch
*Chestnut Soup*
*Herbed Chicken*
*Spiced Cranberry and Apple Pie*

### Tea
*Walnut Squares*
*Honey Fruit Loaf*

### Bedtime Drink
*Mulled Apple Juice*

# Index